SELECTIONS

FROM

WILLIAM MORRIS

(PROSE)

T0381587

SELECTIONS
FROM THE PROSE WORKS OF
WILLIAM MORRIS

Edited by
A. H. R. BALL, M.A.

CAMBRIDGE
AT THE UNIVERSITY PRESS
1931

CAMBRIDGE
UNIVERSITY PRESS

University Printing House, Cambridge CB2 8BS, United Kingdom

Cambridge University Press is part of the University of Cambridge.

It furthers the University's mission by disseminating knowledge in the pursuit of education, learning and research at the highest international levels of excellence.

www.cambridge.org
Information on this title: www.cambridge.org/9781107437609

© Cambridge University Press 1931

First published 1931
First paperback edition 2014

A catalogue record for this publication is available from the British Library

ISBN 978-1-107-43760-9 Paperback

PREFACE

Previous volumes in this series have represented the work of Carlyle and Ruskin, the great allies against the utilitarian philosophy of the nineteenth century. This book, to borrow a term from the drama, completes the trilogy, for William Morris preached the gospels of humanity and beauty no less arduously and convincingly than the two older prophets. Each of them has still a vital message, and not only in social reform: they are all distinguished by their mastery over a surprising variety of subjects. We can build up from them a background of culture and philosophy not accessible elsewhere in so small a compass. In this respect Morris is not the least of the three, and certainly he is the one who comes nearest to our own experience, who speaks to us most intimately.

Morris's work falls naturally into three divisions: his vision of the past, his hopes and fears for the present, his dream of the future; and this volume is intended to give an adequate conception of each. In the first we have intuitions more sure, detail more realistic, and imagination more powerful than in any historic record. Of the second it is sufficient to say that though most of his fears have proved true, only a few of his hopes have been realised, and his thoughts on life and art are as applicable to-day as in the nineteenth century. And though we may not see eye to eye with him in his portrayal of Utopia, it is a splendid stimulant to thought and a dream of beauty over which it is pleasant to brood. Lastly there is the inspiration of a great spirit, a mind and courage akin to those of the Norsemen he loved so well, a life which is a perpetual reminder of the possibilities of human endeavour.

I am indebted to Mr S. C. Cockerell, the trustees of William Morris, and Messrs Longmans, Green and Company, for permission to print these extracts, all of which are copyright; and, like its predecessors, this volume owes much to Mr W. Holdgate, of Liverpool, for his valuable advice and criticism.

A. H. R. B.

Manchester
1931

CONTENTS

PREFACE . . . . *page* v

INTRODUCTION
William Morris xi
Art and Social Reform: Ruskin and Morris . . xx
Style xxxiii

THE MIDDLE AGES

THE ROOF OF THE WOLFINGS . . . 1
The House of the Wolfings, chap. i

GOTHS AND ROMANS 5
The House of the Wolfings, chap. xv

THE HALL OF THE RAVAGERS . . . 15
The Story of the Glittering Plain, chap. vii

THE SPRING MARKET AT BURGSTEAD . 24
The Roots of the Mountains, chap. xxxii

THE WEAPON-SHOW 26
The Roots of the Mountains, chap. xxxi

THE OPENING OF THE FOLK-MOTE . . 35
The Roots of the Mountains, chap. xxxviii

THE MAIDEN WARD 40
The Roots of the Mountains, chap. lviii

THE UNKNOWN CHURCH 45
The Story of the Unknown Church

THE CHURCHES OF NORTH FRANCE . . 48
Shadows of Amiens

viii CONTENTS

A KENTISH VILLAGE . . . . . *page* 49
  A Dream of John Ball, chap. i

JOHN BALL'S SPEECH AT THE CROSS . 53
  A Dream of John Ball, chap. iv

THE BATTLE AT THE TOWNSHIP'S END. 60
  A Dream of John Ball, chap. vi

THE VISION OF THE FUTURE . . . 66
  A Dream of John Ball, chap. xii

ART AND SOCIAL REFORM

MEDIEVAL ARTS AND CRAFTS . . . 76
  Lectures on Art and Industry: Art and the Beauty of the Earth

ART AND THE BEAUTY OF LIFE . . 81
  Hopes and Fears for Art: The Beauty of Life

THE ART OF THE PEOPLE 88
  Hopes and Fears for Art: The Art of the People

THE STUDY OF ANCIENT ART . . . 92
  Hopes and Fears for Art: The Lesser Arts

NEGLECT OF ART 97
  Hopes and Fears for Art: The Prospects of Architecture

THE BEAUTY OF ENGLAND 103
  Lectures on Art and Industry: Art and the Beauty of the Earth

THE MODERN CITY 108
  Lectures on Socialism: Art under Plutocracy

ARCHITECTURE 111
  Hopes and Fears for Art: The Beauty of Life, The Art of the People, The Prospects of Architecture

MACHINERY 121
  Signs of Change: The Aims of Art

THE NECESSITIES OF LIFE 123
  Signs of Change: How we live and how we might live

MEANS OF IMPROVEMENT . . . *page* 129
  Signs of Change: Useful Work v. Useless Toil

THE DECORATIVE ARTS 138
  Hopes and Fears for Art: The Lesser Arts

ART AND MORALS 143
  Hopes and Fears for Art: The Lesser Arts, The Art of the People

THE BEST ART 148
  Lectures on Art and Industry: Some Hints on Pattern-Designing

GARDENS 152
  Hopes and Fears for Art: Making the Best of It

FURNITURE 157
  *Hopes and Fears for Art: The Beauty of Life, Making the Best
  of It*
  Lectures on Art and Industry: The Lesser Arts of Life

POTTERY 162
  Lectures on Art and Industry: The Lesser Arts of Life

ART FOR ALL 168
  Hopes and Fears for Art: The Lesser Arts

UTOPIAN ENGLAND

THE GUEST HOUSE 171
  News from Nowhere, chap. iii

HAMMERSMITH MARKET 176
  News from Nowhere, chap. iv

EDUCATION 180
  News from Nowhere, chap. v

SHOPPING IN PICCADILLY . . . 184
  News from Nowhere, chap. vi

GOVERNMENT 188
  News from Nowhere, chap. xii

x   CONTENTS

ART AND INDUSTRY . . . . . *page* 194
  News from Nowhere, chap. xv

THE CHANGE IN INDUSTRY 196
  News from Nowhere, chap. xxvii

THE TOWNS 200
  News from Nowhere, chap. x

HAMPTON COURT 208
  News from Nowhere, chap. xxii

THE UPPER THAMES 212
  News from Nowhere, chaps. xxix, xxx

GLOSSARY 215

INDEX 221

INTRODUCTION

WILLIAM MORRIS

THE genius of William Morris was determined less by inherited talents than by the social, intellectual and spiritual movements of his day. He grew to manhood amid the general unrest of England in the 'fifties. The period from 1837 to 1850 was one of acute economic depression: wages were at their lowest; with the coming of machines sweated industries were common; hours of work, especially for women and children, were long and unbroken; and the lot of the poor was aggravated by the insanitary conditions under which they were compelled to live. Little was done by the ruling classes to mitigate these evils, in fact the doctrines of the Utilitarian philosophers, the dominant school of thinkers, not only blessed the industrial system, but made it a necessity. Carlyle began the recoil. He set up a ferment in the youth of the 'fifties, a total disgust with the commercialism of the age, which found expression in the philosophy and intellectual radicalism of his ally, though not disciple, Charles Kingsley. *Politics for the People*, the series of tracts issued by Kingsley and his friends in support of the working classes, who were concentrating their efforts for social reform into obtaining the 'points' of the great Charter which came before Parliament in 1848, and the two novels of 1849, *Alton Locke* and *Yeast*, provided a pregnant commentary on the plight of the poor in the heyday of Victorian prosperity.

No less disturbing were the new movements in art and spiritual life. In the same year as the Workers' Charter, 1848, Rossetti, Millais, and Holman Hunt formed their pre-Raphaelite brotherhood, launching a new movement in art with an object like that achieved by Wordsworth in poetry: to go to nature, to be accurate and truthful in studying her, and to open the mind of the painter to that sympathetic and religious tone of feeling which distinguishes the later medieval painters of Italy. In 1848 the movement started, in 1850 its artistic creed was formulated in *The Germ*, and in 1851 Ruskin's *Pre-Raphaelitism* set it on its feet, making it a potent force in art. The Anglican movement, too, the leaders of which Carlyle had dismissed contemptuously from his mind as having but the brains of rabbits, although it had been eclipsed at Oxford by Newman's secession, was favourable to these ideas. It had little immediate or serious effect on English letters, but it exercised profound influence on the minds of men. Even Tennyson shared the general unrest, and *Maud* in 1855 voices the desire to get away from the smug security of the time and to mix with action.

William Morris was born at Walthamstow on March 24th, 1834, the son of a prosperous City bill-broker, whose fortune, through timely investments, had grown rapidly, and from whom the boy inherited a remarkable business capacity. After a happy childhood, lived on the edge of Epping Forest, he went to Marlborough, and, in 1853, to Oxford. As a boy he was not precocious, but he had a genial humour and a tempestuous anger. He enjoyed solitary pleasures with a self-sufficiency which remained his chief characteristic, and in a quiet, almost secret way, before he left school he collected a minute and intimate knowledge of the life of medieval England. The library at Marlborough was rich in archaeological works, and he taught himself most of what was to be known of English Gothic. Even as a boy, a Gothic church was to him more than a building: it was the key to a whole vision of life and society. To see a church once was to remember it always; and he could never look at one without a gush of love towards the men who had built it.

The Anglo-Catholic Movement had great influence on the staff at Marlborough and coloured the religious services there. It attracted Morris, and when he left for Oxford in 1853, ostensibly to take orders, he went to Exeter College. There he met Edward Burne-Jones, a man of similar nature who also intended to take orders, and they began a friendship which lasted till death. They found little congenial society at Exeter, and Oxford, as Burne-Jones said, seemed "languid and indifferent", so they joined a group at Pembroke which developed into the most sensitive nerve in the University at the time. In the memories of two of these friends, Dixon and Faulkner, Morris survives in the Oxford years as an overgrown boy. Only gradually did they discover his firmness and decisiveness of character, his enormous and accurate knowledge of unfamiliar things. The religious interest in his mind had begun to wear off and was rapidly being exchanged for an interest in art. He knew now what he wanted in life; his loves and hates were firmly fixed. Two of them dominated his whole career—his great passions for the life and faith of the Scandinavian Sagas, and for the spirit and society of thirteenth-century England. These two interests determined the doctrines he was to preach, and they were confirmed in 1853 by the publication of Ruskin's *Stones of Venice*, which, to Morris, seemed to open up a new road along which the humanity of the future might travel.

In the vacations of 1854 and 1855, he visited Northern France and Belgium and saw the great Gothic churches of Chartres, Amiens and Rouen. To the end he retained an intense love for this district: it was the true setting of old romance; and in the article "On the Cathedral of Amiens" he speaks of these churches as "the grandest, the most beautiful, the kindest and most loving of all the buildings that the earth has ever borne; and thinking of their passed-away builders, I can see through them, very faintly, dimly, some little of the mediaeval times, else dead, and gone from me for ever; voiceless for ever". About this time the thoughts of the friends turned towards the future. One of the most memorable hours of Morris's life was in 1855 when he was walking along the quay at Havre with Burne-Jones. They solemnly vowed their lives to art: Morris to architecture, Burne-Jones to painting. Burne-Jones did not swerve from his resolution; Morris never built a house. But to Morris architecture meant not only building; it bore a transcendental meaning. It was the tangible expression of all the order and sweetness which sustains man's world and makes his life what it is. In this sense Morris, too, was faithful. He wanted to turn all life into art, and he enjoyed art's triumph most when it glorified the things of use. Meanwhile he had discovered the poet in himself. Canon Dixon describes how, in 1854, they heard Morris read his poem *The Willow and the Red Cliff*, and found that he was a poet. It seemed to them a poetry the like of which had never been heard before, but Morris assured them that he found it very easy to write. Indeed he reached his perfection in this form almost at once, and from this time wrote profusely in poetry. In 1855 the friends determined to start a magazine, with a view to applying their literary ability to the reform of English social life. *The Oxford and Cambridge Magazine* of 1856, a literary and philosophical journal financed by Morris, was the result. It was not a success, barely surviving the year, though Morris wrote for it a number of poems and prose stories, a review of Browning's *Men and Women*, and the paper "On the Cathedral at Amiens".

In 1855 Morris took his degree and went into the world an independent man with a comfortable private income. He entered the office of George Edmund Street, a famous architect of the Gothic revival, and worked there for a year. In 1857 he met Rossetti, then at the height of his power, and under the influence of the strong spell which the great artist and poet cast upon all who knew him well, he took rooms in London and turned himself into a pre-Raphaelite painter. But here again he was not satisfied. He achieved some success, but he could not forget that a picture is enclosed in a frame. Painting seemed a solitary and independent art, produced only for the rich and purchased only by them. For Morris art was nothing if not a social thing, and he deviated rapidly into the decorative arts, illuminating manuscripts on vellum and designing furniture for his rooms.

Then suddenly Morris saw the purpose for which he was born—to revive the practical arts. He married Miss Jane Burden at Oxford in 1859, and he had to find a satisfactory house and furnish it, at a time when public taste in all the domestic arts in England had reached its lowest ebb. Houses, if not built of stone, were built of brick and stucco, and the stucco disguise had become an object of pride and a sign of gentility. Furniture, decoration, and all the applied arts had fallen entirely into the hands of the dealer, and existed on his notion of the market prospect. The costly was everywhere preferred to the beautiful. Morris could not buy a single article with which he would consent to live. Moreover the complacency with ugliness was to him a deeper thing, it was the symbol of something debased and mean in the general mind. The standard was not merely degraded, but the whole nation was deliberately living down to it. And though, like his master Ruskin, Morris came in for much ridicule for this moralistic theory of art, he preached it to the end of his time.

The house was built by Philip Webb on Bexley Heath in Kent, and all the fittings were designed by Morris and executed under his own eye. Here he saw that he had discovered a need. He gathered his friends together—Rossetti,

Burne-Jones, Madox Brown, Peter Marshall, and Faulkner
—and founded the industrial company of Morris, Marshall,
Faulkner and Co., which was dissolved in 1865 and re-
constituted as the more familiar Morris and Co. The firm
undertook to supply furniture and pictures, mural decora-
tions, stained glass, metal, jewellery, and many other articles
for domestic use, produced by skilled workmen in close
co-operation with the artist and designer. Morris was the
sole manager and chief designer, and he produced over six
hundred patterns, chiefly for wallpapers. His sense of
colour tones was mysterious and wonderful, and he had
remarkable intuitions of the composition of shades. Moreover, in this gigantic labour he unearthed a number of
applied arts which had been lost since the middle ages—
vegetable dying, artistic printing, tapestry weaving—and
taught them to his workmen. Such works could not be
produced cheaply—the necessity of teaching the processes
of production as he went along precluded that—but, as a
good business man, Morris found a market for his wares,
and the firm prospered.

The happy life of labour at the Red House on Bexley
Heath was soon to end. "It was the most beautiful sight
in the world", said one of his friends, "to see Morris
coming up from the cellar before dinner, beaming with joy,
with his hands full of bottles of wine and others tucked
under his arm." But a period of illness which made the
frequent journeys to London arduous, and the growing
business of the firm, made him decide to leave the Red
House and settle in town. He took a house in Queen
Square, Bloomsbury, in 1865, and, appointing a new
manager for his business, turned again in his leisure to
writing poetry. *The Life and Death of Jason*, a romantic
narrative in Chaucerian form but classical spirit was published in 1867; the two sections of *The Earthly Paradise*,
a storehouse of ancient and medieval tales, in 1868 and

1870; and *Love is Enough*, a morality poem, in 1872. In these works to the romantic spirit of his earlier poems, *The Defence of Guenevere, King Arthur's Tomb, Summer Dawn*, he adds a mastery of narrative only equalled by Chaucer; he wrote of other days and medieval scenes as one who walked about in them. The fault, if it is one, is that they were written too easily; much is mere pleasure-giving poetry, both to the poet and to the reader. Meanwhile, in addition to making translations of the *Aeneid* and *Odyssey*, he had learned Icelandic, and in 1876 he published his most ambitious work, the epic *Sigurd the Volsung*, founded upon the prose *Volsunga Saga*.

Sigurd was the last of Morris's ambitious poems. In 1871 he had bought the beautiful manor house of Kelmscott, near Letchford on the Upper Thames, and this became his chosen rest and paradise until his death. In London, the firm was progressing, and rapidly bringing about a revolution in public taste. The work was moved in 1881 to Merton Abbey, and here were executed painted glass, tapestries, carpets, embroidery, tiles, furniture, paper-hangings, velvets, cloths and upholstery. Much later he designed for his prose romances a new type, and set up a printing press of his own, the products of which equalled the art of the old calligraphists.

In 1881 and 1882, the beliefs he had cherished that art would never be good without a social revolution overmastered his other interests, and from this time until 1896 he wore himself out in continual agitation. It began indirectly with his interest in the Society for the Protection of Ancient Buildings, which Morris, moved by indignation at the restoration of Lichfield Cathedral, founded in 1877. He had been an official of the National Liberal League, but in 1881 he decided that a complete political change was the only way to accomplish the social one, and he became an active Socialist. Though he never suffered

them, he felt the wrongs of the poor, and he preached
political revolt only as a means to improve economic conditions. In 1883 he enlisted in the Democratic Federation,
and rapidly became one of its leaders, contributing money
and articles to its magazine *Justice*, writing Socialist songs
and lectures, even speaking at street corner meetings. In
1884 Morris and his party split from the parent body to
form the Socialist League, and he continued the work
whole-heartedly. "The simplicity with which he did this
was fine to see", Lady Burne-Jones tells us. "Consider
what it must have meant for him to leave the Grange
unsped by sympathy, and to speak, as he frequently did,
either at a street corner near his own house—where he
was but a prophet in his own country—or perhaps miles
away at Ball's Pond, where he was not of as much importance in the neighbourhood as a cheap-jack." In 1890,
he was driven out of the League by internal quarrels, and
he founded the Hammersmith Socialist Society, which
attracted men like John Burns, Bernard Shaw, Sidney
Webb, and Lord Haldane, but in 1896 a serious illness
put an end to his public career.

Two lasting results in literature mark this period of
social propaganda: the prose romances *News from Nowhere*
and *A Dream of John Ball*, both of which were written
for a political purpose. The former is a serious essay in
political theory, written in reply to Bellamy's *Looking
Backward*, which describes the world of the future as
purely mechanical. Morris's is a pastoral Utopia, a picture
of Europe as it may be a couple of centuries hence, beyond
the combination of the trade unions, when all men live
in perfect equality. In *A Dream of John Ball*, as in the
early *Story of the Unknown Church*, we come back to the
sweet landscapes of the fourteenth century: it is Morris
closing his eyes to this world and escaping to a better. The
writer strays into a Kentish village in the middle of the

rising of the peasants under Richard II. The arrival of John Ball, and their subsequent discussions, give Morris the opportunity of speaking his mind through the mouth of the democratic priest more clearly than through any other of his characters. But the sweet savour of the book is the picture of English village life and the beautiful medieval setting.

In 1889, worn out with his social labours, Morris returned to romantic prose stories. *The House of the Wolfings* and *The Roots of the Mountains* deal with the Germanic migrations of the second century. In the former the Goths are in conflict with the Romans at the time of the decline of the Empire; the latter is a tale of a pastoral community threatened by a race of Dusky Men, presumably the Huns. Both are romantic tales of the simple life and stern conflicts of olden times, told as by one who is present and sees it all, in a peculiar but fitting musical prose, interspersed with poetry. *The Story of the Glittering Plain, The Wood beyond the World, The Water of the Wondrous Isles* and *The Sundering Flood* followed in quick succession. They are all marked by the same qualities: somewhat indefinite character-drawing, general vagueness of locality together with strange clearness of detail, unbounded imagination, isolated scenes and episodes of memorable clearness and beauty, and a not unpleasing archaic language. Above all there is immense power in the tales; though often prolix, they are never wearisome. The characters really live and inhabit the medieval towns with a communicable love.

A few poems occupied the intervals of these later years, and in *The Pilgrims of Hope* and *Poems by the Way*, he reaches his highest level as a lyric poet. In 1896 the results of the continuous tax on his vitality began to be obvious to his friends. A trip to Norway was ordered, but he got back in August too ill to reach Kelmscott. On the 3rd October he died. His disease, as a doctor said, "was simply being William Morris, and having done more work than most ten men".

ART AND SOCIAL REFORM

Ruskin & Morris

It is important to remember that in his social philosophy of art, Morris treads closely on the steps of his master, Ruskin, who, in all political matters, is the reverential disciple of Carlyle. But whereas Carlyle is dominated altogether by the utilitarian philosophers, who developed him, but warped him, tying him down to political issues and keeping him away from the wider things of culture and life, Ruskin and Morris come to social reform through art. To combat the utilitarians Carlyle goes back to the theories of the German philosophers, to Saint-Simon, and the first French socialists; the socialism of Ruskin and Morris is never far from its aesthetic basis. Ruskin had a critical reputation which made him the monarch of the moment in matters of art, and the work of Morris was rapidly bringing about a revolution in public taste, when consciousness of the evils of the social system seized them, and they joined the struggle because they felt that great art was no longer possible in England until things were set right. In 1839, Carlyle's *Chartism* opened the attack in the name of morals; in 1847 Ruskin's *Seven Lamps of Architecture*, with *The Stones of Venice* in 1850, mark the beginning of the aesthetic revolt. The chapter on "The Nature of Gothic" was hailed as a new light by William Morris and his friends—"Then this man John Ruskin rose, seeming to us like a Luther of the arts". It may be said to have founded a new sociological school.

A distinction has been drawn between the static and dynamic theories of social reform. The latter takes the circumstances of society as always changing, and derives its morality from extracting the greatest opportunities from these circumstances as they come. All modern inventions thus become moral opportunities, the life of the modern city for instance, though it brings losses and dangers and demands a great deal of accommodation in the human mind, more than compensates us for these things in the development of the faculties. Ruskin is the archetype of the static theory which believes in a norm of human happiness. Man has heaped up the comforts of civilization until they tend to stifle his spirit, and so we must call a halt in the progress, or undo what has been done and get back to the norm. Ruskin, Morris, and Tolstoi are thinkers of this type. Ruskin believed passionately that he lived in a debased time, and that in the thirteenth century there was an age when the human faculty was larger and human conduct nobler. This age may thus be a test of our own: a standard and a clue to our betterment. We must find out how they did things then, compare them with our own methods, and remould these where they differ.

Ruskin's social philosophy and positive ideal of reconstructed society follow from his aesthetic theories in *Modern Painters* and *The Stones of Venice*. In the artist there is need for sympathy with the Divine and a quiet conscience: his function is to recognize and apprehend the qualities and attributes of the Divine in nature, and render them again with no alteration or improvement but the colouring of his imaginative faculty. Thus one of the main points of *Modern Painters* is an appreciation of the artistic height and dignity of the 'Primitives', the fourteenth and early fifteenth-century artists of Italy—Giotto, Fra Angelico, Fra Filippo Lippi, and Botticelli. Ruskin divides art into four periods. The first is the Greek, noble in its way, but pagan and unspiritual, lacking any self-abandoning affection or majesty of feeling. In the second the primitives are nobler because religious in feeling, but imperfect yet in execution.

Their successors in the fifteenth century, the third period,—Michael Angelo, Raphael, Tintoretto—unite the best elements of the two civilizations, classic finish and Christian interpretation. The primitives represent earth and man as purer and better than reality; they are purists. The great masters of the fifteenth century face and accept all the evil in the world, but redeem it by finding in it some promise of good. They join perfect technique to the felicity of heart and the beauty which descended from the primitives, and we get an age of art never equalled since. But this perfection itself becomes a bane; their successors inherit the technique, but not the inward feeling. They go back to the Greeks and substitute mere intellect for spiritual light. The fourth period is thus the long decay after the fifteenth century, a succession of artists who delight in evil for its own sake, who descend to the common and the utilitarian, and who lead on to the base copying of the Dutch masters and the conventional beauties of the French school.

If the history of painting is to Ruskin the story of the Christian spirit, exalted and then fallen, still more clearly is this the case with architecture. The early Gothic of the fourteenth century is instinct with the spirit of Christianity. In its rudeness, love of variety, delight in nature, forceful regenesis and exuberance of ornament, it represents a heart strong and affectionable—humble also, because it is not too proud to try and to confess its failures. But the most single expression of this spirit is that while the Gothic church is full of ornament, this is not only executed, but designed by the working mason. It is left to him to put out the poetry of his soul. The Gothic Church is thus offered to God by the whole community with a joy and will, as in no other type of architecture. There is, for instance, no such opportunity in Classic or Renaissance buildings, where ornament is sparse, geometrical, and easily executed. The workman here is a mere mechanic.

There are inferences, both moral and practical, which Ruskin draws from these facts. It is obvious, for one thing, that no great art was ever created by bad men, and Ruskin never swerved from this belief—you must be good or you cannot paint. And it follows that the coldness to beauty and the indifference to art characteristic of English puritanism is a bad sign, the sign of a religion cranked and narrow, for nothing but art is moral, and industry without art is brutal, since art depends on and is fed by love. The state of the arts is thus an index of national wealth. Even if an efflorescence of art does sometimes accompany corruption in society, it does not alter the fact that art comes from goodness—the evil in society is just a challenge to the good, and brings it out.

This is the bridge that leads Ruskin to social questions. He looked round and saw that the sense of beauty had disappeared in the lower as well as the higher arts. The loss of beauty in English furniture and household goods dates from about 1790. In the eighteenth century there was some sense of it in the Queen Anne and Chippendale styles, but about 1790 public taste began to gravitate towards the Victorian modes. They learned to put up with things ugly and ill made, with no honesty in making, no solidity or strength of workmanship, and, worst of all, they did not notice the change. With these things came the economic stress of the time, and Ruskin connects the two. Injustice and ugliness, he says, proceed from the same root, and injustice comes first. If you wish to lead a beautiful and moral life, you must remove the social injustices and so get back to beauty. And here he looks to his great periods of art.

The secret of the noble life of these early ages he found to consist largely in the absence of machinery from industry, whereby much of the life of man was permeated with the joy of creative art. Ruskin's most important pages, and those which exerted greatest influence on Morris, are those in *The Stones of Venice* where he speaks of the enslavement of the modern mason in architecture, and the importance of allowing him to offer the rude gift of his own mind and spirit. The lust after the perfection of machine-made work is alien to the spirit of beauty. Moreover the conditions under which the men of the great ages lived differ from ours in that we lack the fixity, permanence and security that they had—the restfulness of lives set to one sphere and one work, without vanities or social ambition. Their cities bear witness to this; they were built for posterity, they were small and might easily be left, and the men of that time lived more in the open air and in the country. Our sins, on the other hand, are pride and hurry; we strike our roots shallowly into the soil. This is visible in our houses, those "pitiful concretions of lime and clay", and the whole of *The Seven Lamps of Architecture* is a pleading for the old substantial style of building, for houses built to last, and for a way of living that will harmonize with them.

Ruskin goes on to draw drastic conclusions for the reconstruction of our social and political system. The principle of the Gothic builders cannot be confined to architecture; we must extend it to all branches of life, and it damns three-quarters of our modern industrial methods. There must be no machines—Ruskin has always a great hatred of steel and iron,—and nothing must be made by power which can, without undue drudgery, be made by hand and with a free brain. Mills must be driven by water, not steam, and there must be no railways, or at least, only trunk lines. No cities—or only small ones, girdled with gardens and streams. And it follows that the state of things must go back to feudalism, to the strict hierarchy of rank and class, to habits of loyalty and obedience. Our hopes of salvation depend on the nobility and strength of the governing classes.

So, being steeped in the past, and enthusiastic for the present, Ruskin goes off into a vision of the systematic reconstruction of the middle ages, the old times brought back with the best a little better. But the theories are pressed too far and in the later social works, *Time and Tide* and *The Crown of Wild Olive*, the ideas become fantastic. The element of dream-like archaism in his speculation— the treatment of war in *The Crown of Wild Olive* is a flagrant instance of a man dreaming aloud,—the view of his own day as a monstrosity to be put aside, the theory that development is a deformation, can only end in a for-lorn hope. His social ideas are too purely Utopian, too alien from the brute facts and forces of life. It was left for his ally and disciple, Morris, to propound a more practical ideal.

It has been shown that Morris's political faith, like that of Ruskin, flowed from his theory of art and life. Its most concise expression is in the lectures delivered between 1878 and 1882, collected as *Hopes and Fears for Art*, *Signs of Change* and *Architecture, Industry and Wealth*. Like Ruskin he lived much in the world of the middle ages, and he continually said that the new era could come to us only through the intense and reverential study of those times. But in contrast to Ruskin the art Morris desires is a living and modern one, not a repetition of medieval art, but fraught with the full experience of to-day. Morris, in fact, was too unaffected to make his work purely medieval, and there was at one time a controversy as to whether his windows were really suitable for the medieval churches in which they were placed. "Let us study ancient art wisely," he said, "be taught by it, kindled by it; all the while determining not to imitate or repeat it; to have either no art at all, or an art which we have made our own."[1]

The religious leaders and social reformers of the day,

[1] *Hopes and Fears for Art: The Lesser Arts.*

c

whose ultimate aspirations he could see really tallied with his own, appeared to Morris, as to Ruskin, as enemies of beauty, and it was one of his inward trials that this should be so. To convert them, as he always wished to do, he appealed to history and showed them that at one time art was popular, and conversely that labour unsweetened by art leads to discontent, unrest, and despair, which will at last swallow up all society. All great art of medieval times, he says, is made "by the people and for the people, as a happiness to the maker and user"; it is "the expression of man's happiness in his labour".[1] But now art is made for the rich, and by the genius who lives in luxury and solitude, shut off in the contemplation of the past glories of the world from the everyday squalors that the most of men move in.[2] On these terms, he says, "I do not wish art to live. I protest that it should be a shame to an honest artist to enjoy what he has huddled up to himself of such art, as it would be for a rich man to sit and eat dainty food amongst starving soldiers in a beleaguered fort. I do not want art for a few, any more than education for a few, or freedom for a few".[3] The expression of beauty must be the greatest among the forces of life, and universal. Works of craftsmanship are now divided into two kinds, works of art and non-works of art, whereas all things made by man's hand should be beautiful. The artist cannot wrap himself up in his special gifts and high cultivation and live apart from other men: he must share in the general discomfort, and he gains by it.[4] The wonders of the South Kensington Museum are just the common household goods of past days, made by men who worked, not unhappily, most days and the most part of the day, and the design and ornament of the treasures of architecture were accomplished not by the great architect, but more often by the monk,

[1] *Hopes and Fears for Art: The Art of the People.*
[2] *Ibid.: The Lesser Arts.* [3] *Ibid.* [4] *Ibid.: The Beauty of Life.*

the village carpenter, smith and mason.[1] In those days, there was full sympathy between the works of men and the land they were made for, and, with an art striving little to impress by pomp or ingenuity, not unseldom commonplace, but never oppressive and always inventive and individual, men sought to adorn the unromantic, uneventful-looking land of England. And this art was sweet because it came from the heart, given freely and equally to the yeoman's house, the humble village church, the lord's palace, or the mighty cathedral.[2]

This vital connection between their work and the happiness of the people was Morris's chief argument for those who looked on art as a trifling thing and not in the line of the social question. In his own workshops he lived to make art popular, and largely banished the estrangement between execution and design. His daily work brought him into contact with ordinary artisans, and he had no delusions about the British workman. But he knew that there is no man who cannot be taught some measure of skill and who cannot participate in his own degree in a work of art. In his factory he became a worker like his own men, for, he said, "you cannot design perfectly unless you have handled the material on which your design is to be printed". He believed firmly that art would come to earth among the handicrafts, and would take up the chain where it fell from the hands of the craft guilds in the fifteenth century. The great artist, he thought, had become divorced from the crafts, to the general loss. The artist lost the criticism of the common folk, the accompaniment of an abundance of that commoner work in which all men share, without which the highest art cannot exist, and the people lost by the withdrawal of the artist's fellowship and sympathy. It was this that made Morris realize that the

[1] *Hopes and Fears for Art: The Art of the People.*
[2] *Ibid.: The Lesser Arts.*

great despotic artists of the Renaissance were the last fruits of the old era, not the beginning of the new. Sporadic art in the brains of a few imaginative men must be replaced by another and universal art. And if this art is to be revived, the crafts must be revived with it. The bond between high and low must be re-established.

In 1884 Morris visited an exhibition at the Royal Academy, and he wrote a review in the socialist organ *The Day* in which he asserts that "Those only do work worth while whose minds have managed to leap back into the middle ages; anyone who wants beauty must be always crying out 'Look back!'". He goes on to show that art has always reconciled the poor man to his lot. Morris did not regard the middle ages as a paradise. Men sat, he said, "under such grinding tyrannies, amongst violence and fear so great, that nowadays we wonder how they lived through twenty-four hours of it". But each man had his pleasure in his work—the daily labour was sweetened by the daily creation of Art.[1] There was much going on to make life endurable in those times: "Not every day, you may be sure, was a day of slaughter and tumult, though the histories read almost as if it were so; but every day the hammer clinked on the anvil, and the chisel played about the oak-beam, and never without some beauty and invention being born of it, and consequently some human happiness".[2] Only in these later days has man rejected the universal gift of striving to make his work happy, and before we can rescue civilization we must recapture the gift and seek to labour in this way.

Morris was not unfair to the commercial civilization of his time, and in the lecture on "The Beauty of Life" he gives a just account of the progress made by the old commercialism. "It has broken down many a prejudice and taught many a lesson that the world has hitherto been slow

[1] *Hopes and Fears for Art: The Art of the People.*   [2] *Ibid.*

to learn: it has made it possible for many a man to live free, who would in other times have been a slave, body or soul, or both." But he shows that much of the work has been roughly done, that recklessness has commonly gone with energy and blindness too often with haste. If the nineteenth has been the Century of Commerce, he looks forward to the twentieth as the Century of Education. Only you cannot educate or civilize men, unless you give them a share in art, and before we can have art, many changes have to come to pass. Most things must be made by hand. The workman must have not merely enough wages to free him from anxiety, but leisure in which to read and to enjoy. We must achieve "simplicity of life, begetting simplicity of taste, that is, a love for sweet and lofty things; simplicity everywhere, in the palace as well as in the cottage".[1] We must get rid of the superfluity of our luxuries, articles depressing to maker and user, for which the workman labours with a sense of degradation and under the mass of which the rich user unwittingly stifles his own life. Art, Morris declares, can only flourish apart from luxury. "The silk curtains in my Lord's drawing-room are no more a matter of art to him than the powder in his footman's hair; the kitchen in a country farmhouse is most commonly a pleasant and homelike place, the parlour dreary and useless."[2]

Morris believed that this change would come, but sometimes the fear beset him that he trusted in a kind of mystical optimism, that the world was going to relapse into indifference to beauty, and so to goodness and peace. "I do not mean to say that our own eyes will look upon it: it may be so far off, as indeed it seems to some, that many would scarcely think it worth while thinking of: but there are some of us who cannot turn our faces to the wall, or sit deedless because our hope seems somewhat

[1] *Hopes and Fears for Art: The Lesser Arts.*   [2] *Ibid.*

dim."[1] The change, he thought, might all go amiss. In *News from Nowhere* he prophesied that the perfect communism would begin by great combinations of trade unions which would win recognition and control through general strikes, oppression, and civil war. But it was possible that the members of the unions, by extorting high wages, might easily develop into a new middle class and leave their poorer fellows worse than before. Morris never doubted that the social revolution would be at first materialistic, but he hoped for a revolt from materialism. Nor did he anticipate that the revolution would be a pleasant thing for the men of culture: "That necessary change may make life poorer for the rich, rougher for the refined, and, it may be, duller for the gifted—for a while; it may even take such forms that not the best or wisest of us shall always be able to know it for a friend, but may at whiles fight it as a foe".[2] Patience and prudence must not be lacking, and courage still less. The men of Kent lie in the little church after the Battle at the Township's End; the mysterious visitor prophesies great and grievous strife, many failures of the wise and much despair of the valiant, backsliding and doubt and contest before the better days come; and John Ball goes forth to his death.[3]

Here we must remember the second great interest of Morris's life, his love for the Scandinavian Sagas, which almost equalled his delight in thirteenth-century England. He visited Iceland in 1871, and in the Preface to the translation of the *Volsunga Saga*, which he completed in conjunction with his teacher, Magnússon, he speaks of the qualities that appealed to him in these ancient stories. "We cannot doubt", he says, "that the reader will be intensely touched by finding, amidst all its wildness and remoteness, such startling realism, such subtilty, such close sympathy

[1] *Hopes and Fears for Art: The Lesser Arts.*
[2] *Ibid.: Making the Best of It.* [3] *A Dream of John Ball*, ch. xii.

with all the passions that may move himself today." But it was the faith behind these qualities which drew Morris's spirit northwards. There is here a nether world of dragons and giants, figures of ruin and evil, and an upper world, peopled by the gods of order and of light. Gradually the lower world gains on the other, one by one the gods die as they accomplish their work and extinguish some dread or misery that has brooded over life, until it comes to a sort of divine Armageddon, when the higher world is engulfed. Then after a time is formed a new heaven and earth, more glorious than before. And whether or not men live again to share in it, it is enough to have helped to make this unnameable glory, to have lived not altogether deedless. These thoughts were often present to Morris. The Norsemen believed that such was the order of things, that the powers of darkness must have their day, yet they lived joyfully in their courage. Courage thus becomes to Morris the dower of great art. "Imaginative work", he says, "is the very blossom of civilisation triumphant and hopeful; it would fain lead men to aspire towards perfection: each hope that it fulfils gives birth to yet another hope: it bears in its bosom the worth and the meaning of life and the counsel to strive to understand everything; to fear nothing and to hate nothing: in a word 'tis the symbol and sacrament of the Courage of the World."[1] For such art Morris craves, whatever the cost of national disgrace, and for this reason the Germanic nations who overthrew the Roman Empire were to him great deliverers.

It is in this simple, practical philosophy of happiness that Morris is in advance of the other artistic socialists of the nineteenth century. Carlyle gives us many plain and practical suggestions, but they remain a number of hints. He cannot apply them to the situation, and he neither shows us how the better world may come nor persuades us that

[1] *Hopes and Fears for Art: Architecture in Civilisation.*

it will be a more desirable place when it does come. He, too, preaches the nobility of labour; but his labour is a grim moral duty; to Morris man's work is impregnated with the joy of variety, creation and beauty. Ruskin feels keenly, but he had no experience of the brute facts of the problem and he leaves us with pictures of fantastic archaism or arguments of forlorn hope. Morris's solution is sane and possible, exampled in his own life and work, within the reach of all. The ideal world he dreams of, and paints for us at times, is at least one in which it would seem very happy to live. It is one we can comprehend; men and women move about in it, sport and make love in attractive simplicity. And Morris never loses his sense of proportion. In one of his noblest passages he says:

When all is gained that we so long for, what shall we do then? That great change that we are working for, each in his own way, will come like other changes, as a thief in the night, and will be with us before we know it; but let us imagine that it has come suddenly and dramatically, acknowledged and hailed by all right minded people; and what shall we do then lest we begin once more to heap up fresh corruption for the woeful labour of ages once again? I say, as we turn away from the flagstaff where the new banner has been just run up, as we depart, our ears yet ringing with the blare of the heralds' trumpets that have proclaimed the new order of things, what shall we turn to then, what must we turn to then? To what else save our work, our daily labour?[1]

He calls men back to the way of happiness which they have missed in the labyrinth of modern life, to honest work and sound taste, to joy in the work of man's hands, to courage and to hope.

[1] *Hopes and Fears for Art: The Art of the People.*

STYLE

Morris has no place in any sequence of English prose, nor is he a great innovator, one who moulds the medium into new and strange forms. In style, Carlyle stands alone among the prose-writers of the nineteenth century, the counterpart of Browning in poetry. His rugged, irregular manner, with its strong tincture of Germanism and its effects of throwing powerful words into high relief, is a thing essentially individual and new in England. Ruskin's work is in the line of periodic prose which comes down to him from Jeremy Taylor and Sir Thomas Browne, through Burke, Gibbon and De Quincey. The style of Morris owes little to any preceding prose dynasty. "I cannot think", he said, "that I ever consciously aimed at any particular style." There are a few hints of Malory, but the general effect is an atmosphere like that of the ballads of Chatterton and Coleridge. It was not exactly the language of the middle ages, which it reproduces so vividly, nor was it an entire copy of the Icelandic, on which much of it was modelled. It was a style and diction entirely individual, yet not ostentatiously so, produced by a more than usually intimate combination of natural gifts and practical interests.

Morris was, from the beginning, well endowed with the qualities of the great stylists. He had always the rare and superb gift of fearless sincerity; his words are the expression of a great mind and a noble temper. All his life, with an intensity not less than that of Carlyle and Ruskin, he preached the doctrine of sincerity. His eloquence is that of a man enthusiastic for truth and beauty, scornful of the false and base, whose earnest desire is to convince others of the truths he has not easily learned. His descriptions of himself, "dreamer of dreams, born out of my due time", "the idle singer of an empty day", can be but whimsically applied to his language and manner. There is no affectation in him; his words are poured forth with a splendid spontaneity. They are unusually free from the tricks of style and are marked by a fine clearness of expression. In spite of his archaic diction, Morris had the gift of saying what he had to say clearly, cogently and persuasively. It is rarely that one has to read a paragraph twice to ascertain its meaning, and the plots of his stories are laid out with a fine technique. Moreover the material of his work is enriched by the multitude of beautiful legends woven into it. Morris began with a vivid imagination; he was unusually sensitive to colour and sound and scenery; and the atmosphere of his pictures is built up with convincing truth of detail. Lastly there is his power of producing musical prose. Morris is among the small group of writers—Southey, Moore, Coleridge, Shelley, Landor—who attain mastery of both poetry and prose. His manner is not that of Ruskin, one which often avoids the definite forms of poetry only by being clad in the apparel of prose, but it is a new style of poetic prose, a form of singular charm which steals upon the soul with music, dies off, and leaves it satisfied.

Though there is a long period of poetry between the early and late prose of Morris, there is a singular unity in his work. He had no period of development, of youthful exuberance and experiment. The boyish articles and romances of the *Oxford and Cambridge Magazine* are the lineal ancestors of his later work. In his lifetime Morris persistently refused to reprint this early prose, but in the imaginative detail of the unknown church,[1] the dramatic descriptions of the dreary forest in *Lindenborg Pool*, the medieval detail of *The Hollow Land*, and the warfare of *Gertha's Lovers*, there is all his characteristic, dreamy, sensitive sympathy with the middle ages. Here his mind is a combination of Anglo-Norman medieval and classical spirit, and the difference between this and the style of his

[1] See p. 45.

second period is due to his deep study of Icelandic literature after 1860. The influence of the Norse spirit and manner, caught so well in the translations, is carried into the texture of the poems of these years: *Love is Enough* is almost purely Northern in style. At the same time he learned much from these old stories in the art of narration, and in *Sigurd* the plot is constructed more carefully, the characters are nearer the heroic strain, and the effect of tragic intensity is increased.

This Icelandic influence on Morris's later prose resulted in a style which has received the ignorant appellation of "Wardour Street English". The following is perhaps a fair example of the type intended:

> The day after, by the rede of the shepherd-folk, they turned up into the hills again, for they had no wish to raise the country against them; and to say sooth, Sir Godrick was somewhat pensive that he found enmity so far off his own land. So they rode the hills for five days, falling in with few folk, and going slowly because of the rough ways. Thereafter they needed victual, and had been fain of better lodging might they get it; and whereas they saw a fair plain well builded and tilled, with good roads through the same, and knew that this was the nighest way to the Wood Masterless, they turned down thither at all adventure, and found no evil haps there, but that the folk were well enough pleased to make their market of the riders, and had neither fear of them nor harboured enmity against them. Thus then they rode for two days, and at the end of the second day entered a good cheaping-town, unfenced save by timber pales. There they abode a whole day, yet warily, since, though there were no waged men-at-arms in the stead, there went about many stout carles, who all bore long whittles, and looked as if their bills and bows had not been far to seek. But no strife betid.   *The Sundering Flood.*

The essential quality of this style is the deliberate use of an archaic diction which is not found in Morris's early prose or poems. His reading of early English gave him a natural preference for the native language, for short words rather than long ones; but his teacher and collaborator, Mr Magnússon, points out that the peculiarity of Morris's diction is that his old-time words are not romance words, but Teutonic. It is not, he says, pseudo Middle-English, but a deliberate attempt to bring about a harmony between the Teutonic element in English and the language of the Icelandic sagas. The strange and unfamiliar diction—*by-men* for *towns' folk*, *shoe-swain* for *page*, *cheaping* for *trading-town*, *stead* for *homestead*,—is confined to particular expressions in the sagas, and they are very limited in number. The important point is that this style, by continual reading in the sagas, became natural to Morris and he used it in prose without effort or affectation. What we take for the shadow is the very substance. Moreover it is a diction picturesque and concrete, a definite enrichment of the language, and it falls at times into strangely beautiful cadences:

"Surely thou goest to thy death." He smiled very sweetly, yet proudly, as he said: "Yea, the road is long, but the end cometh at last. Friend, many a day have I been dying; for my sister, with whom I have played and been merry in the autumn tide about the edges of the stubble-fields; and we gathered the nuts and brambleberries there, and started thence the missel-thrush, and wondered at his voice and thought him big; and the sparrow-hawk wheeled and turned over the hedges and the weasel ran across the path, and the sound of the sheep-bells came to us from the downs as we sat happy on the grass; and she is dead and gone from the earth, for she pined from famine after the years of the great sickness; and my brother was slain in the French wars, and none thanked him for dying save he that stripped him of his gear; and my unwedded wife with whom I dwelt in love after I had taken the tonsure, and all men said she was good and fair, and true she was and lovely; she also is dead and gone from the earth; and why should I abide save for the deeds of the flesh which must be done? Truly, friend, this is but an old tale that men must die; and I will tell thee another, to wit, that they live: and I live now and shall live. Tell me then what shall befall"

A Dream of John Ball.

We cease to complain of Morris's archaism when we contrast such passages with the most modern varieties of literary prose, like the following:

The Mabbot street entrance of nighttown, before which stretches an uncobbled tramsiding set with skeleton tracks, red and green will-o'-the-wisps and danger signals. Rows of flimsy houses with gaping doors. Rare lamps with faint rainbow-fans. Round Rabaiotti's halted ice gondola stunted men and women squabble. They grab wafers between which are wedged lumps of coal and copper snow. Sucking, they scatter slowly. Children. The swancomb of the gondola, highreared, forges on through the murk, white and blue under a lighthouse. Whistles call and answer.
                                        JAMES JOYCE, *Ulysses*.

All Morris's mature prose is not in his archaic style: the lectures, pamphlets and leaflets of the period of social activity are marked by a simpler but not less emphatic form. Morris does not, like Ruskin in his social works, put on the whole armour of controversy. There is none of the banter, extravagance and harlequinade which mingle with the rhetoric, raillery and invective of *Fors Clavigera*; no hurricanes of dictatorial passion, sparkling vituperation, and scintillating humour. Morris's lectures are manly, outspoken attacks in homely English, simple and unadorned. He reasons with conclusiveness and intensity of thought on an amazing variety of practical subjects, and the ideas are held together without effort, giving a definiteness of motive and unity of impression equal to the best of expository writers. The art is not delicate or subtle; it is plain, simple English, rising, when the theme demands exaltation of style, into poignant poetic passages, or lapsing into moods of tender thoughtfulness.

The prose romances fall into three divisions, in the first of which *A Dream of John Ball* and *News from Nowhere* stand apart. They are, for one thing, strongly impregnated with the social feeling of the lectures, and they gain in gravity and serenity as they deal with our own land. All Morris's best qualities of style unite here. The language is simple and pure, and in itself gives the keynote of the stories—the beauty of England when pleasure in work and delight in physical life upon the earth are regarded as the natural state of man. The picturesque is occasionally over-done, and we get glimpses of yeomen's cottages which could only exist in an Earthly Paradise of Morris's own, but there is much compensation. There are virile and pleasant pages, as in "The Battle at the Township's End";[1] startling realism of detail in the vision of medieval England—the Kentish village of *John Ball*[2] and the renovated Thames country of *News from Nowhere*;[3] characteristic delight in the representation of the quiet moods of landscape, the meadows, villages, and streams of olden times; beauty, sanity, and strength in the passages of social argument— the speech of John Ball at the Cross,[4] the convincing sketch of "How the Change Came" in *News from Nowhere*; a stronger hold of characterization, particularly in the figures of John Ball, and the beautiful but tragic Ellen, typical of the New England; a tender and resigned melancholy, frequently reminiscent of Athenian writers; all held to-gether by an attractive simplicity of plan.

The other romances fall into two classes: *The House of the Wolfings* and *The Roots of the Mountains*, which were the two earliest, and the series of fairy-like tales of Morris's last years. The first two are a wonderful mingling of mythology and fact. *The House of the Wolfings*, a story of the conflict between Romans and Goths, is entirely in the atmosphere of the sagas. There is dignity in the treat-ment of the subject, heroic characters like the Hall-Sun, tragic quality in the death of the leader, Thiodolf, and an interest in action and elaboration of battle-incident worthy

| [1] See p. 60. | [2] See p. 49. |
| [3] See p. 212. | [4] See p. 53. |

of Homer. Moreover the prose of the Goth who tells the
tale is of rare beauty, passing in moments of emotional
exaltation into poetry, with a subtle transition that is hardly
noticed. In *The Roots of the Mountains*, the same people,
at a much later date, are in conflict with the Huns, in a
region close to the great Mountains of Southern Europe.
Though the location is vague, the scenery of both books
is vividly and longingly described. The poetic pitch of the
style is much less exalted than that of *The House of the
Wolfings*, but the work gains in human interest. The
emotion and the love motive are on a more normal plane;
they are personal and intimate. But the handling of the
theme is no less forcible, and the delineation of characters,
places, costumes and institutions is vivid and convincing.[1]
It is this more definite historical atmosphere which distinguishes these two books from the later romances.

"Literary inspiration in my father's early life", Miss
May Morris tells us, "came upon him, as it seems to me,
in two very different moods: one produced the nerve-
racked prose tales and poems of bitter loves and clouded
lives; the other led him to deal with a simpler view of life,
simpler passions and motives, though the play is played in
a land on which the enchanted light lies always." In the
latter mood, she says, "he stands as the modern type of
the medieval teller of tales and wonders, and as the years
closed in, the old impulse towards pure romance came over
him afresh, came in a sort of flood of invention, and kept
him busy for all the time that could be spared from the
claims of actual life". This is a fitting description of the
later romances, *The Story of the Glittering Plain*, *The Wood
beyond the World*, *The Well at the World's End*, *The Water
of the Wondrous Isles* and *The Sundering Flood*. They are
vivid narrations of the doings of men and women of various
ages, set in an atmosphere of medieval fairyland. They are

[1] See p. 26.

stories, as Ruskin would have said, of imagination not fancy. They catch the very spirit and language of the time. But if they lived in fairyland, a fairyland which, with a knowledge of the middle ages we can apprehend, the characters are living men and women, speaking a familiar tongue, but in a fresh and invigorated style. The Maid of *The Wood beyond the World* and the woman who has drunk of the well in *The Well at the World's End*, who has to go out of the tale to allow Morris to get down to the human interests, are worthy of places among the famous female characters of fiction. And the stories are told with admirable clearness. Few books so lengthy can hold the interest of the reader to the end as these do by the poetic detail and multitude of beautiful legends. If Morris's fiction were the only prose of his left to us, it would ensure him a place among the literary artists of the world.

SELECTIONS

THE MIDDLE AGES

THE ROOF OF THE WOLFINGS

As to the Roof of the Wolfings,[1] it was a great hall and
goodly, after the fashion of their folk and their day; not
built of stone and lime, but framed of the goodliest trees
of the wild-wood squared with the adze, and betwixt the
framing filled with clay wattled with reeds. Long was that
house, and at one end anigh the gable was the Man's-door,
not so high that a man might stand on the threshold and
his helmcrest clear the lintel; for such was the custom, that
a tall man must bow himself as he came into the hall;
which custom maybe was a memory of the days of onslaught when the foemen were mostly wont to beset the
hall; whereas in the days whereof the tale tells they drew
out into the fields and fought unfenced; unless at whiles
when the odds were over great, and then they drew their
wains about them and were fenced by the wainburg. At
least it was from no niggardry that the door was made
thus low, as might be seen by the fair and manifold carving
of knots and dragons that was wrought above the lintel
of the door for some three foot's space. But a like door
was there anigh the other gable-end, whereby the women
entered, and it was called the Woman's-door.

Near to the house on all sides except toward the wood
were there many bowers and cots round about the penfolds

[1] A typical Gothic tribe living about the foot of the Italian Alps,
at the time of the breaking up of the Roman Empire.

and the byres: and these were booths for the stowage of
wares, and for crafts and smithying that were unhandy to
do in the house; and withal they were the dwelling-places
of the thralls. And the lads and young men often abode
there many days and were cherished there of the thralls
that loved them, since at whiles they shunned the Great
Roof that they might be the freer to come and go at their
pleasure, and deal as they would. Thus was there a clustering
on the slopes and bents betwixt the acres of the Wolfings
and the wild-wood wherein dwelt the wolves.

As to the house within, two rows of pillars went down
it end-long, fashioned of the mightiest trees that might be
found, and each one fairly wrought with base and chapiter,
and wreaths and knots, and fighting men and dragons; so
that it was like a church of later days that has a nave and
aisles; windows there were above the aisles, and a passage
underneath the said windows in their roofs. In the aisles
were the sleeping-places of the Folk, and down the nave
under the crown of the roof were three hearths for the
fires, and above each hearth a luffer or smoke-bearer to
draw the smoke up when the fires were lighted. Forsooth
on a bright winter afternoon it was strange to see the three
columns of smoke going wavering up to the dimness of
the mighty roof, and one maybe smitten athwart by the
sunbeams. As for the timber of the roof itself and its
framing, so exceeding great and high it was, that the tale
tells how that none might see the fashion of it from the
hall-floor unless he were to raise aloft a blazing faggot on
a long pole: since no lack of timber was there among the
men of the Mark.[1]

At the end of the hall anigh the Man's-door was the
dais, and a table thereon set thwartwise of the hall; and
in front of the dais was the noblest and greatest of the

[1] AS. *mearc*, G. *mark*, territory; used for the village land held in
common by the tribe, and so for the village.

hearths; (but of the others one was in the very midmost, and another in the Woman's Chamber) and round about the dais, along the gable-wall, and hung from pillar to pillar were woven cloths pictured with images of ancient tales and the deeds of the Wolfings, and the deeds of the Gods from whence they came. And this was the fairest place of all the house and the best-beloved of the folk, and especially of the older and the mightier men: and there were tales told, and songs sung, especially if they were new: and thereto also were messengers brought if any tidings were abroad: there also would the elders talk together about matters concerning the House or the Mid-mark or the whole Folk of the Markmen.

Yet you must not think that their solemn councils were held there, the folk-motes whereat it must be determined what to do and what to forbear doing; for according as such councils, (which they called Things) were of the House or of the Mid-mark or of the whole Folk, were they held each at the due Thing-steads in the Wood aloof from either acre or meadow, (as was the custom of our forefathers for long after) and at such Things would all the men of the House or the Mid-mark or the Folk be present man by man. And in each of these steads was there a Doom-ring wherein Doom was given by the neighbours chosen, (whom now we call the Jury) in matters between man and man; and no such doom of neighbours was given, and no such voice of the Folk proclaimed in any house or under any roof, nor even as aforesaid on the tilled acres or the depastured meadows. This was the custom of our forefathers, in memory, belike, of the days when as yet there was neither house nor tillage, nor flocks and herds, but the Earth's face only and what freely grew thereon.

But over the dais there hung by chains and pulleys fastened to a tie-beam of the roof high aloft a wondrous lamp fashioned of glass; yet of no such glass as the folk made then and there, but of a fair and clear green like an emerald, and all done with figures and knots in gold, and strange beasts, and a warrior slaying a dragon, and the sun rising on the earth: nor did any tale tell whence this lamp came, but it was held as an ancient and holy thing by all the Markmen, and the kindred of the Wolf had it in charge to keep a light burning in it night and day for ever; and they appointed a maiden of their own kindred to that office; which damsel must needs be unwedded, since no wedded woman dwelling under that roof could be a Wolfing woman, but would needs be of the houses wherein the Wolfings wedded.

This lamp which burned ever was called the Hall-Sun, and the woman who had charge of it, and who was the fairest that might be found was called after it the Hall-Sun also.

At the other end of the hall was the Woman's Chamber, and therein were the looms and other gear for the carding and spinning of wool and the weaving of cloth.

Such was the Roof under which dwelt the kindred of the Wolfings; and the other kindreds of the Mid-mark had roofs like to it; and of these the chiefest were the Elkings, the Vallings, the Alftings, the Beamings, the Galtings, and the Bearings; who bore on their banners the Elk, the Falcon, the Swan, the Tree, the Boar, and the Bear. But other lesser and newer kindreds there were than these: as for the Hartings, they were a kindred of the Upper-mark.

The House of the Wolfings, chap. i.

GOTHS AND ROMANS

THEN Egil clomb the Speech-Hill, and said:
"Ye have heard how the Daylings were appointed to
go to help Thiodolf[1] in driving the folk-spear home to the
heart of the Roman host. So they went; but six hours
thereafter comes one to Otter[2] bidding him send a great
part of the kindreds to him; for that he had had tidings that
a great host of Romans were drawing near the wood-edge,
but were not entered therein, and that fain would he meet
them in the open field.

"So the kindreds drew lots, and the lot fell first to the
Elkings, who are a great company, as ye know; and then
to the Hartings, the Beamings, the Alftings, the Vallings
(also a great company), the Galtings (and they no lesser),
each in their turn; and last of all to the Laxings; and the
Oselings prayed to go with the Elkings, and this Otter
deemed good, whereas a many of them be bowmen.

"All these then to the number of a thousand or more
entered the wood; and I was with them, for in sooth I was
the messenger.

"No delay made we in the wood, nor went we over
warily, trusting to the warding of the wood by Thiodolf;
and there were men with us who knew the paths well,
whereof I was one; so we speedily came through into the
open country.

"Shortly we came upon our folk and the War-duke
lying at the foot of a little hill that went up as a buttress
to a long ridge high above us, whereon we set a watch; and
a little brook came down the dale for our drink.

"Night fell as we came thither; so we slept for a while,
but abode not the morning, and we were afoot (for we

[1] Chief of the Wolfings and chosen leader of the Markmen against
the Romans.
[2] The second leader of the Markmen.

had no horses with us) before the moon grew white. We took the road in good order, albeit our folk-banners we had left behind in the burg; so each kindred raised aloft a shield of its token to be for a banner. So we went forth, and some swift footmen, with Fox, who hath seen the Roman war-garth, had been sent on before to spy out the ways of the foemen.

"Two hours after sunrise cometh one of these, and telleth how he hath seen the Romans, and how that they are but a short mile hence breaking their fast, not looking for any onslaught; 'but', saith he, 'they are on a high ridge whence they can see wide about, and be in no danger of ambush, because the place is bare for the most part, nor is there any cover except here and there down in the dales a few hazels and blackthorn bushes, and the rushes of the becks in the marshy bottoms, wherein a snipe may hide, or a hare, but scarce a man; and note that there is no way up to that ridge but by a spur thereof as bare as my hand; so ye will be well seen as ye wend up thereto'.

"So spake he in my hearing. But Thiodolf bade him lead on to that spur, and old Heriulf, who was standing nigh, laughed merrily and said: 'Yea, lead on, and speedily, lest the day wane and nothing be done save the hunting of snipes'.

"So on we went, and coming to the hither side of that spur beheld those others and Fox with them; and he held in his hand an arrow of the Aliens, and his face was all astir with half-hidden laughter, and he breathed hard, and pointed to the ridge, and somewhat low down on it we saw a steel cap and three spear-heads showing white from out a little hollow in its side, but the men hidden by the hollow: so we knew that Fox had been chased, and that the Romans were warned and wary.

"No delay made the War-duke, but led us up that spur, which was somewhat steep; and as we rose higher we saw a band of men on the ridge, a little way down it, not a many; archers and slingers mostly, who abode us till we were within shot, and then sent a few shots at us, and so fled. But two men were hurt with the sling-plummets, and one, and he not grievously, with an arrow, and not one slain.

"Thus we came up on to the ridge, so that there was nothing between us and the bare heavens; thence we looked south-east and saw the Romans wisely posted on the ridge not far from where it fell down steeply to the north; but on the south, that is to say on their left hands, and all along the ridge past where we were stayed, the ground sloped gently to the south-west for a good way, before it fell, somewhat steeply, into another long dale. Looking north we saw the outer edge of Mirkwood but a little way from us, and we were glad thereof; because ere we left our sleeping-place that morn Thiodolf had sent to Otter another messenger bidding him send yet more men on to us in case we should be hard-pressed in the battle; for he had had a late rumour that the Romans were many. And now when he had looked on the Roman array and noted how wise it was, he sent three swift-foot ones to take stand on a high knoll which we had passed on the way, that they might take heed where our folk came out from the wood and give signal to them by the horn, and lead them to where the battle should be.

"So we stood awhile and breathed us, and handled our weapons some half a furlong from the alien host. They had no earth rampart around them, for that ridge is water-less, and they could not abide there long, but they had pitched sharp pales in front of them and they stood in very good order, as if abiding an onslaught, and moved not when they saw us; for that band of shooters had joined themselves to them already. Taken one with another we deemed them to be more than we were; but their hauberked footmen with the heavy cast-spears not so many as we by a good deal.

"Now we were of mind to fall on them ere they should fall on us; so all such of us as had shot-weapons spread out from our company and went forth a little; and of the others Heriulf stood foremost along with the leaders of the Beamings and the Elkings; but as yet Thiodolf held aback and led the midmost company, as his wont was, and the more part of the Wolfings were with him.

"Thus we ordered ourselves, and waited a little while yet what the Aliens should do; and presently a war-horn blew amongst them, and from each flank of their mailed footmen came forth a many bowmen and slingers and a band of horsemen; and drew within bowshot, the shooters in open array yet wisely, and so fell to on us, and the horsemen hung aback a little as yet.

"Their arrow-shot was of little avail, their bowmen fell fast before ours; but deadly was their sling-shot, and hurt and slew many and some even in our main battle; for they slung round leaden balls and not stones, and they aimed true and shot quick; and the men withal were so light and lithe, never still, but crouching and creeping and bounding here and there, that they were no easier to hit than coneys amidst of the fern, unless they were very nigh.

"Howbeit when this storm had endured awhile, and we moved but little, and not an inch aback, and gave them shot for shot, then was another horn winded from amongst the Aliens; and thereat the bowmen cast down their bows, and the slingers wound their slings about their heads, and they all came on with swords and short spears and feathered darts, running and leaping lustily, making for our flanks, and the horsemen set spurs to their horses and fell on in the very front of our folk like good and valiant men-at-arms.

"That saw Heriulf and his men, and they set up the war-whoop, and ran forth to meet them, axe and sword aloft, terribly yet maybe somewhat unwarily. The archers and slingers never came within sword-stroke of them, but fell away before them on all sides; but the slingers fled not far, but began again with their shot, and slew a many. Then was a horn winded, as if to call back the horsemen, who, if they heard, heeded not, but rode hard on our kindred like valiant warriors who feared not death. Sooth to say, neither were the horses big or good, or the men fit for the work, saving for their hardihood; and their spears were short withal and their bucklers unhandy to wield.

"Now could it be seen how the Goths gave way before them to let them into the trap, and then closed around again, and the axes and edge weapons went awork hewing as in a wood; and Heriulf towered over all the press, and the Wolf's-sister[1] flashed over his head in the summer morning.

"Soon was that storm over, and we saw the Goths tossing up their spears over the slain, and horses running loose and masterless adown over the westward-lying slopes, and a few with their riders still clinging to them. Yet some, sore hurt by seeming, galloping toward the main battle of the Romans.

"Unwarily then fared the children of Tyr[2] that were with Heriulf; for by this time they were well nigh within shot of the spears of those mighty footmen of the Romans: and on their flanks were the slingers, and the bowmen, who had now gotten their bows again; and our bowmen, though they shot well and strong, were too few to quell them; and indeed some of them had cast by their bows to join in Heriulf's storm. Also the lie of the ground was against us, for it sloped up toward the Roman array at first very gently, but afterwards steeply enough to breathe a

---

[1] Heriulf's twibill, or double axe.
[2] In Northern mythology, the god of war and victory.

short-winded man. Also behind them were we of the other kindreds, whom Thiodolf had ordered into the wedge-array; and we were all ready to move forward, so that had they abided somewhat, all had been well and better.

"So did they not, but straightway set up the Victory-whoop and ran forward on the Roman host. And these were so ordered that, as aforesaid, they had before them sharp piles stuck into the earth and pointed against us, as we found afterwards to our cost; and within these piles stood the men some way apart from each other, so as to handle their casting spears, and in three ranks were they ordered and many spears could be cast at once, and if any in the front were slain, his fellow behind him took his place.

"So now the storm of war fell at once upon our folk, and swift and fierce as was their onslaught yet were a many slain and hurt or ever they came to the piles aforesaid. Then saw they death before them and heeded it nought, but tore up the piles and dashed through them, and fell in on those valiant footmen. Short is the tale to tell: wheresoever a sword or spear of the Goths was upraised there were three upon him, and saith Toti of the Beamings, who was hurt and crawled away and yet lives, that on Heriulf there were six at first and then more; and he took no thought of shielding himself, but raised up the Wolf's-sister and hewed as the woodman in the thicket, when night cometh and hunger is on him. There fell Heriulf the Ancient and many a man of the Beamings and the Elkings with him, and many a Roman.

"But amidst the slain and the hurt our wedge-array moved forward slowly now, warily shielded against the plummets and shafts on either side; and when the Romans saw our unbroken array, and Thiodolf the first with Throng-plough[1] naked in his hand, they chased not such

[1] Thiodolf's sword.

men of ours unhurt or little hurt, as drew aback from before them: so these we took amongst us, and when we had gotten all we might, and held a grim face to the foe, we drew aback little by little, still facing them till we were out of shot of their spears, though the shot of the arrows and the sling-plummets ceased not wholly from us. Thus ended Heriulf's Storm".

Then he rested from his speaking for a while, and none said aught, but they gazed on him as if he bore with him a picture of the battle, and many of the women wept silently for Heriulf, and yet more of the younger ones were wounded to the heart when they thought of the young men of the Elkings, and the Beamings, since with both those houses they had affinity; and they lamented the loves that they had lost, and would have asked concerning their own speech-friends had they durst. But they held their peace till the tale was told out to an end.

Then Egil spake again:

"No long while had worn by in Heriulf's Storm, and though men's hearts were nothing daunted, but rather angered by what had befallen, yet would Thiodolf wear away the time somewhat more, since he hoped for succour from the Wain-burg and the Wood; and he would not that any of these Romans should escape us, but would give them all to Tyr, and to be a following to Heriulf the Old and the Great.

"So there we abided a while moving nought, and Thiodolf stood with Throng-plough on his shoulder, unhelmed, unbyrnied, as though he trusted to the kindred for all defence. Nor for their part did the Romans dare to leave their vantage-ground, when they beheld what grim countenance we made them.

"Albeit, when we had thrice made as if we would fall on, and yet they moved not, whereas it trieth a man sorely to stand long before the foeman, and do nought but endure, and whereas many of our bowmen were slain or hurt, and the rest too few to make head against the shot-weapons of the Aliens, then at last we began to draw nearer and a little nearer, not breaking the wedge-array; and at last, just before we were within shot of the cast-spears of their main battle, loud roared our war-horn: then indeed we broke the wedge-array, but orderly as we knew how, spreading out from right and left of the War-duke till we were facing them in a long line: one minute we abode thus, and then ran forth through the spear-storm: and even therewith we heard, as it were, the echo of our own horn, and whoso had time to think betwixt the first of the storm and the handstrokes of the Romans deemed that now would be coming fresh kindreds for our helping.

"Not long endured the spear-rain, so swift we were, neither were we in one throng as betid in Heriulf's Storm, but spread abroad, each trusting in the other that none thought of the backward way.

"Though we had the ground against us we dashed like fresh men at their pales, and were under the weapons at once. Then was the battle grim; they could not thrust us back, nor did we break their array with our first storm; man hewed at man as if there were no foes in the world but they two: sword met sword, and sax met sax; it was thrusting and hewing with point and edge, and no long-shafted weapons were of any avail; there we fought hand to hand and no man knew by eyesight how the battle went two yards from where he fought, and each one put all his heart in the stroke he was then striking, and thought of nothing else.

"Yet at the last we felt that they were faltering and that our work was easier and our hope higher; then we cried our cries and pressed on harder, and in that very nick of time there arose close behind us the roar of the Markmen's horn and the cries of the kindreds answering ours. Then such of the Romans as were not in the very act of smiting, or thrusting, or clinging or shielding, turned and fled, and the whoop of victory rang around us, and the earth shook, and past the place of the slaughter rushed the riders of the Goths; for they had sent horsemen to us, and the paths were grown easier for our much treading of them. Then I beheld Thiodolf, that he had just slain a foe, and clear was the space around him, and he rushed sideways and caught hold of the stirrup of Angantyr of the Bearings, and ran ten strides beside him, and then bounded on afoot swifter than the red horses of the Bearings, urging on the chase, as his wont was.

"But we who were wearier, when we had done our work, stood still between the living and the dead, between the freemen of the Mark and their war-thralls. And in no long while there came back to us Thiodolf and the chasers, and we made a great ring on the field of the slain, and sang the Song of Triumph; and it was the Wolfing Song that we sang.

"'Thus then ended Thiodolf's Storm'".

When he held his peace there was but little noise among the stay-at-homes, for still were they thinking about the deaths of their kindred and their lovers. But Egil spoke again:

"Yet within that ring lay the sorrow of our hearts; for Odin had called a many home, and there lay their bodies; and the mightiest was Heriulf; and the Romans had taken him up from where he fell, and cast him down out of the way, but they had not stripped him, and his hand still gripped the Wolf's-sister. His shield was full of shafts of arrows and spears; his byrny was rent in many places, his helm battered out of form. He had been grievously hurt in the side and in the thigh by cast-spears or ever he came to hand-blows with the Romans, but moreover he had three great wounds from the point of the sax, in the throat, in the side, in the belly, each enough for his bane. His face was yet fair to look on, and we deemed that he had died smiling.

"At his feet lay a young man of the Beamings in a gay green coat, and beside him was the head of another of his House, but his green-clad body lay some yards aloof. There lay of the Elkings a many. Well may ye weep, maidens, for them that loved you. Now fare they to the Gods a goodly company, but a goodly company is with them.

"Seventy and seven of the Sons of the Goths lay dead within the Roman battle, and fifty-four on the slope before it; and to boot there were twenty-four of us slain by the arrows and plummets of the shooters, and a many hurt withal.

"But there were no hurt men inside the Roman array or before it. All were slain outright, for the hurt men either dragged themselves back to our folk, or onward to the Roman ranks, that they might die with one more stroke smitten.

"Now of the Aliens the dead lay in heaps in that place, for grim was the slaughter when the riders of the Bearings and the Wormings fell on the Aliens; and a many of the foemen scorned to flee, but died where they stood, craving no peace; and to few of them was peace given. There fell of the Roman footmen five hundred and eighty and five, and the remnant that fled was but little: but of the slingers and bowmen but eighty and six were slain, for they were there to shoot and not to stand; and they were nimble and fleet of foot, men round of limb, very dark-skinned, but not foul of favour".

Then he said:

"There are men through the dusk a-faring, our speech-
    friends and our kin,
No more shall they crave our helping, nor ask what work
    to win;

They have done their deeds and departed when they had
    holpen the House,
So high their heads are holden, and their hurts are glorious
With the story of strokes stricken, and new weapons to
    be met,
And new scowling of foes' faces, and new curses un-
    known yet.
Lo, they dight the feast in Godhome, and fair are the
    tables spread,
Late come, but well-belovèd is every war-worn head,
And the Godfolk and the Fathers, as these cross the
    tinkling bridge,
Crowd round and crave for stories of the Battle on the
    Ridge".

Therewith he came down from the Speech-Hill and the
women-folk came round about him, and they brought him
to the Hall, and washed him, and gave him meat and drink;
and then would he sleep, for he was weary.

The House of the Wolfings, chap. xv.

THE HALL OF THE RAVAGERS

So Hallblithe[1] went back into the main hall, and the sun
had gotten round now, and was shining into the hall,
through the clerestory windows, so that he saw clearly all
that was therein. And he deemed the hall fairer within
than without; and especially over the shut-beds were many
stories carven in the panelling, and Hallblithe beheld them
gladly. But of one thing he marvelled, that whereas he
was in an island of the strong-thieves of the waters, and
in their very home and chiefest habitation, there were no

---

[1] A young man of the House of the Raven, whose promised bride,
the Hostage, is carried off by the Ravagers. The book describes his
adventures while searching for her.

ships or seas pictured in that imagery, but fair groves and gardens, with flowery grass and fruited trees all about. And there were fair women abiding therein, and lovely young men, and warriors, and strange beasts and many marvels, and the ending of wrath and beginning of pleasure and the crowning of love. And amidst these was pictured oft and again a mighty king with a sword by his side and a crown on his head; and ever was he smiling and joyous, so that Hallblithe, when he looked on him, felt of better heart and smiled back on the carven image.

So while Hallblithe looked on these things, and pondered his case carefully, all alone as he was in that alien hall, he heard a noise without of talking and laughter, and presently the pattering of feet therewith, and then women came into the hall, a score or more, some young, some old, some fair enough, and some hard-featured and uncomely, but all above the stature of the women whom he had seen in his own land.

So he stood amidst the hall-floor and abided them; and they saw him and his shining war-gear, and ceased their talking and laughter, and drew round about him, and gazed at him; but none said aught till an old crone came forth from the ring, and said: "Who art thou, standing under weapons in our hall?"

He knew not what to answer, and held his peace; and she spake again: "Whither wouldest thou, what seekest thou?"

Then answered Hallblithe: "THE HOUSE OF THE UNDYING".[1]

None answered, and the other women all fell away from him at once, and went about their business hither and

[1] The Ravagers are subjects of the Undying King, who rules over the Glittering Plain. One old man of the Ravagers is allowed each year to journey to the Glittering Plain, there to be restored to eternal youth.

thither through the hall. But the old crone took him by the hand, and led him up to the dais, and set him next to the midmost high-seat. Then she made as if she would do off his war-gear, and he would not gainsay her, though he deemed that foes might be anear; for in sooth he trusted in the old carle that he would not bewray him, and moreover he deemed it would be unmanly not to take the risks of the guesting, according to the custom of that country.

So she took his armour and his weapons and bore them off to a shut-bed next to that wherein lay the ancient man, and she laid the gear within it, all save the spear, which she laid on the wall-pins above; and she made signs to him that therein he was to lie; but she spake no word to him. Then she brought him the hand-washing water in a basin of latten, and a goodly towel therewith, and when he had washed she went away from him, but not far.

This while the other women were busy about the hall; some swept the floor down, and when it was swept strawed thereon rushes and handfuls of wild thyme: some went into the buttery and bore forth the boards and the trestles: some went to the chests and brought out the rich hangings, the goodly bankers and dorsars, and did them on the walls: some bore in the stoups and horns and beakers, and some went their ways and came not back a while, for they were busied about the cooking. But whatever they did, none hailed him, or heeded him more than if he had been an image, as he sat there looking on. None save the old woman who brought him the fore-supper, to wit a great horn of mead, and cakes and dried fish.

So was the hall arrayed for the feast very fairly, and Hallblithe sat there while the sun westered and the house grew dim, and dark at last, and they lighted the candles up and down the hall. But a little after these were lit, a great horn was winded close without, and thereafter came the clatter of arms about the door, and exceeding tall weaponed men came in, one score and five, and strode two by two up to the foot of the dais, and stood there in a row. And Hallblithe deemed their war-gear exceeding good; they were all clad in ring-locked byrnies, and had steel helms on their heads with garlands of gold wrought about them and they bore spears in their hands, and white shields hung at their backs. Now came the women to them and unarmed them; and under their armour their raiment was black; but they had gold rings on their arms, and golden collars about their necks. So they strode up to the dais and took their places on the high-seat, not heeding Hallblithe any more than if he were an image of wood. Nevertheless that man sat next to him who was the chieftain of all and sat in the midmost high-seat; and he bore his sheathed sword in his hand and laid it on the board before him, and he was the only man of those chieftains who had a weapon.

But when these were set down there was again a noise without, and there came in a throng of men armed and unarmed who took their places on the endlong benches up and down the hall; with these came women also, who most of them sat amongst the men, but some busied them with the serving: all these men were great of stature, but none so big as the chieftains on the high-seat.

Now came the women in from the kitchen bearing the meat, whereof no little was flesh-meat, and all was of the best. Hallblithe was duly served like the others, but still none spake to him or even looked on him; though amongst themselves they spoke in big, rough voices so that the rafters of the hall rang again.

When they had eaten their fill the women filled round the cups and the horns to them, and those vessels were both great and goodly. But ere they fell to drinking uprose the chieftain who sat furthest from the midmost high-seat on the right and cried a health: "THE TREASURE OF

THE SEA!" Then they all stood up and shouted, women as well as men, and emptied their horns and cups to that health. Then stood up the man furthest on the left and cried out, "Drink a health to the Undying King!" And again all men rose up and shouted ere they drank. Other healths they drank, as the "Cold Keel", the "Windworn Sail", the "Quivering Ash" and the "Furrowed Beach". And the wine and mead flowed like rivers in that hall of the Wild Men. As for Hallblithe, he drank what he would but stood not up, nor raised his cup to his lips when a health was drunk; for he knew not whether these men were his friends or his foes, and he deemed it would be little-minded to drink to their healths, lest he might be drinking death and confusion to his own kindred.

But when men had drunk a while, again a horn blew at the nether end of the hall, and straightway folk arose from the endlong tables, and took away the boards and trestles, and cleared the floor and stood against the wall; then the big chieftain beside Hallblithe arose and cried out: "Now let man dance with maid, and be we merry! Music, strike up!" Then flew the fiddle-bows and twanged the harps, and the carles and queens stood forth on the floor; and all the women were clad in black raiment, albeit embroidered with knots and wreaths of flowers. A while they danced and then suddenly the music fell, and they all went back to their places. Then the chieftain in the high-seat arose and took a horn from his side, and blew a great blast on it that filled the hall; then he cried in a loud voice: "Be we merry! Let the champions come forth!"

Men shouted gleefully thereat, and straightway ran into the hall from out the screens three tall men clad all in black armour with naked swords in their hands, and stood amidst the hall-floor, somewhat on one side, and clashed their swords on their shields and cried out: "Come forth ye Champions of the Raven!"

Then leapt Hallblithe from his seat and set his hand to his left side, but no sword was there; so he sat down again, remembering the warning of the Elder, and none heeded him.

Then there came into the hall slowly and mournfully three men-at-arms, clad and weaponed like the warriors of his folk, with the image of the Raven on their helms and shields. So Hallblithe refrained him, for besides that this seemed like to be a fair battle of three against three, he doubted some snare, and he determined to look on and abide.

So the champions fell to laying on strokes that were no child's play, though Hallblithe doubted if the edges bit, and it was but a little while before the Champions of the Raven fell one after another before the Wild Men, and folk drew them by the heels out into the buttery. Then arose great laughter and jeering, and exceeding wroth was Hallblithe; howbeit he refrained him because he remembered all he had to do. But the three Champions of the Sea strode round the hall, tossing up their swords and catching them as they fell, while the horns blew up behind them.

After a while the hall grew hushed, and the chieftain arose and cried: "Bring in now some sheaves of the harvest we win, we lads of the oar and the arrow!" Then was there a stir at the screen doors, and folk pressed forward to see, and, lo, there came forward a string of women, led in by two weaponed carles; and the women were a score in number, and they were barefoot and their hair hung loose and their gowns were ungirt, and they were chained together wrist to wrist; yet had they gold at arm and neck: there was silence in the hall when they stood amidst of the floor.

Then indeed Hallblithe could not refrain himself, and he leapt from his seat and on to the board, and over it, and ran down the hall, and came to those women and looked them in the face one by one, while no man spake in the hall. But the Hostage was not amongst them; nay forsooth, they none of them favoured of the daughters of his people, though they were comely and fair; so that again Hallblithe doubted if this were aught but a feast-hall play done to anger him; whereas there was but little grief in the faces of those damsels, and more than one of them smiled wantonly in his face as he looked on them.

So he turned about and went back to his seat, having said no word, and behind him arose much mocking and jeering; but it angered him little now; for he remembered the rede of the Elder and how that he had done according to his bidding, so that he deemed the gain was his. So sprang up talk in the hall betwixt man and man, and folk drank about and were merry, till the chieftain arose again and smote the board with the flat of his sword, and cried out in a loud and angry voice, so that all could hear: "Now let there be music and minstrelsy ere we wend bedward!"

Therewith fell the hubbub of voices, and there came forth three men with great harps, and a fourth man with them, who was the minstrel; and the harpers smote their harps so that the roof rang therewith, and the noise, though it was great, was tuneable, and when they had played thus a little while, they abated their loudness somewhat, and the minstrel lifted his voice and sang:

> The land lies black
> With winter's lack,
> The wind blows cold
> Round field and fold;
> All folk are within,
> And but weaving they win.
>
> Where from finger to finger the shuttle flies fast,
> And the eyes of the singer look fain on the cast,
> As he singeth the story of summer undone
> And the barley sheaves hoary ripe under the sun.

Then the maidens stay
The light-hung sley,
And the shuttles bide
By the blue web's side,
While hand in hand
With the carles they stand.

But ere to the measure the fiddles strike up
And the elders yet treasure the last of the cup,
There stand they a-hearkening the blast from the lift,
And e'en night is a-darkening more under the drift.

There safe in the hall
They bless the wall,
And the roof o'er head
Of the valiant stead;
And the hands they praise
Of the olden days.

Then through the storm's roaring the fiddles break out,
And they think not of warring, but cast away doubt,
And, man before maiden, their feet tread the floor,
And their hearts are unladen of all that they bore.

But what winds are o'er-cold
For the heart of the bold?
What seas are o'er-high
For the undoomed to die?
Dark night and dread wind,
But the haven we find.

Then ashore mid the flurry of stone-washing surf!
Cloud-hounds the moon worry, but light lies the turf;
Lo the long dale before us! the lights at the end,
Though the night darkens o'er us, bid whither to wend.

Who beateth the door
By the foot-smitten floor?
What guests are these
From over the seas?

Take shield and sword
For their greeting-word.
Lo, lo, the dance ended! Lo, midst of the hall
The fallow blades blended! Lo, blood on the wall!
Who liveth, who dieth? O men of the sea,
For peace the folk crieth; our masters are ye.

Now the dale lies grey
At the dawn of day;
And fair feet pass
O'er the wind-worn grass;
And they turn back to gaze
On the roof of old days.
Come tread ye the oaken-floored hall of the sea!
Be your hearts yet unbroken; so fair as ye be,
That kings are abiding unwedded to gain
The news of our riding the steeds of the main.

Much shouting and laughter arose at the song's end;
and men sprang up and waved their swords above the cups,
while Hallblithe sat scowling down on their merriment.
Lastly arose the chieftain and called out loudly for the
good-night cup, and it went round and all men drank.
Then the horn blew for bed, and the chieftains went to
their chambers, and the others went to the out-bowers or
laid them down on the hall-floor, and in a little while
none stood upright thereon. So Hallblithe arose, and went
to the shut-bed appointed for him, and laid him down and
slept dreamlessly till the morning.

The Story of the Glittering Plain, chap. vii.

THE SPRING MARKET AT BURGSTEAD

On the morrow betimes in the morning the Westland chapmen, who were now all come, went out from the House of the Face,[1] where they were ever wont to be lodged, and set up their booths adown the street betwixt gate and bridge. Gay was the show; for the booths were tilted over with painted cloths, and the merchants themselves were clad in long gowns of fine cloth; scarlet, and blue, and white, and green, and black, with broidered welts of gold and silver; and their knaves were gaily attired in short coats of divers hues, with silver rings about their arms, and short swords girt to their sides. People began to gather about these chapmen at once when they fell to opening their bales and their packs, and unloading their wains. There had they iron, both in pigs and forged scrap and nails; steel they had, and silver, both in ingots and vessel; pearls from over sea; cinnabar and other colours for staining, such as were not in the mountains: madder from the marshes, and purple of the sea, and scarlet grain from the holm-oaks by its edge, and woad from the deep clayey fields of the plain; silken thread also from the outer ocean, and rare webs of silk, and jars of olive oil, and fine pottery, and scented woods, and sugar of the cane. But gold they had none with them, for that they took there; and for weapons, save a few silver-gilt toys, they had no market.

So presently they fell to chaffer; for the carles brought them little bags of the river-borne gold, so that the weights and scales were at work; others had with them scrolls and tallies to tell the number of the beasts which they had to sell, and the chapmen gave them wares therefor without beholding the beasts; for they wotted that the Dalesmen

[1] *The Roots of the Mountains* deals with the adventures of Face-of-god, son of Iron-face, the Alderman of the Dalesmen and head of the House of the Face.

lied not in chaffer. While the day was yet young withal came the Dalesmen from the mid and nether Dale with their wares and set up their booths; and they had with them flasks and kegs of the wine which they had to sell; and bales of the good winter-woven cloth, some grey, some dyed, and pieces of fine linen; and blades of swords, and knives, and axes of such fashion as the Westland men used; and golden cups and chains, and fair rings set with mountain-blue stones, and copper bowls, and vessels gilt and parcel-gilt, and mountain-blue for staining. There were men of the Shepherds also with such fleeces as they could spare from the daily chaffer with the neighbours. And of the Woodlanders were four carles and a woman with peltries and dressed deer-skins, and a few pieces of well-carven wood-work for bedsteads and chairs and such like.

Soon was the Burg thronged with folk in all its open places, and all were eager and merry, and it could not have been told from their demeanour and countenance that the shadow of a grievous trouble hung over them. True it was that every man of the Dale and the neighbours was girt with his sword, or bore spear or axe or other weapon in his hand, and that most had their bucklers at their backs and their helms on their heads; but this was ever their custom at all meetings of men, not because they dreaded war or were fain of strife, but in token that they were free men, from whom none should take the weapons without battle.

Such were the folk of the land: as for the chapmen, they were well-spoken and courteous, and blithe with the folk, as they well might be, for they had good pennyworths of them; yet they dealt with them without using measureless lying, as behoved folk dealing with simple and proud people; and many was the tale they told of the tidings of the Cities and the Plain.

The Roots of the Mountains, chap. xxxii.

THE WEAPON-SHOW

Now on the day appointed for the Weapon-show came the Folk flock-meal to the great and wide meadow that was cleft by Wildlake as it ran to join the Weltering Water. Early in the morning, even before sunrise, had the wains full of women and children begun to come thither. Also there came little horses and asses from the Shepherd country with one or two or three damsels or children sitting on each, and by wain-side or by beast strode the men of the house, merry and fair in their war-gear. The Woodlanders, moreover, man and woman, elder and swain and young damsel, streamed out of the wood from Carlstead, eager to make the day begin before the sunrise, and end before his setting.

Then all men fell to pitching of tents and tilting over of wains; for the April sun was hot in the Dale, and when he arose the meads were gay with more than the spring flowers; for the tents and the tilts were stained and broidered with many colours, and there was none who had not furbished up his war-gear so that all shone and glittered. And many wore gay surcoats over their armour, and the women were clad in all their bravery, and the Houses mostly of a suit; for one bore blue and another corn-colour, and another green, and another brazil, and so forth, and all gleaming and glowing with broidery of gold and bright hues. But the women of the Shepherds were all clad in white, embroidered with green boughs and red blossoms, and the Woodland women wore dark red kirtles. Moreover, the women had set garlands of flowers on their heads and the helms of the men, and for the most part they were slim of body and tall and light-limbed, and as dainty to look upon as the willow-boughs that waved on the brook-side.

Thither had the goodmen who were guesting the Runaways brought their guests, even now much bettered by their new soft days; and much the poor folk marvelled at all this joyance, and they scarce knew where they were; but to some it brought back to their minds days of joyance before the thralldom and all that they had lost, so that their hearts were heavy a while, till they saw the warriors of the kindreds streaming into the mead and bethought them why they carried steel.

Now by then the sun was fully up there was a great throng on the Portway, and this was the folk of the Burg on their way to the Weapon-mead. The men-at-arms were in the midst of the throng, and at the head of them was the War-leader, with the banner of the Face before him, wherein was done the image of the God with the ray-ringed head. But at the rearward of the warriors went the Alderman and the Burg-wardens, before whom was borne the banner of the Burg pictured with the Gate and its Towers; but in the midst betwixt those two was the banner of the Steer, a white beast on a green field.

So when the Dale-wardens who were down in the meadow heard the music and beheld who were coming, they bade the companies of the Dale and the Shepherds and the Woodlanders who were down there to pitch their banners in a half circle about the ingle of the meadow which was made by the streams of Wildlake and the Weltering Water, and gather to them to be ordered there under their leaders of scores and half-hundreds and hundreds; and even so they did. But the banners of the Dale without the Burg were the Bridge, and the Bull, and the Vine, and the Sickle. And the Shepherds had three banners, to wit Greenbury, and the Fleece, and the Thorn.

As for the Woodlanders, they said that they were abiding their great banner, but it should come in good time; "and meantime", said they, "here are the war-tokens that we shall fight under; for they are good enough banners for us poor men, the remnant of the valiant of time past".

Therewith they showed two great spears, and athwart the one was tied an arrow, its point dipped in blood, its feathers singed with fire; and they said, "This is the banner of the War-shaft".

On the other spear there was nought; but the head thereof was great and long, and they had so burnished the steel that the sun smote out a ray of light from it, so that it might be seen from afar. And they said: "This is the Banner of the Spear! Down yonder where the ravens are gathering ye shall see a banner flying over us. There shall fall many a mother's son".

Smiled the Dale-wardens, and said that these were good banners to fight under; and those that stood nearby shouted for the valiancy of the Woodland Carles.

Now the Dale-wardens went to the entrance from the Portway to the meadow, and there met the Men of the Burg, and two of them went one on either side of the War-leader to show him to his seat, and the others abode till the Alderman and Burg-wardens came up, and then joined themselves to them, and the horns blew up both in the meadow and on the road, and the new-comers went their ways to their appointed places amidst the shouts of the Dalesmen; and the women and children and old men from the Burg followed after, till all the mead was covered with bright raiment and glittering gear, save within the ring of men at the further end.

So came the War-leader to his seat of green turf raised in the ingle aforesaid; and he stood beside it till the Alderman and Wardens had taken their places on a seat behind him raised higher than his; below him on the step of his seat sat the Scrivener with his pen and ink-horn and scroll of parchment, and men had brought him a smooth shield whereon to write.

On the left side of Face-of-god stood the men of the Face all glittering in their arms, and amongst them were

Wolfstone and his two fellows, but Dallach was not yet whole of his hurts. On his right were the folk of the House of the Steer: the leader of that House was an old white-bearded man, grandfather of the Bride, for her father was dead; and who but the Bride herself stood beside him in her glorious war-gear, looking as if she were new come from the City of the Gods, thought most men; but those who beheld her closely deemed that she looked heavy-eyed and haggard, as if she was aweary. Nevertheless, wheresoever she passed, and whosoever looked on her (and all men looked on her), there arose a murmur of praise and love; and the women, and especially the young ones, said how fair her deed was, and how meet she was for it; and some of them were for doing on war-gear and faring to battle with the carles; and of these some were sober and solemn, as was well seen afterwards, and some spake lightly: some also fell to boasting of how they could run and climb and swim and shoot in the bow, and fell to baring of their arms to show how strong they were: and indeed they were no weaklings, though their arms were fair.

There then stood the ring of men, each company under its banner; and beyond them stood the women and children and men unmeet for battle; and beyond them again the tilted wains and the tents.

Now Face-of-god sat him down on the turf-seat with his bright helm on his head and his naked sword across his knees, while the horns blew up loudly, and when they had done, the elder of the Dale-wardens cried out for silence. Then again arose Face-of-god and said:

"Men of the Dale, and ye friends of the Shepherds, and ye, O valiant Woodlanders; we are not assembled here to take counsel, for in three days' time shall the Great Folk-mote be holden, whereat shall be counsel enough. But since I have been appointed your Chief and War-leader, till such time as the Folk-mote shall either yeasay or naysay my leadership, I have sent for you that we may look each other in the face and number our host and behold our weapons, and see if we be meet for battle and for the dealing with a great host of foemen. For now no longer can it be said that we are going to war, but rather that war is on our borders, and we are blended with it; as many have learned to their cost; for some have been slain and some sorely hurt. Therefore I bid you now, all ye that are weaponed, wend past us that the tale of you may be taken. But first let every hundred-leader and half-hundred-leader and score-leader make sure that he hath his tale aright, and give his word to the captain of his banner that he in turn may give it out to the Scrivener with his name and the House and Company that he leadeth".

So he spake and sat him adown; and the horns blew again in token that the companies should go past; and the first that came was Hall-ward of the House of the Steer, and the first of those that went after him was the Bride, going as if she were his son.

So he cried out his name, and the name of his House, and said, "An hundred and a half", and passed forth, his men following him in most goodly array. Each man was girt with a good sword and bore a long heavy spear over his shoulder, save a score who bare bows; and no man lacked a helm, a shield, and a coat of fence.

Then came a goodly man of thirty winters, and stayed before the Scrivener and cried out:

"Write down the House of the Bridge of the Upper Dale at one hundred, and War-well their leader".

And he strode on, and his men followed clad and weaponed like those of the Steer, save that some had axes hanging to their girdles instead of swords; and most bore casting-spears instead of the long spears, and half a score were bowmen.

Then came Fox of Upton leading the men of the Bull

of Mid-dale, an hundred and a half lacking two; very great and tall were his men, and they also bore long spears, and one score and two were bowmen.

Then Folk-beard of Lea, a man well on in years, led on the men of the Vine, an hundred and a half and five men thereto; two score of them bare bow in hand and were girt with sword; the rest bore their swords naked in their right hands, and their shields (which were but small bucklers) hanging at their backs, and in the left hand each bore two casting-spears. With these went two doughty women-at-arms among the bowmen, tall and well-knit, already growing brown with the spring sun, for their work lay among the stocks of the vines on the southward-looking bents.

Next came a tall young man, yellow-haired, with a thin red beard, and gave himself out for Red-beard of the Knolls; he bore his father's name, as the custom of their house was, but the old man, who had long been head man of the House of the Sickle, was late dead in his bed, and the young man had not seen twenty winters. He bade the Scrivener write the tale of the Men of the Sickle at an hundred and a half, and his folk fared past the War-leader joyously, being one half of them bowmen; and fell shooters they were; the other half were girt with long swords, and bore withal long ashen staves armed with great blades curved inwards, which weapon they called heft-sax.

All these bands, as the name and the tale of them was declared, were greeted with loud shouts from their fellows and the bystanders; but now arose a greater shout still, as Stone-face, clad in goodly glittering array, came forth and said:

"I am Stone-face of the House of the Face, and I bring with me two hundreds of men with their best war-gear and weapons: write it down, Scrivener!"

And he strode on like a young man after those who had

gone past, and after him came the tall Hall-face and his men, a gallant sight to see: two score bowmen girt with swords, and the others with naked swords waving aloft, and each bearing two casting-spears in his left hand.

Then came a man of middle age, broad-shouldered, yellow-haired, blue-eyed, of wide and ruddy countenance, and after him a goodly company; and again great was the shout that went up to the heavens; for he said:

"Scrivener, write down that Hound-under-Greenbury, from amongst the dwellers in the hills where the sheep feed, leadeth the men who go under the banner of Greenbury, to the tale of an hundred and four score".

Therewith he passed on, and his men followed, stout, stark, and merry-faced, girt with swords, and bearing over their shoulders long-staved axes, and spears not so long as those which the Dalesmen bore; and they had but a half score of arrow-shot with them.

Next came a young man, blue-eyed also, with hair the colour of flax on the distaff, broad-faced and short-nosed, low of stature, but very strong-built, who cried out in a loud, cheerful voice:

"I am Strongitharm of the Shepherds, and these valiant men are of the Fleece and the Thorn blended together, for so they would have it; and their tale is one hundred and two score and ten".

Then the men of those kindreds went past merry and shouting, and they were clad and weaponed like to them of Greenbury, but had with them a score of bowmen. And all these Shepherd-folk wore over their hauberks white woollen surcoats broidered with green and red.

Now again uprose the cry, and there stood before the War-leader a very tall man of fifty winters, dark-faced and grey-eyed, and he spake slowly and somewhat softly, and said:

"War-leader, this is Red-wolf of the Woodlanders

leading the men who go under the sign of the War-shaft, to the number of an hundred and two".

Then he passed on, and his men after him, tall, lean, and silent amidst the shouting. All these men bare bows, for they were keen hunters; each had at his girdle a little axe and a wood-knife, and some had long swords withal. They wore, everyone of the carles, short green surcoats over their coats of fence; but amongst them were three women who bore like weapons to the men, but were clad in red kirtles under their hauberks, which were of good ring-mail gleaming over them from throat to knee.

Last came another tall man, but young, of twenty-five winters, and spake:

"Scrivener, I am Bears-bane of the Woodlanders, and these that come after me wend under the sign of the Spear, and they are of the tale of one hundred and seven".

And he passed by at once, and his men followed him, clad and weaponed no otherwise than they of the War-shaft, and with them were two women.

Now went all those companies back to their banners, and stood there; and there arose among the bystanders much talk concerning the Weapon-show, and who were the best arrayed of the Houses. And of the old men, some spake of past weapon-shows which they had seen in their youth, and they set them beside this one, and praised and blamed. So it went on a little while till the horns blew again, and once more there was silence. Then arose Face-of-god and said:

"Men of Burgdale, and ye Shepherd-folk, and ye of the Woodland, now shall ye wot how many weaponed men we may bring together for this war. Scrivener, arise and give forth the tale of the companies, as they have been told unto you".

Then the Scrivener stood up on the turf-bench beside

Face-of-god, and spake in a loud voice, reading from his scroll:

"Of the Men of Burgdale there have passed by me nine hundreds and six; of the Shepherds three hundreds and eight and ten; and of the Woodlanders two hundreds and nine; so that all told our men are fourteen hundreds and thirty and three".

Now in those days men reckoned by long hundreds, so that the whole tale of the host was one thousand, five hundred, and four score and one, telling the tale in short hundreds.

When the tale had been given forth and heard, men shouted again, and they rejoiced that they were so many. For it exceeded the reckoning which the Alderman had given out at the Gate-thing. But Face-of-god said:

"Neighbours, we have held our Weapon-show; but now hold you ready, each man, for the Hosting toward very battle; for belike within seven days shall the leaders of hundreds and twenties summon you to be ready in arms to take whatso fortune may befall. Now is sundered the Weapon-show. Be ye as merry to-day as your hearts bid you to be".

Therewith he came down from his seat with the Alderman and the Wardens, and they mingled with the good folk of the Dale and the Shepherds and the Woodlanders, and merry was their converse there. It yet lacked an hour of noon; so presently they fell to and feasted in the green meadow, drinking from wain to wain and from tent to tent; and thereafter they played and sported in the meads, shooting at the butts and wrestling, and trying other masteries. Then they fell to dancing one and all, and so at last to supper on the green grass in great merriment. Nor might you have known from the demeanour of any that any threat of evil overhung the Dale. Nay, so glad were they, and so friendly, that you might rather have

deemed that this was the land whereof tales tell, wherein
people die not, but live for ever, without growing any older
than when they first come thither, unless they be born
into the land itself, and then they grow into fair manhood,
and so abide. In sooth, both the land and the folk were
fair enough to be that land and the folk thereof.

But a little after sunset they sundered, and some fared
home; but many of them abode in the tents and tilted
wains, because the morrow was the first day of the Spring
Market: and already were some of the Westland chapmen
come; yea, two of them were with the bystanders in the
meadow; and more were looked for ere the night was far
spent.   *The Roots of the Mountains*, chap. xxxi.

THE OPENING OF THE FOLK-MOTE

Amidst the clamour uprose the Alderman; for it was
clear to all men that the Folk-mote should be holden at
once, and the matters of the War, and the Fellowship, and
the choosing of the War-leader, speedily dealt with. So
the Alderman fell to hallowing-in the Folk-mote: he went
up to the Altar of the Gods, and took the Gold-ring off
it, and did it on his arm; then he drew his sword and waved
it toward the four airts, and spake; and the noise and
shouting fell, and there was silence but for him:

"Herewith I hallow-in this Folk-mote of the Men of the
Dale and the Sheepcotes and the Woodland, in the name
of the Warrior and the Earth-god and the Fathers of the
kindreds. Now let not the peace of the Mote be broken.
Let not man rise against man, or bear blade or hand, or
stick or stone against any. If any man break the Peace
of the Holy Mote, let him be a man accursed, a wild-beast
in the Holy Places; an outcast from home and hearth,
from bed and board, from mead and acre; not to be holpen

3-2

with bread, nor flesh, nor wine; nor flax, nor wool, nor any cloth; nor with sword, nor shield, nor axe, nor plough-share; nor with horse, nor ox, nor ass; with no saddle-beast nor draught-beast; nor with wain, nor boat, nor way-leading; nor with fire nor water; nor with any world's wealth. Thus let him who hath cast out man be cast out by man. Now is hallowed-in the Folk-mote of the Men of the Dale and the Sheepcotes and the Wood-lands".

Therewith he waved his sword again toward the four airts, and went and sat down in his place. But presently he arose again, and said:

"Now if man hath aught to say against man, and claimeth boot of any, or would lay guilt on any man's head, let him come forth and declare it; and the judges shall be named, and the case shall be tried this afternoon or to-morrow. Yet first I shall tell you that I, the Alder-man of the Dalesmen, doomed one Iron-face[1] of the House of the Face to pay a double fine, for that he drew a sword at the Gate-thing of Burgstead with the intent to break the peace thereof. Thou, Green-sleeve, bring forth the peace-breaker's fine, that Iron-face may lay the same on the Altar".

Then came forth a man from the men of the Face bearing a bag, and he brought it to Iron-face, who went up to the Altar and poured forth weighed gold from the bag thereon, and said:

"Warden of the Dale, come thou and weigh it!"

"Nay," quoth the Warden, "it needeth not, no man here doubteth thee, Alderman Iron-face."

A murmur of yeasay went up, and none had a word to say against the Alderman, but they praised him rather: also men were eager to hear of the war, and the fellowship, and

[1] The Alderman himself, who drew his sword in anger against his son, so breaking the Peace of the Holy Thing.

to be done with these petty matters. Then the Alderman
rose again and said:

"Hath any man a grief against any other of the Kindreds
of the Dale, or the Sheepcotes, or the Woodlands?"

None answered or stirred; so after he had waited a
while, he said:

"Is there any who hath any guilt to lay against a
Stranger, an Outlander, being such a man as he deems we
can come at?"

Thereat was a stir amongst the Men of the Fleece of
the Shepherds, and their ranks opened, and there came
forth an ill-favoured lean old man, long-nebbed, blear-
eyed, and bent, girt with a rusty old sword, but not otherwise armed. And all men knew Penny-thumb, who had
been ransacked last autumn. As he came forth, it seemed
as if his neighbours had been trying to hold him back; but
a stout, broad-shouldered man, black-haired and red-
bearded, made way for the old man, and led him out of
the throng, and stood by him; and this man was well
armed at all points, and looked a doughty carle. He stood
side by side with Penny-thumb, right in front of the men
of his house, and looked about him at first somewhat un-
easily, as though he were ashamed of his fellow; but
though many smiled, none laughed aloud; and they for-
bore, partly because they knew the man to be a good man,
partly because of the solemn tide of the Folk-mote, and
partly in sooth because they wished all this to be over, and
were as men who had no time for empty mirth.

Then said the Alderman: "What wouldest thou, Penny-
thumb, and thou, Bristler, son of Brightling?"

Then Penny-thumb began to speak in a high squeaky
voice: "Alderman, and Lord of the Folk!"—But therewithal Bristler pulled him back, and said:

"I am the man who hath taken this quarrel upon me,
and have sworn upon the Holy Boar to carry this feud

through; and we deem, Alderman, that if they who slew Rusty and ransacked Penny-thumb be not known now, yet they soon may be".

As he spake, came forth those three men of the Shepherds and the two Dalesmen who had sworn with him on the Holy Boar. Then up stood Folk-might, and came forth into the field, and said:

"Bristler, son of Brightling, and ye other good men and true, it is but sooth that the ransackers and the slayer may soon be known; and here I declare them unto you: I it was and none other who slew Rusty; and I was the leader of those who ransacked Penny-thumb, and cowed Harts-bane of Greentofts. As for the slaying of Rusty, I slew him because he chased me, and would not forbear, so that I must either slay or be slain, as hath befallen me erewhile, and will befall again, methinks. As for the ransacking of Penny-thumb, I needed the goods that I took, and he needed them not, since he neither used them, nor gave them away, and, they being gone, he hath lived no worser than aforetime. Now I say, that if ye will take the outlawry off me, which, as I hear, ye laid upon me, not knowing me, then will I handsel self-doom to thee, Bristler, if thou wilt bear thy grief to purse, and I will pay thee what thou wilt out of hand; or if perchance thou wilt call me to Holm, thither will I go, if thou and I come unslain out of this war. As to the ransacking and cowing of Harts-bane, I say that I am sackless therein, because the man is but a ruffler and a man of violence, and hath cowed many men of the Dale; and if he gainsay me, then do I call him to the Holm after this war is over; either him or any man who will take his place before my sword".

Then he held his peace, and man spake to man, and a murmur arose, as they said for the more part that it was a fair and manly offer. But Bristler called his fellows and Penny-thumb to him, and they spake together; and sometimes Penny-thumb's shrill squeak was heard above the deep-voiced talk of the others; for he was a man that harboured malice. But at last Bristler spake out and said:

"Tall man, we know that thou art a chieftain and of good will to the men of the Dale and their friends, and that want drave thee to the ransacking, and need to the manslaying, and neither the living nor the dead to whom thou art guilty are to be called good men; therefore will I bring the matter to purse, if thou wilt handsel me self-doom".

"Yea, even so let it be", quoth Folk-might; and stepped forward and took Bristler by the hand, and handselled him self-doom. Then said Bristler:

"Though Rusty was no good man, and though he followed thee to slay thee, yet was he in his right therein, since he was following up his goodman's gear; therefore shalt thou pay a full blood-wite for him, that is to say, the worth of three hundreds in weed-stuff in whatso goods thou wilt. As for the ransacking of Penny-thumb, he shall deem himself well paid if thou give him four hundreds in weed-stuff for that which thou didst borrow of him".

Then Penny-thumb set up his squeak again, but no man hearkened to him, and each man said to his neighbour that it was well doomed of Bristler, and neither too much nor too little. But Folk-might bade Wood-wont to bring thither to him that which he had borne to the Mote; and he brought forth a big sack, and Folk-might emptied it on the earth, and lo! the silver rings of the slain felons, and they lay in a heap on the green field, and they were the best of silver. Then the Elder of the Dale-wardens weighed out from the heap the blood-wite for Rusty, according to the due measure of the hundred in weed-stuff, and delivered it unto Bristler. And Folk-might said:

"Draw nigh now, Penny-thumb, and take what thou

wilt of this gear, which I need not, and grudge not at me henceforward".

But Penny-thumb was afraid, and abode where he was; and Bristler laughed, and said: "Take it, goodman, take it; spare not other men's goods as thou dost thine own".

And Folk-might stood by, smiling faintly: so Penny-thumb plucked up a heart, and drew nigh trembling, and took what he durst from that heap; and all that stood by said that he had gotten a full double of what had been awarded to him. But as for him, he went his ways straight from the Mote-stead, and made no stay till he had gotten him home, and laid the silver up in a strong coffer; and thereafter he bewailed him sorely that he had not taken the double of that which he took, since none would have said him nay.

When he was gone, the Alderman arose and said:

"Now, since the fines have been paid duly and freely, according to the dooming of Bristler, take we off the outlawry from Folk-might and his fellows, and account them to be sackless before us".

Then he called for other cases; but no man had aught more to bring forward against any man, either of the Kindreds or the Strangers.

The Roots of the Mountains, chap. xxxviii.

THE MAIDEN WARD

So wore the days toward Midsummer, when the wheat was getting past the blossoming, and the grass in the mown fields was growing deep green again after the shearing of the scythe; when the leaves were most and biggest; when the roses were beginning to fall; when the apples were reddening, and the skins of the grape-berries gathering bloom. High aloft floated the light clouds over the Dale;

deep blue showed the distant fells below the ice-mountains; the waters dwindled; all things sought the shadow by day-time, and the twilight of even and the twilight of dawn were but sundered by three hours of half-dark night.

So in the bright forenoon were seventeen brides as-sembled in the Gate of Burgstead (but of the rest of the Dale were twenty and three looked for), and with these was the Sun-beam, her face as calm as the mountain lake under a summer sunset, while of the others many were restless, and babbling like April throstles; and not a few talked to her eagerly, and in their restless love of her dragged her about hither and thither.

No men were to be seen that morning; for such was the custom, that the carles either departed to the fields and the acres, or abode within doors on the morn of the day of the Maiden Ward; but there was a throng of women about the Gate and down the street of Burgstead, and it may well be deemed that they kept not silence that hour.

So fared the Brides of Burgstead to the place of the Maiden Ward on the causeway, whereto were come already the other brides from steads up and down the Dale, or were even then close at hand on the way; and among them were Long-coat and her two fellows, with whom Face-of-god had held converse on that morning whereon he had fol-lowed his fate to the Mountain.

There then were they gathered under the cliff-wall of the Portway; and by the road-side had their grooms built them up bowers of green boughs to shelter them from the sun's burning, which were thatched with bulrushes, and decked with garlands of the fairest flowers of the meadows and the gardens.

Forsooth they were a lovely sight to look on, for no fairer women might be seen in the world; and the eldest of them was scant of five and twenty winters. Every maiden was clad in as goodly raiment as she might compass;

their sleeves and gown-hems and girdles, yea, their very shoes and sandals were embroidered so fairly and closely, that as they shifted in the sun they changed colour like the king-fisher shooting from shadow to sunshine. According to due custom every maiden bore some weapon. A few had bows in their hands and quivers at their backs; some had nought but a sword girt to their sides; some bore slender-shafted spears, so as not to overburden their shapely hands; but to some it seemed a merry game to carry long and heavy thrust-spears, or to bear great war-axes over their shoulders. Most had their flowing hair coifed with bright helms; some had burdened their arms with shields; some bore steel hauberks over their linen smocks: almost all had some piece of war-gear on their bodies; and one, to wit, Steed-linden of the Sickle, a tall and fair damsel, was so arrayed that no garment could be seen on her but bright steel war-gear.

As for the Sun-beam, she was clad in a white kirtle embroidered from throat to hem with work of green boughs and flowers of the goodliest fashion, and a garland of roses on her head. Dale-warden himself was girt to her side by a girdle fair-wrought of golden wire, and she bore no other weapon or war-gear; and she let him lie quiet in his scabbard, nor touched the hilts once; whereas some of the other damsels would be ever drawing their swords out and thrusting them back. But all noted that goodly weapon, the yoke-fellow of so many great deeds.

There then on the Portway, between the water and the rock-wall, rose up plenteous and gleeful talk of clear voices shrill and soft; and whiles the maidens sang, and whiles they told tales of old days, and whiles they joined hands and danced together on the sweet summer dust of the high-way. Then they mostly grew aweary, and sat down on the banks of the road or under their leafy bowers.

Noon came, and therewithal goodwives of the neighbouring Dale, who brought them meat and drink, and fruit and fresh flowers from the teeming gardens; and thereafter for a while they nursed their joy in their bosoms, and spake but little and softly while the day was at its hottest in the early afternoon.

Then came out of Burgstead men making semblance of chapmen with a wain bearing wares, and they made as though they were wending down the Portway westward to go out of the Dale. Then arose the weaponed maidens and barred the way to them, and turned them back amidst fresh-springing merriment.

Again in a while, when the sun was westering and the shadows growing long, came herdsmen from down the Dale driving neat, and making as though they would pass by into Burgstead, but to them also did the maidens gainsay the road, so that needs must they turn back amidst laughter and mockery, they themselves also laughing and mocking.

And so at last, when the maidens had been all alone a while, and it was now hard on sunset, they drew together and stood in a ring, and fell to singing; and one Gold-may of the House of the Bridge, a most sweet singer, stood amidst their ring and led them. And this is somewhat of the meaning of their words:

The sun will not tarry; now changeth the light,
Fail the colours that marry the Day to the Night.

Amid the sun's burning bright weapons we bore,
For this eve of our earning comes once and no more.

For to-day hath no brother in yesterday's tide,
And to-morrow no other alike it doth hide.

This day is the token of oath and behest
That ne'er shall be broken through ill days and best.

Here the troth hath been given, the oath hath been done,
To the Folk that hath thriven well under the sun.

And the gifts of its giving our troth-day shall win
Are the Dale for our living and dear days therein.

O Sun, now thou wanest! yet come back and see
Amidst all that thou gainest how gainful are we.

O witness of sorrow wide over the earth,
Rise up on the morrow to look on our mirth!

Thy blooms art thou bringing back ever for men,
And thy birds are a-singing each summer again.

But to men little-hearted what winter is worse
Than thy summers departed that bore them the curse?

And e'en such art thou knowing where thriveth the year,
And good is all growing save thralldom and fear.

Nought such be our lovers' hearts drawing anigh,
While yet thy light hovers aloft in the sky.

Lo the seeker, the finder of Death in the Blade!
What lips shall be kinder on lips of mine laid?

Lo he that hath driven back tribes of the South!
Sweet-breathed is thine even, but sweeter his mouth.

Come back from the sea then, O sun! come aback,
Look adown, look on me then, and ask what I lack!

Come many a morrow to gaze on the Dale,
And if e'er thou seest sorrow remember its tale!

For 'twill be of a story to tell how men died
In the garnering of glory that no man may hide.

O sun sinking under! O fragrance of earth!
O heart! O the wonder whence longing has birth!

So they sang, and the sun sank indeed; and amidst their
singing the eve was still about them, though there came a

happy murmur from the face of the meadows and the houses of the Thorp aloof. But as their song fell they heard the sound of footsteps a many on the road; so they turned and stood with beating hearts in such order as when a band of the valiant draw together to meet many foes coming on them from all sides, and they stand back to back to face all comers. And even therewith, their raiment gleaming amidst the gathering dusk, came on them the young men of the Dale newly delivered from the grief of war.

Then in very deed the fierce mouths of the raisers of the war-shout were kind on the faces of tender maidens. Then went spear and axe and helm and shield clattering to the earth, as the arms of the new-comers went round about the bodies of the Brides, weary with the long day of sunshine, and glee and loving speech, and the maidens suffered the young men to lead them whither they would, and twilight began to draw round about them as the Maiden Band was sundered.

The Roots of the Mountains, chap. lviii.

THE UNKNOWN CHURCH

I was the master-mason of a church that was built more than six hundred years ago; it is now two hundred years since that church vanished from the face of the earth; it was destroyed utterly,—no fragment of it was left; not even the great pillars that bore up the tower at the cross, where the choir used to join the nave. No one knows now even where it stood, only in this very autumn-tide, if you knew the place, you would see the heaps made by the earth-covered ruins heaving the yellow corn into glorious waves, so that the place where my church used to be is as beautiful now as when it stood in all its splendour. I do not remember very much about the land where my

church was; I have quite forgotten the name of it, but
I know it was very beautiful, and even now, while I am
thinking of it, comes a flood of old memories, and I almost
seem to see it again...that old beautiful land! Only dimly
do I see it in spring and summer and winter, but I see it
in autumn-tide clearly now; yes, clearer, clearer, oh! so
bright and glorious! yet it was beautiful too in spring,
when the brown earth began to grow green: beautiful in
summer, when the blue sky looked so much bluer, if you
could hem a piece of it in between the new white carving;
beautiful in the solemn starry nights, so solemn that it
almost reached agony—the awe and joy one had in their
great beauty. But of all these beautiful times, I remember
the whole only of autumn-tide; the others come in bits to
me; I can think only of parts of them but of all autumn;
and of all days and nights in autumn, I remember one more
particularly. That autumn day the church was nearly
finished, and the monks, for whom we were building the
church, and the people, who lived in the town hard by,
crowded round us often-times to watch us carving.

Now the great Church, and the buildings of the Abbey
where the monks lived, were about three miles from the
town, and the town stood on a hill overlooking the rich
autumn country: it was girt about with great walls that
had overhanging battlements, and towers at certain places
all along the walls, and often we could see from the church
yard or the Abbey garden the flash of helmets and spears,
and the dim shadowy waving of banners, as the knights
and lords and men-at-arms passed to and fro along the
battlements; and we could see too in the town the three
spires of the three churches; and the spire of the Cathedral,
which was the tallest of the three, was gilt all over with
gold, and always at night-time a great lamp shone from it
that hung in the spire midway between the roof of the
church and the cross at the top of the spire.

The Abbey where we built the Church was not girt by stone walls, but by a circle of poplar trees, and whenever a wind passed over them, were it ever so little a breath, it set them all a-ripple; and when the wind was high, they bowed and swayed very low, and the wind, as it lifted the leaves, and showed their silvery white sides, or as again in the lulls of it, it let them drop, kept on changing the trees from green to white, and white to green; moreover, through the boughs and trunks of the poplars we caught glimpses of the great golden corn sea, waving, waving, waving for leagues and leagues; and among the corn grew burning scarlet poppies, and blue corn-flowers; and the corn-flowers were so blue, that they gleamed, and seemed to burn with a steady light, as they grew beside the poppies among the gold of the wheat. Through the corn sea ran a blue river, and always green meadows and lines of tall poplars followed its windings.

The old Church had been burned, and that was the reason why the monks caused me to build the new one; the buildings of the Abbey were built at the same time as the burned-down Church, more than a hundred years before I was born, and they were on the north side of the Church, and joined to it by a cloister of round arches, and in the midst of the cloister was a lawn, and in the midst of that lawn, a fountain of marble, carved round about with flowers and strange beasts; and at the edge of the lawn, near the round arches, were a great many sun-flowers that were all in blossom on that autumn day; and up many of the pillars of the cloister crept passion-flowers and roses. Then farther from the Church, and past the cloister and its buildings, were many detached buildings, and a great garden round them, all within the circle of the poplar trees; in the garden were trellises covered over with roses, and convolvulus, and the great-leaved fiery nasturtium; and specially all along by the poplar trees were there trellises, but on these grew nothing but deep crimson roses; the hollyhocks too were all out in blossom at that time, great spires of pink, and orange, and red, and white, with their soft, downy leaves. I said that nothing grew on the trellises by the poplars but crimson roses, but I was not quite right, for in many places the wild flowers had crept into the garden from without; lush green briony, with green-white blossoms, that grows so fast, one could almost think that we see it grow, and deadly nightshade, La bella donna, oh! so beautiful; red berry, and purple, yellow-spiked flower, and deadly, cruel-looking, dark green leaf, all growing together in the glorious days of early autumn. And in the midst of the great garden was a conduit, with its sides carved with histories from the Bible, and there was on it too, as on the fountain in the cloister, much carving of flowers and strange beasts.

Now the Church itself was surrounded on every side but the north by the cemetery, and there were many graves there, both of monks and of laymen, and often the friends of those whose bodies lay there, had planted flowers about the graves of those they loved. I remember one such particularly, for at the head of it was a cross of carved wood, and at the foot of it, facing the cross, three tall sun-flowers; then in the midst of the cemetery was a cross of stone, carved on one side with the Crucifixion of our Lord Jesus Christ, and on the other with Our Lady holding the Divine Child.

The Story of the Unknown Church.

THE CHURCHES OF NORTH FRANCE

I will say here that I think those same churches of North France the grandest, the most beautiful, the kindest and most loving of all the buildings that the earth has ever borne; and thinking of their passed-away builders I can see through them very faintly, dimly, some little of the mediaeval times, else dead and gone from me for ever; voiceless for ever. And those same builders, still surely living, still real men and capable of receiving love, I love no less than the great men, poets and painters and such like, who are on earth now; no less than my breathing friends whom I can see looking kindly on me now. Ah, do I not love them with just cause who certainly loved me, thinking of me sometimes between the strokes of their chisels? And for this love of all men that they had, and moreover for the great love of God which they certainly had too; for this, and for this work of theirs, the upraising of the great Cathedral front, with its beating heart of the thoughts of men wrought into the leaves and flowers of the fair earth, wrought into the faces of good men and true, fighters against the wrong, of angels who upheld them, of God who rules all things; wrought through the lapse of years and years and years by the dint of chisel and stroke of hammer into stories of life and death, the second life, the second death, stories of God's dealing in love and wrath with the nations of the earth, stories of the faith and love of man that dies not: for their love, and the deeds through which it worked, I think they will not lose their reward.

Shadows of Amiens.

A KENTISH VILLAGE

I GOT up and rubbed my eyes and looked about me, and the landscape seemed unfamiliar to me, though it was, as to the lie of the land, an ordinary English low-country, swelling into rising ground here and there. The road was narrow, and I was convinced that it was a piece of Roman road from its straightness. Copses were scattered over the country, and there were signs of two or three villages and

hamlets in sight besides the one near me, between which
and me there was some orchard-land, where the early
apples were beginning to redden on the trees. Also, just
on the other side of the road and the ditch which ran along
it, was a small close of about a quarter of an acre, neatly
hedged with quick, which was nearly full of white poppies,
and, as far as I could see for the hedge, had also a good
few rose-bushes of the bright-red nearly single kind, which
I had heard are the ones from which rose-water used to
be distilled. Otherwise the land was quite unhedged, but all
under tillage of various kinds, mostly in small strips. From
the other side of a copse not far off rose a tall spire white
and brand-new, but at once bold in outline and unaffectedly
graceful and also distinctly English in character. This,
together with the unhedged tillage and a certain unwonted
trimness and handiness about the enclosures of the garden
and orchards, puzzled me for a minute or two, as I did not
understand, new as the spire was, how it could have been
designed by a modern architect; and I was of course used
to the hedged tillage and tumble-down bankrupt-looking
surroundings of our modern agriculture. So that the garden-
like neatness and trimness of everything surprised me.
But after a minute or two that surprise left me entirely;
and if what I saw and heard afterwards seems strange to
you, remember that it did not seem strange to me at the
time, except where now and again I shall tell you of it.
Also, once for all, if I were to give you the very words
of those who spoke to me you would scarcely understand
them, although their language was English too, and at the
time I could understand them at once.

Well, as I stretched myself and turned my face toward
the village, I heard horse-hoofs on the road, and presently
a man and horse showed on the other end of the stretch
of road and drew near at a swinging trot with plenty of
clash of metal. The man soon came up to me, but paid

me no more heed than throwing me a nod. He was clad in armour of mingled steel and leather, a sword girt to his side, and over his shoulder a long-handled bill-hook. His armour was fantastic in form and well wrought; but by this time I was quite used to the strangeness of him, and merely muttered to myself, "He is coming to summon the squire to the leet"; so I turned toward the village in good earnest. Nor, again, was I surprised at my own garments, although I might well have been from their unwontedness. I was dressed in a black cloth gown reaching to my ankles, neatly embroidered about the collar and cuffs, with wide sleeves gathered in at the wrists; a hood with a sort of bag hanging down from it was on my head, a broad red leather girdle round my waist, on one side of which hung a pouch embroidered very prettily and a case made of hard leather chased with a hunting scene, which I knew to be a pen and ink case; on the other side a small sheath-knife, only an arm in case of dire necessity.

Well, I came into the village, where I did not see (nor by this time expected to see) a single modern building, although many of them were nearly new, notably the church, which was large, and quite ravished my heart with its extreme beauty, elegance, and fitness. The chancel of this was so new that the dust of the stone still lay white on the midsummer grass beneath the carvings of the windows. The houses were almost all built of oak frame-work filled with cob or plaster well whitewashed; though some had their lower stories of rubble-stone, with their windows and doors of well-moulded free-stone. There was much curious and inventive carving about most of them; and though some were old and much worn, there was the same look of deftness and trimness, and even beauty, about every detail in them which I noticed before in the field-work. They were all roofed with oak shingles, mostly grown as grey as stone; but one was so newly built that its roof was yet pale and yellow. This was a corner house, and the corner post of it had a carved niche wherein stood a gaily painted figure holding an anchor—St Clement[1] to wit, as the dweller in the house was a blacksmith. Half a stone's throw from the east end of the churchyard wall was a tall cross of stone, new like the church, the head beautifully carved with a crucifix amidst leafage. It stood on a set of wide stone steps, octagonal in shape, where three roads from other villages met and formed a wide open space on which a thousand people or more could stand together with no great crowding.

All this I saw, and also that there was a goodish many people about, women and children, and a few old men at the doors, many of them somewhat gaily clad, and that men were coming into the village street by the other end to that by which I had entered, by twos and threes, most of them carrying what I could see were bows in cases of linen yellow with wax or oil; they had quivers at their backs, and most of them a short sword by their left side, and a pouch and knife on the right; they were mostly dressed in red or brightish green or blue cloth jerkins, with a hood on the head generally of another colour. As they came nearer I saw that the cloth of their garments was somewhat coarse, but stout and serviceable. I knew, somehow, that they had been shooting at the butts, and, indeed, I could still hear a noise of men thereabout, and even now and again when the wind set from that quarter the twang of the bowstring and the plump of the shaft in the target.

I leaned against the churchyard wall and watched these men, some of whom went straight into their houses and some loitered about still; they were rough-looking fellows,

---

[1] The patron saint of blacksmiths was St Peter, not St Clement, who was the patron of tanners. St Clement's symbol was an anchor, as he was said to have been martyred by being thrown into the sea with an anchor round his neck.

tall and stout, very black some of them, and some red-
haired, but most had hair burnt by the sun into the colour
of tow; and, indeed, they were all burned and tanned and
freckled variously. Their arms and buckles and belts and
the finishings and hems of their garments were all what
we should now call beautiful, rough as the men were;
nor in their speech was any of that drawling snarl or thick
vulgarity which one is used to hear from labourers in
civilization; not that they talked like gentlemen either, but
full and round and bold, and they were merry and good-
tempered enough; I could see that, though I felt shy and
timid amongst them.   *A Dream of John Ball*, chap. i.

JOHN BALL'S SPEECH AT THE CROSS

WHILE I pondered all these things, and how men fight
and lose the battle, and the thing that they fought for
comes about in spite of their defeat, and when it comes
turns out not to be what they meant, and other men have
to fight for what they meant under another name—while
I pondered all this, John Ball[1] began to speak again in the
same soft and clear voice with which he had left off.

"Good fellows, it was your fellowship and your kindness
that took me out of the archbishop's prison three days
agone, though God wot ye had nought to gain by it save
outlawry and the gallows; yet lacked I not your fellowship
before ye drew near me in the body, and when between
me and Canterbury street was yet a strong wall, and the
turnkeys and sergeants and bailiffs.

[1] An English priest who took a prominent part in Wat Tyler's
rebellion in 1381. He made himself popular by preaching the equality
of all classes. He was several times committed to the Archbishop's
prison at Maidstone, and was set free by the insurgents in June, 1381.
After the death of Wat Tyler, John Ball was executed at St Albans
in July, 1381.

"For hearken, my friends and helpers; many days ago, when April was yet young, I lay there, and the heart that I had strung up to bear all things because of the fellowship of men and the blessed saints and the angels and those that are, and those that are to be, this heart, that I had strung up like a strong bow, fell into feebleness, so that I lay there a-longing for the green fields and white-thorn bushes and the lark singing over the corn, and the talk of good fellows round the ale-house bench, and the babble of the little children, and the team on the road and the beasts afield, and all the life of earth; and I alone all the while, near my foes and afar from my friends, mocked and flouted and starved with cold and hunger; and so weak was my heart that though I longed for all these things yet I saw them not, nor knew them but as names; and I longed so sore to be gone that I chided myself that I had once done well; and I said to myself:

"Forsooth, hadst thou kept thy tongue between thy teeth thou mightest have been something, if it had been but a parson of a town, and comfortable to many a poor man; and then mightest thou have clad here and there the naked back, and filled the empty belly, and holpen many, and men would have spoken well of thee, and of thyself thou hadst thought well; and all this hast thou lost for lack of a word here and there to some great man, and a little winking of the eyes amidst murder and wrong and unruth; and now thou art nought and helpless, and the hemp for thee is sown and grown and heckled and spun, and lo there, the rope for thy gallows-tree!—all for nought, for nought.

"Forsooth, my friends, thus I thought and sorrowed in my feebleness that I had not been a traitor to the Fellowship of the Church, for e'en so evil was my foolish imagination.

"Yet, forsooth, as I fell a-pondering over all the comfort and help that I might have been and that I might have had, if I had been but a little of a trembling cur to creep and crawl before abbot and bishop and baron and bailiff, came the thought over me of the evil of the world wherewith I, John Ball, the rascal hedge-priest, had fought and striven in the Fellowship of the saints in heaven and poor men upon earth.

"Yea, forsooth, once again I saw as of old, the great treading down the little, and the strong beating down the weak, and cruel men fearing not, and kind men daring not, and wise men caring not; and the saints in heaven forbearing and yet bidding me not to forbear; forsooth, I knew once more that he who doeth well in fellowship, and because of fellowship, shall not fail though he seem to fail to-day, but in days hereafter shall he and his work yet be alive, and men be holpen by them to strive again and yet again; and yet indeed even that was little, since, forsooth, to strive was my pleasure and my life.

"So I became a man once more, and I rose up to my feet and went up and down my prison what I could for my hopples, and into my mouth came words of good cheer, even such as we to-day have sung, and stoutly I sang them, even as we now have sung them; and then did I rest me, and once more thought of those pleasant fields where I would be, and all the life of man and beast about them, and I said to myself that I should see them once more before I died, if but once it were.

"Forsooth, this was strange, that whereas before I longed for them and yet saw them not, now that my longing was slaked my vision was cleared, and I saw them as though the prison walls opened to me and I was out of Canterbury street and amidst the green meadows of April; and therewithal along with me folk that I have known and who are dead, and folk that are living; yea, and all those of the Fellowship on earth and in heaven; yea, and all that are here this day. Overlong were the tale to tell of them, and of the time that is gone.

"So thenceforward I wore through the days with no such faint heart, until one day the prison opened verily and in the daylight, and there were ye, my fellows, in the door —your faces glad, your hearts light with hope, and your hands heavy with wrath; then I saw and understood what was to do. Now, therefore, do ye understand it!"

His voice was changed, and grew louder than loud now, as he cast his hands abroad towards that company with those last words of his; and I could feel that all shame and fear was falling from those men, and that mere fiery manhood was shining through their wonted English shamefast stubbornness, and that they were moved indeed and saw the road before them. Yet no man spoke, rather the silence of the men-folk deepened, as the sun's rays grew more level and more golden, and the swifts wheeled about shriller and louder than before.

Then again John Ball spoke and said, "In good sooth, I deem ye wot no worse than I do what is to do—and first that somewhat we shall do—since it is for him that is lonely or in prison to dream of fellowship, but for him that is of a fellowship to do and not to dream.

"And next, ye know who is the foeman, and that is the proud man, the oppressor, who scorneth fellowship, and himself is a world to himself and needeth no helper nor helpeth any, but, heeding no law, layeth law on other men because he is rich; and surely every one that is rich is such an one, nor may be other.

"Forsooth, in the belly of every rich man dwelleth a devil of hell, and when the man would give his goods to the poor, the devil within him gainsayeth it, and saith, 'Wilt thou then be of the poor, and suffer cold and hunger and mocking as they suffer, then give thou thy goods to them, and keep them not'. And when he would be compassionate, again saith the devil to him, 'If thou heed these losels and turn on them a face like to their faces, and deem of them as men, then shall they scorn thee, and evil shall come of it, and even one day they shall fall on thee to slay thee when they have learned that thou art but as they be'.

"Ah, woe worth the while! too oft he sayeth sooth, as the wont of the devil is, that lies may be born of the barren truth; and sooth it is that the poor deemeth the rich to be other than he, and meet to be his master, as though, forsooth, the poor were come of Adam, and the rich of him that made Adam, that is God; and thus the poor man oppresseth the poor man, because he feareth the oppressor. Nought such are ye, my brethren; or else why are ye gathered here in harness to bid all bear witness of you that ye are the sons of one man and one mother, begotten of the earth?"

As he said the words there came a stir among the weapons of the throng, and they pressed closer round the cross, yet withheld the shout as yet which seemed gathering in their bosoms.

And again he said:

"Forsooth, too many rich men there are in this realm; and yet if there were but one, there would be one too many, for all should be his thralls. Hearken, then, ye men of Kent. For overlong belike have I held you with words; but the love of you constrained me, and the joy that a man hath to babble to his friends and his fellows whom he hath not seen for a long season.

"Now, hearken, I bid you: To the rich men that eat up a realm there cometh a time when they whom they eat up, that is the poor, seem poorer than of wont, and their complaint goeth up louder to the heavens; yet it is no riddle to say that oft at such times the fellowship of the poor is waxing stronger, else would no man have heard his cry. Also at such times is the rich man become fearful, and so waxeth in cruelty, and of that cruelty do people misdeem that it is power and might waxing. Forsooth, ye are stronger than your fathers, because ye are more grieved than they, and ye should have been less grieved than they had ye been horses and swine; and then, forsooth, would ye have been stronger to bear; but ye, ye are not strong to bear, but to do.

"And wot ye why we are come to you this fair eve of holiday? and wot ye why I have been telling of fellowship to you? Yea, forsooth, I deem ye wot well, that it is for this cause, that ye might bethink you of your fellowship with the men of Essex".

His last word let loose the shout that had been long on all men's lips, and great and fierce it was as it rang shattering through the quiet upland village. But John Ball held up his hand, and the shout was one and no more.

Then he spoke again:

"Men of Kent, I wot well that ye are not so hard bested as those of other shires, by the token of the day when behind the screen of leafy boughs ye met Duke William with bill and bow as he wended Londonward from that woeful field of Senlac;[1] but I have told of fellowship, and ye have hearkened and understood what the Holy Church is, whereby ye know that ye are fellows of the saints in heaven and the poor men of Essex; and as one day the saints shall call you to the heavenly feast, so now do the poor men call you to the battle.

"Men of Kent, ye dwell fairly here, and your houses are framed of stout oak beams, and your own lands ye till; unless some accursed lawyer with his false lying sheep-skin

[1] There is a story that after the battle of Senlac (Hastings) the Kentishmen hid themselves and their arms with branches of trees, so that they looked like a walking wood. Then suddenly they threw aside the branches, and stood before William, to his surprise, as an army ready for battle. In his alarm William confirmed their ancient law and customs in return for their submission. There is no basis for the story (cf. Birnam Wood in *Macbeth*), and actually the Kentishmen, who had suffered severely at Senlac, submitted more easily than the rest of the kingdom.

and forged custom of the Devil's Manor hath stolen it from you; but in Essex slaves they be and villeins, and worse they shall be, and the lords swear that ere a year be over ox and horse shall go free in Essex, and man and woman shall draw the team and the plough; and north away in the east countries dwell men in poor halls of wattled reeds and mud, and the north-east wind from off the fen whistles through them; and poor they be to the letter; and there him whom the lord spareth, the bailiff squeezeth, and him whom the bailiff forgetteth, the Easterling[1] Chapman sheareth; yet be these stout men and valiant, and your very brethren.

"And yet if there be any man here so base as to think that a small matter, let him look to it that if these necks abide under the yoke, Kent shall sweat for it ere it be long; and ye shall lose acre and close and woodland, and be servants in your own houses, and your sons shall be the lords' lads, and your daughters their lemans, and ye shall buy a bold word with many stripes, and an honest deed with a leap from the gallows-tree.

"Bethink ye, too, that ye have no longer to deal with Duke William, who, if he were a thief and a cruel lord, was yet a prudent man and a wise warrior; but cruel are these, and headstrong, yea, thieves and fools in one—and ye shall lay their heads in the dust".

A shout would have arisen again, but his eager voice rising higher yet, restrained it as he said:

"And how shall it be then when these are gone? What else shall ye lack when ye lack masters? Ye shall not lack for the fields ye have tilled, nor the houses ye have built, nor the cloth ye have woven; all these shall be yours, and whatso ye will of all that the earth beareth; then shall no man mow the deep grass for another, while his own kine lack cow-meat; and he that soweth shall reap, and the

---

[1] Relating to the easterlings, or Baltic traders.

reaper shall eat in fellowship the harvest that in fellowship
he hath won; and he that buildeth a house shall dwell in
it with those that he biddeth of his free will; and the tithe
barn shall garner the wheat for all men to eat of when the
seasons are untoward, and the rain-drift hideth the sheaves
in August; and all shall be without money and without
price. Faithfully and merrily then shall all men keep the
holidays of the Church in peace of body and joy of heart.
And man shall help man, and the saints in heaven shall
be glad, because men no more fear each other; and the
churl shall be ashamed, and shall hide his churlishness till
it be gone, and he be no more a churl; and fellowship shall
be established in heaven and on the earth ".

A Dream of John Ball, chap. iv.

THE BATTLE AT THE TOWNSHIP'S END

As we waited there, every bowman with his shaft nocked
on the string, there was a movement in the line opposite,
and presently came from it a little knot of three men, the
middle one on horseback, the other two armed with long-
handled glaives; all three well muffled up in armour. As
they came nearer I could see that the horseman had a
tabard over his armour, gaily embroidered with a green tree
on a gold ground, and in his hand a trumpet.

"They are come to summon us. Wilt thou that he speak,
Jack?" said Will Green.

"Nay," said the other; "yet shall he have warning first.
Shoot when my horn blows!"

And therewith he came up to the hedge, climbed over,
slowly because of his armour, and stood some dozen yards
out in the field. The man on horseback put his trumpet to
his mouth and blew a long blast, and then took a scroll

into his hand and made as if he were going to read; but Jack Straw[1] lifted up his voice and cried out:

"Do it not, or thou art but dead! We will have no accursed lawyers and their sheep-skins here! Go back to those that sent thee—"

But the man broke in in a loud harsh voice:

"Ho! YE PEOPLE! what will ye gathering in arms?"

Then cried Jack Straw:

"Sir Fool, hold your peace till ye have heard me, or else we shoot at once. Go back to those that sent thee, and tell them that we free men of Kent are on the way to London to speak with King Richard, and to tell him that which he wots not; to wit, that there is a certain sort of fools and traitors to the realm who would put collars on our necks and make beasts of us, and that it is his right and his devoir to do as he swore when he was crowned and anointed at Westminster on the Stone of Doom,[2] and gainsay these thieves and traitors; and if he be too weak, then shall we help him; and if he will not be king, then shall we have one who will be, and that is the King's Son of Heaven. Now, therefore, if any withstand us on our lawful errand as we go to speak with our own king and lord, let him look to it. Bear back this word to them that sent thee. But for thee, hearken, get thee gone and tarry not; three times shall I lift up my hand, and the third time look to thyself, for then shalt thou hear the loose of our bowstrings, and after that nought else till thou hearest the devil bidding thee welcome to hell!"

[1] Described as Tyler's most prominent lieutenant, but little is known of him except that he led the men of Essex to London. The name is probably an emblematic one.

[2] Traditionally, the stone used by Jacob as a pillow at Bethel. It passed to Ireland, where it received the name *Lia Fail*, Stone of Destiny, and in 1296 it was embodied in the chair in Westminster Abbey on which the kings of England are crowned.

Our fellows shouted, but the summoner began again, yet in a quavering voice:

"Ho! ye People! what will ye gathering in arms? Wot ye not that ye are doing or shall do great harm, loss, and hurt to the king's lieges—"

He stopped; Jack Straw's hand was lowered for the second time. He looked to his men right and left, and then turned rein and turned tail, and scuttled back to the main body at his swiftest. Huge laughter rattled out all along our line as Jack Straw climbed back into the orchard grinning also.

Then we noted more movement in the enemy's line. They were spreading the archers and arbalestiers to our left, and the men-at-arms and others also spread somewhat under the three pennons of which Long Gregory had told us, and which were plain enough to us in the clear evening. Presently the moving line faced us, and the archers set off at a smart pace toward us, the men-at-arms holding back a little behind them. I knew now that they had been within bow-shot all along, but our men were loth to shoot before their first shots would tell, like those half-dozen in the road when, as they told me afterwards, a plump of their men-at-arms had made a show of falling on.

But now as soon as those men began to move on us directly in face, Jack Straw put his horn to his lips and blew a loud rough blast that was echoed by five or six others along the orchard hedge. Every man had his shaft nocked on the string; I watched them, and Will Green specially; he and his bow and its string seemed all of a piece, so easily by seeming did he draw the nock of the arrow to his ear. A moment, as he took his aim, and then—O then did I understand the meaning of the awe with which the ancient poet speaks of the loose of the god Apollo's bow;[1] for terrible indeed was the mingled sound of the

[1] Homer, *Iliad*, I, 43–52.

twanging bowstring and the whirring shaft so close to me.

I was now on my knees right in front of Will and saw all clearly; the arbalestiers (for no long-bow men were over against our stead) had all of them bright headpieces, and stout body-armour of boiled leather with metal studs, and as they came towards us, I could see over their shoulders great wooden shields hanging at their backs. Further to our left their long-bow men had shot almost as soon as ours, and I heard or seemed to hear the rush of the arrows through the apple-boughs and a man's cry therewith; but with us the long-bow had been before the cross-bow; one of the arbalestiers fell outright, his great shield clattering down on him, and moved no more; while three others were hit and were crawling to the rear. The rest had shouldered their bows and were aiming, but I thought unsteadily; and before the triggers were drawn again Will Green had nocked and loosed, and not a few others of our folk; then came the wooden hail of the bolts rattling through the boughs, but all overhead and no one hit.

The next time Will Green nocked his arrow he drew with a great shout, which all our fellows took up; for the arbalestiers instead of turning about in their places covered by their great shields and winding up their cross-bows for a second shot, as is the custom of such soldiers, ran huddling together toward their men-at-arms, our arrows driving thump-thump into their shields as they ran: I saw four lying on the field dead or sore wounded.

But our archers shouted again, and kept on each plucking the arrows from the ground, and nocking and loosing swiftly but deliberately at the line before them; indeed now was the time for these terrible bowmen, for as Will Green told me afterwards they always reckoned to kill through cloth or leather at five hundred yards, and they had let the cross-bow men come nearly within three hundred, and

these were now all mingled and muddled up with the men-
at-arms at scant five hundred yards' distance; and belike,
too, the latter were not treating them too well, but seemed
to be belabouring them with their spear-staves in their
anger at the poorness of the play; so that as Will Green
said it was like shooting at hay-ricks.

All this you must understand lasted but a few minutes,
and when our men had been shooting quite coolly, like
good workmen at peaceful work, for a few minutes more,
the enemy's line seemed to clear somewhat; the pennon
with the three red kine showed in front and three men
armed from head to foot in gleaming steel, except for their
short coats bright with heraldry, were with it. One of
them (and he bore the three kine on his coat) turned round
and gave some word of command, and an angry shout went
up from them, and they came on steadily towards us, the
man with the red kine on his coat leading them, a great
naked sword in his hand: you must note that they were
all on foot; but as they drew nearer I saw their horses
led by grooms and pages coming on slowly behind them.

Sooth said Will Green that the men-at-arms run not
fast either to or fro the fray; they came on no faster than
a hasty walk, their arms clashing about them and the twang
of the bows and whistle of the arrows never failing all the
while, but going on like the push of the westerly gale, as
from time to time the men-at-arms shouted, "Ha! ha!
out! out! Kentish thieves!"

But when they began to fall on, Jack Straw shouted out,
"Bills to the field! bills to the field!"

Then all our billmen ran up and leapt over the hedge
into the meadow and stood stoutly along the ditch under
our bows, Jack Straw in the forefront handling his great
axe. Then he cast it into his left hand, caught up his horn
and winded it loudly. The men-at-arms drew near steadily,
some fell under the arrow-storm, but not a many; for

though the target was big, it was hard, since not even the cloth-yard shaft could pierce well-wrought armour of plate, and there was much armour among them. Withal the arbalestiers were shooting again, but high and at a venture, so they did us no hurt.

But as these soldiers made wise by the French war were now drawing near, and our bowmen were casting down their bows and drawing their short swords, or handling their axes, as did Will Green, muttering, "Now must Hob Wright's gear[1] end this play"—while this was a-doing, lo, on a sudden a flight of arrows from our right on the flank of the sergeants' array, which stayed them somewhat; not because it slew many men, but because they began to bethink them that their foes were many and all around them; then the road-hedge on the right seemed alive with armed men, for whatever could hold sword or staff amongst us was there; every bowman also leapt our orchard-hedge sword or axe in hand, and with a great shout, billmen, archers, and all, ran in on them; half-armed, yea, and half-naked some of them; strong and stout and lithe and light withal, the wrath of battle and the hope of better times lifting up their hearts till nothing could withstand them. So was all mingled together, and for a minute or two was a confused clamour over which rose a clatter like the riveting of iron plates, or the noise of the street of coppersmiths at Florence; then the throng burst open and the steel-clad sergeants and squires and knights ran huddling and shuffling towards their horses; but some cast down their weapons and threw up their hands and cried for peace and ransom; and some stood and fought desperately, and slew some till they were hammered down by many strokes, and of these were the bailiffs and tipstaves, and the lawyers and their men, who could not run and hoped for no mercy.

[1] Hand weapons. Hob Wright, mentioned earlier as a follower of Jack Straw, was the village wheelwright and smith.

I looked as on a picture and wondered, and my mind was at strain to remember something forgotten, which yet had left its mark on it. I heard the noise of the horse-hoofs of the fleeing men-at-arms (the archers and arbalestiers had scattered before the last minutes of the play), I heard the confused sound of laughter and rejoicing down in the meadow, and close by me the evening wind lifting the lighter twigs of the trees, and far away the many noises of the quiet country, till light and sound both began to fade from me and I saw and heard nothing.

A Dream of John Ball, chap. vi.

THE VISION OF THE FUTURE

H E said: "Many strange things hast thou told me that I could not understand; yea, some my wit so failed to compass, that I cannot so much as ask thee questions concerning them; but of some matters would I ask thee, and I must hasten, for in very sooth the night is worn old and grey. Whereas thou sayest that in the days to come, when there shall be no labouring men who are not thralls after their new fashion, that their lords shall be many and very many, it seemeth to me that these same lords, if they be many, shall hardly be rich, or but very few of them, since they must verily feed and clothe and house their thralls, so that that which they take from them, since it will have to be dealt out amongst many, will not be enough to make many rich; since out of one man ye may get but one man's work; and pinch him never so sorely, still as aforesaid ye may not pinch him so sorely as not to feed him. Therefore, though the eyes of my mind may see a few lords and many slaves, yet can they not see many lords as well as many slaves; and if the slaves be many and the lords few, then some day shall the slaves make an end of that mastery by the force of their bodies. How then shall thy mastership of the latter days endure?"

"John Ball," said I, "mastership hath many shifts whereby it striveth to keep itself alive in the world. And now hear a marvel: whereas thou sayest these two times that out of one man ye may get but one man's work, in days to come one man shall do the work of a hundred men —yea, of a thousand or more: and this is the shift of mastership that shall make many masters and many rich men."

John Ball laughed. "Great is my harvest of riddles to-night," said he; "for even if a man sleep not, and eat and drink while he is a-working, ye shall but make two men, or three at the most, out of him."

Said I: "Sawest thou ever a weaver at his loom?"

"Yea," said he, "many a time."

He was silent a little, and then said: "Yet I marvelled not at it; but now I marvel, because I know what thou wouldst say. Time was when the shuttle was thrust in and out of all the thousand threads of the warp, and it was long to do; but now the spring-staves go up and down as the man's feet move, and this and that leaf of the warp cometh forward and the shuttle goeth in one shot through all the thousand warps. Yea, so it is that this multiplieth a man many times. But look you, he is so multiplied already; and so hath he been, meseemeth, for many hundred years".

"Yea", said I, "but what hitherto needed the masters to multiply him more? For many hundred years the workman was a thrall bought and sold at the cross; and for other hundreds of years he hath been a villein—that is, a working-beast and a part of the stock of the manor on which he liveth; but then thou and the like of thee shall free him, and then is mastership put to its shifts; for what should avail the mastery then, when the master no longer owneth the man by law as his chattel, nor any longer by law owneth him as stock of his land, if the master hath not that which he on whom he liveth may not lack and live withal, and cannot have without selling himself?"

He said nothing, but I saw his brow knitted and his lips pressed together as though in anger; and again I said:

"Thou hast seen the weaver at his loom: think how it should be if he sit no longer before the web and cast the shuttle and draw home the sley, but if the shed open of itself and the shuttle of itself speed through it as swift as the eye can follow, and the sley come home of itself; and the weaver standing by and whistling *The Hunt's Up!* the while, or looking to half-a-dozen looms and bidding them what to do. And as with the weaver so with the potter, and the smith, and every worker in metals, and all other crafts, that it shall be for them looking on and tending, as with the man that sitteth in the cart while the horse draws. Yea, at last so shall it be even with those who are mere husbandmen; and no longer shall the reaper fare afield in the morning with his hook over his shoulder, and smite and bind and smite again till the sun is down and the moon is up; but he shall draw a thing made by men into the field with one or two horses, and shall say the word and the horses shall go up and down, and the thing shall reap and gather and bind, and do the work of many men. Imagine all this in thy mind if thou canst, at least as ye may imagine a tale of enchantment told by a minstrel, and then tell me what shouldst thou deem that the life of men would be amidst all this, men such as these men of the township here, or the men of the Canterbury gilds".[1]

"Yea," said he; "but before I tell thee my thoughts of thy tale of wonder, I would ask thee this: In those days when men work so easily, surely they shall make more wares than they can use in one country-side, or one good town, whereas in another, where things have not gone as

[1] Canterbury was the cradle of Wat Tyler's rebellion.

well, they shall have less than they need; and even so it is with us now, and thereof cometh scarcity and famine; and if people may not come at each other's goods, it availeth the whole land little that one country-side hath more than enough while another hath less; for the goods shall abide there in the storehouses of the rich place till they perish. So if that be so in the days of wonder ye tell of (and I see not how it can be otherwise), then shall men be but little holpen by making all their wares so easily and with so little labour."

I smiled again and said: "Yea, but it shall not be so; not only shall men be multiplied a hundred and a thousand fold, but the distance of one place from another shall be as nothing; so that the wares which lie ready for market in Durham in the evening may be in London on the morrow morning; and the men of Wales may eat corn of Essex and the men of Essex wear wool of Wales; so that, so far as the flitting of goods to market goes, all the land shall be as one parish. Nay, what say I? Not as to this land only shall it be so, but even the Indies, and far countries of which thou knowest not, shall be, so to say, at every man's door, and wares which now ye account precious and dear-bought, shall then be common things bought and sold for little price at every huckster's stall. Say then, John, shall not those days be merry, and plentiful of ease and contentment for all men?"

"Brother," said he, "meseemeth some doleful mockery lieth under these joyful tidings of thine; since thou hast already partly told me to my sad bewilderment what the life of man shall be in those days. Yet will I now for a little set all that aside to consider thy strange tale as of a minstrel from over sea, even as thou biddest me. Therefore I say, that if men still abide men as I have known them, and unless these folk of England change as the land changeth—and forsooth of the men, for good and for evil,

I can think no other than I think now, or behold them other than I have known them and loved them—I say if the men be still men, what will happen except that there should be all plenty in the land, and not one poor man therein, unless of his own free will he choose to lack and be poor, as a man in religion or such like; for there would then be such abundance of all good things, that, as greedy as the lords might be, there would be enough to satisfy their greed and yet leave good living for all who laboured with their hands; so that these should labour far less than now, and they would have time to learn knowledge, so that there should be no learned or unlearned, for all should be learned; and they would have time also to learn how to order the matters of the parish and the hundred, and of the parliament of the realm, so that the king should take no more than his own; and to order the rule of the realm, so that all men, rich and unrich, should have part therein; and so by undoing of evil laws and making of good ones, that fashion would come to an end whereof thou speakest, that rich men make laws for their own behoof; for they should no longer be able to do thus when all had part in making the laws; whereby it would soon come about that there would be no men rich and tyrannous, but all should have enough and to spare of the increase of the earth and the work of their own hands. Yea surely, brother, if ever it cometh about that men shall be able to make things, and not men, work for their superfluities, and that the length of travel from one place to another be made of no account, and all the world be a market for all the world, then all shall live in health and wealth; and envy and grudging shall perish. For then shall we have conquered the earth and it shall be enough; and then shall the kingdom of heaven be come down to the earth in very deed. Why lookest thou so sad and sorry? what sayest thou?"

I said: "Hast thou forgotten already what I told thee,

that in those latter days a man who hath nought save his own body (and such men shall be far the most of men) must needs pawn his labour for leave to labour? Can such a man be wealthy? Hast thou not called him a thrall?"

"Yea," he said; "but how could I deem that such things could be when those days should be come wherein men could make things work for them?"

"Poor man!" said I. "Learn that in those very days, when it shall be with the making of things as with the carter in the cart, that there he sitteth and shaketh the reins and the horse draweth and the cart goeth; in those days, I tell thee, many men shall be as poor and wretched always, year by year, as they are with thee when there is famine in the land; nor shall any have plenty and surety of livelihood save those that shall sit by and look on while others labour; and these, I tell thee, shall be a many, so that they shall see to the making of all laws, and in their hands shall be all power, and the labourers shall think that they cannot do without these men that live by robbing them, and shall praise them and wellnigh pray to them as ye pray to the saints, and the best worshipped man in the land shall be he who by forestalling and regrating hath gotten to him the most money."

"Yea," said he, "and shall they who see themselves robbed worship the robber? Then indeed shall men be changed from what they are now, and they shall be slug-gards, dolts, and cowards beyond all the earth hath yet borne. Such are not the men I have known in my life-days, and that now I love in my death."

"Nay," I said, "but the robbery shall they not see; for have I not told thee that they shall hold themselves to be free men? And for why? I will tell thee: but first tell me how it fares with men now; may the labouring man become a lord?"

He said: "The thing hath been seen that churls have

risen from the dortoir of the monastery to the abbot's chair
and the bishop's throne; yet not often; and whiles hath
a bold sergeant become a wise captain, and they have made
him squire and knight; and yet but very seldom. And now
I suppose thou wilt tell me that the Church will open her
arms wider to this poor people, and that many through her
shall rise into lordship. But what availeth that? Nought
were it to me if the Abbot of St Alban's[1] with his golden
mitre sitting guarded by his knights and sergeants, or the
Prior of Merton[2] with his hawks and his hounds, had once
been poor men, if they were now tyrants of poor men; nor
would it better the matter if there were ten times as many
Houses of Religion in the land as now are, and each with
a churl's son for abbot or prior over it".

I smiled and said: "Comfort thyself; for in those days
shall there be neither abbey nor priory in the land, nor
monks nor friars, nor any religious". (He started as I
spoke.) "But thou hast told me that hardly in these days
may a poor man rise to be a lord: now I tell thee that in
the days to come poor men shall be able to become lords
and masters and do-nothings; and oft will it be seen that
they shall do so; and it shall be even for that cause that
their eyes shall be blinded to the robbing of themselves by
others, because they shall hope in their souls that they may
each live to rob others: and this shall be the very safe-
guard of all rule and law in those days."

"Now am I sorrier than thou hast yet made me," said
he; "for when once this is established, how then can it
be changed? Strong shall be the tyranny of the latter
days. And now meseems, if thou sayest sooth, this time

[1] The Abbey of St Albans in Hertfordshire was founded by Offa II,
in 793, and was later built up on a magnificent scale. It was sup-
pressed in 1539.
[2] An important Priory existed at Merton, in Surrey, from 1115
to 1538, and a great council of the nation was held there in 1236
to oppose one of the king's decrees.

of the conquest of the earth shall not bring heaven down
to the earth, as erst I deemed it would, but rather that it
shall bring hell up on to the earth. Woe's me, brother, for
thy sad and weary foretelling! And yet saidst thou that
the men of those days would seek a remedy. Canst thou
yet tell me, brother, what that remedy shall be, lest the
sun rise upon me made hopeless by thy tale of what is to
be? And, lo you, soon shall she rise upon the earth."

In truth the dawn was widening now, and the colours
coming into the pictures on wall and in window; and as
well as I could see through the varied glazing of these last
(and one window before me had as yet nothing but white
glass in it), the ruddy glow, which had but so little a while
quite died out in the west, was now beginning to gather
in the east—the new day was beginning. I looked at the
poppy that I still carried in my hand, and it seemed to me
to have withered and dwindled. I felt anxious to speak
to my companion and tell him much, and withal I felt that
I must hasten, or for some reason or other I should be too
late; so I spoke at last loud and hurriedly:

"John Ball, be of good cheer; for once more thou
knowest, as I know, that the Fellowship of Men shall
endure, however many tribulations it may have to wear
through. Look you, a while ago was the light bright about
us; but it was because of the moon, and the night was deep
notwithstanding, and when the moonlight waned and died
and there was but a little glimmer in place of the bright
light, yet was the world glad because all things knew that
the glimmer was of day and not of night. Lo you, an
image of the times to betide the hope of the Fellowship
of Men. Yet forsooth, it may well be that this bright day
of summer which is now dawning upon us is no image
of the beginning of the day that shall be; but rather shall
that day-dawn be cold and grey and surly; and yet by its
light shall men see things as they verily are, and no longer

enchanted by the gleam of the moon and the glamour of the dreamtide. By such grey light shall wise men and valiant souls see the remedy, and deal with it, a real thing that may be touched and handled, and no glory of the heavens to be worshipped from afar off. And what shall it be, as I told thee before, save that men shall be determined to be free; yea, free as thou wouldst have them, when thine hope rises the highest, and thou art thinking not of the king's uncles, and poll-groat bailiffs, and the villeinage of Essex, but of the end of all, when men shall have the fruits of the earth and the fruits of their toil thereon, without money and without price. The time shall come, John Ball, when that dream of thine that this shall one day be, shall be a thing that men shall talk of soberly, and as a thing soon to come about, as even with thee they talk of the villeins becoming tenants paying their lord quit-rent; therefore, hast thou done well to hope it; and, if thou heedest this also, as I suppose thou heedest it little, thy name shall abide by thy hope in those days to come, and thou shalt not be forgotten".

I heard his voice come out of the twilight, scarcely seeing him, though now the light was growing fast, as he said:

"Brother, thou givest me heart again; yet since now I wot well that thou art a sending from far-off times and far-off things: tell thou, if thou mayest, to a man who is going to his death how this shall come about".

"Only this may I tell thee," said I; "to thee, when thou didst try to conceive of them, the ways of the days to come seemed follies scarce to be thought of; yet shall they come to be familiar things, and an order by which every man liveth, ill as he liveth, so that men shall deem of them, that thus it hath been since the beginning of the world, and that thus it shall be while the world endureth; and in this wise so shall they be thought of a long while; and the complaint of the poor the rich man shall heed, even as much and no more as he who lieth in pleasure under the lime-trees in the summer heedeth the murmur of his toiling bees. Yet in time shall this also grow old, and doubt shall creep in, because men shall scarce be able to live by that order, and the complaint of the poor shall be hearkened, no longer as a tale not utterly grievous, but as a threat of ruin, and a fear. Then shall those things, which to thee seem follies, and to the men between thee and me mere wisdom and the bond of stability, seem follies once again; yet, whereas men have so long lived by them, they shall cling to them yet from blindness and from fear; and those that see, and that have thus much conquered fear that they are furthering the real time that cometh and not the dream that faileth, these men shall the blind and the fearful mock and missay, and torment and murder: and great and grievous shall be the strife in those days, and many the failures of the wise, and too oft sore shall be the despair of the valiant; and back-sliding, and doubt, and contest between friends and fellows lacking time in the hubbub to understand each other, shall grieve many hearts and hinder the Host of the Fellowship: yet shall all bring about the end, till thy deeming of folly and ours shall be one, and thy hope and our hope; and then—the Day will have come."

A Dream of John Ball, chap. xii.

ART & SOCIAL REFORM

MEDIEVAL ARTS AND CRAFTS

Let us look back a little to the early middle ages, the days of barbarism and confusion. As you follow the pages of the keen-eyed, cool-headed Gibbon,[1] you may well think that the genius of the great historian has been wasted over the mean squabbles, the bald self-seeking, the ignoble superstition, the pomp and the cruelty of the kings and scoundrels who are the chief persons named in the story; yet also you cannot fail to know, when you come to think of it, that the story has not been fully told; nay scarce told at all, only a chance hint given, here and there. The palace and the camp were but a small part of their world surely; and outside them you may be sure that faith and heroism and love were at work, or what birth could there have been from those days? For the visible tokens of that birth you must seek in the art that grew up and flourished amid that barbarism and confusion, and you know who wrought it. The tyrants, and pedants, and bullies of the time paid dog's wages for it, and bribed their gods with it, but they were too busy over other things to make it; the nameless people wrought it; for no names of its makers are left, not one. Their work only is left, and all that came of it, and all that is to come of it. What came of it first was the complete freedom of art in the midst of a society that had at least begun to free itself from religious and political fetters. Art was no longer now, as in Egypt of olden time, kept rigidly within certain prescribed bounds that no fancy might play with, no imagination overpass, lest the majesty of the

[1] Edward Gibbon (1737–94), English historian, author of *The Decline and Fall of the Roman Empire*.

beautiful symbols might be clouded and the memory of the awful mysteries they symbolized become dim in the hearts of men. Nor was it any longer as in the Greece of Pericles,[1] wherein no thought might be expressed that could not be expressed in perfect form. Art was free. Whatever a man thought of, that he might bring to light by the labour of his hands, to be praised and wondered at by his fellows. Whatever man had thought in him of any kind, and skill in him of any kind to express it, he was deemed good enough to be used for his own pleasure and the pleasure of his fellows; in this art nothing and nobody was wasted; all people east of the Atlantic felt this art; from Bokhara[2] to Galway, from Iceland to Madras, all the world glittered with its brightness and quivered with its vigour. It cast down the partitions of race and religion also. Christian and Mussulman were made joyful by it; Kelt, Teuton, and Latin raised it up together; Persian, Tartar, and Arab gave and took its gifts from one another. Considering how old the world is it was not too long-lived at its best. In the days when Norwegian, Dane, and Icelander stalked through the streets of Micklegarth,[3] and hedged with their axes the throne of Kirialax[4] the Greek king, it was alive and

[1] Statesman, orator, and principal minister of Athens, 495–429 B.C.; patron of art and literature; he was responsible for the Parthenon and other famous buildings.

[2] Capital of the state of Bokhara, and one of the chief commercial and religious centres of Central Asia. It has numerous mosques and fine bazaars.

[3] Micklegard, the Great City, was the name given by the Northmen to Constantinople. The Varangian Guard, the Imperial Guard of the East Roman emperors at Constantinople, founded by Basil II in 988, was composed of Scandinavians, Anglo-Saxons, and Danes, and long upheld the Byzantine throne.

[4] There was no Greek king named Kirialax. The word is probably a combination of Gr. *Kyrios*, Lord, and Alexius (Alexius I, Comnenus, 1048–1118). Morris was a great reader of Scott in his early days, and *Count Robert of Paris* contains an account of Alexius and his Varangians.

vigorous. When blind Dandolo[1] was led from the Venetian galleys on to the conquered wall of Constantinople, it was near to its best and purest days. When Constantine Palaeologus came back an old and care-worn man from a peacefuller home in the Morea to his doom in the great city, and the last Caesar got the muddle of his life solved, not ingloriously, by Turkish swords on the breached and battered walls of that same Constantinople, there were signs of sickness beginning to show in the art that sprang from there to cover east and west alike with its glory.[2]

And all that time it was the art of free men. Whatever slavery still existed in the world (more than enough, as always), art had no share in it; and still it was only here and there that any great names rose above the host of those that wrought it. These names (and it was mainly in Italy only) came to the front when those branches of it that were the work of collective rather than individual genius, architecture especially, had quite reached their highest perfection. Men began to look round for something more startlingly new than the slow, gradual change of architecture and the attendant lesser arts could give them. This change they found in the glorious work of the painters, and they received it with an out-spoken excitement and joy that seems strange indeed to us in these days when art is held so cheap.

All went better than well for a time; though in Italy architecture began to lose something of the perfection it had gained, yet it was scarcely to be noticed amidst the glory of the light that was increasing in painting and

---

[1] Doge of Venice, 1192–1205. He was ambassador to Constantinople from 1191, and was blinded by the Emperor Manuel. In 1201 he led the Fourth Crusade, capturing Constantinople in 1203, and establishing the Latin empire.

[2] Constantine Palaeologus (1404–53) was the last East Roman emperor at Constantinople. In 1430, he successfully recovered from the Franks the Greek possessions in Peloponnesus (Morea). He died fighting at the capture of Constantinople by Mohammed II.

sculpture. In France and England meantime the change, as it was slower in growing to a head, so it had begun earlier, as witness the sculpture in the great French Churches, and the exquisite drawing of the illuminations of English books; while the Flemings, never very great in the art of building, towards the end of this period had found their true vocation as painters of a sweet and serious external naturalism, illuminated by colour unsurpassed for purity and brightness.

So had the art of the middle ages climbed gradually to the top of the hill, doubtless not without carrying the seeds of the disease that was to end it, threatenings of great change which no doubt no one heeded at the time. Nor was there much to wonder at in their blindness, since still for centuries to come their art was full of life and splendour, and when at last its death drew near, men could see in it nothing but the hope of a new life. For many years, a hundred years at least, before the change really showed itself, the expression of the greater thoughts that art can deal with was being made more difficult to men not specially learned. Without demanding the absolute perfection that was the rule in the days of Greece, people began to look for an intricacy of treatment that the Greeks had never dreamed of; men began to see hopes of realizing scenes of history and poetry in a far more complete way than the best of their forerunners had attempted. Yet for long the severance between artist and artisan (as our nicknames go) was not obvious, though doubtless things were leading up to it; it is, perhaps, noticeable chiefly in the difference between the work of nation and nation rather than among the individual workmen. I mean, for instance, that in the thirteenth century England was going step by step with Italy as far as mere excellence is concerned, while in the middle of the fifteenth England was rude, and Italy cultured; and even while the change was preparing, by one

accident or another came a great access of discoveries of
the art and literature of the ancient world, and, as it were,
fate ran to meet the half-expressed longings of men.

Then, indeed, all hesitation was over, and suddenly, as it
now seems to us, amidst a blaze of glory, the hoped-for
new birth took place. Once, as I have said, the makers
of beautiful things passed away nameless; but under the
Renaissance there are more names of excellent craftsmen
left to us than a good memory can well remember, and
among those names are the greatest the world has ever
known, or perhaps ever will know. No wonder men's
exultation rose high; no wonder that their pride blinded
them and that they did not know where they were; yet
most pitiable and sad the story is. It was one of those
strange times when men seem to themselves to have pierced
through all the space which lies between longing and attainment. They, it seems, and no others, have at last reached
the spot where lie heaped together all the treasures of the
world, vainly sought aforetime. They, it seems, have everything, and no one of those that went before them had anything, nay, not even their fathers whose bones lie yet
unrotted under the turf.

The men of the Renaissance looked at the thousand
years behind them as a deedless blank, and at all that lay
before them as a perpetual triumphal march. We, taught
so much by other people's failures, can see their position
otherwise than that. We can see that while up to that time,
since art first began, it had always looked forward, now it
was looking backward; that whereas once men were taught
to look through the art at that which the art represented,
they were now taught to deem the art an end in itself,
and that it mattered nothing whether the story it told was
believed or not. Once its aim was to see, now its aim was
to be seen only. Once it was done to be understood, and to
be helpful to all men: now the vulgar were beyond the pale,

and the insults which the Greek slave-holders and the Roman tax-sweaters of old cast upon the people, upon all men but a chosen few, were brought forth and tricked up again in fantastic guise to adorn the day of boundless hope.

Not all this, indeed, came at once, but come it did, nor very slowly either, when men once began to look back. At the beginning of the sixteenth century the new birth was in its hey-day. Before the seventeenth had quite begun, what had become of its over-weening hopes? In Venice alone of all Italy was any art being done that was of any worth. The conquered North had gained nothing from Italy save an imitation of its worst extravagance, and all that saved the art of England from nothingness was a tradition of the earlier days still lingering among a people rustic and narrow-minded indeed, but serious, truthful, and of simple habits.

Lectures on Art and Industry: Art and the Beauty of the Earth.

ART AND THE BEAUTY OF LIFE

THE danger that the present course of civilization will destroy the beauty of life—these are hard words, and I wish I could mend them, but I cannot, while I speak what I believe to be the truth.

That the beauty of life is a thing of no moment, I suppose few people would venture to assert, and yet most civilized people act as if it were of none, and in so doing are wronging both themselves and those that are to come after them; for that beauty, which is what is meant by *art*, using the word in its widest sense, is, I contend, no mere accident to human life, which people can take or leave as they choose, but a positive necessity of life, if we are to live as nature meant us to; that is, unless we are content to be less than men.

Now I ask you, as I have been asking myself this long while, what proportion of the population in civilized countries has any share at all in that necessity of life?

I say that the answer which must be made to that question justifies my fear that modern civilization is on the road to trample out all the beauty of life, and to make us less than men.

Now if there should be any here who will say: It was always so; there always was a mass of rough ignorance that knew and cared nothing about art; I answer first, that if that be the case, then it was always wrong, and we, as soon as we have become conscious of that wrong, are bound to set it right if we can.

But moreover, strange to say, and in spite of all the suffering that the world has wantonly made for itself, and has in all ages so persistently clung to, as if it were a good and holy thing, this wrong of the mass of men being regardless of art was *not* always so.

So much is now known of the periods of art that have left abundant examples of their work behind them, that we can judge of the art of all periods by comparing these with the remains of times of which less has been left us; and we cannot fail to come to the conclusion that down to very recent days everything that the hand of man touched was more or less beautiful: so that in those days all people who made anything shared in art, as well as all people who used the things so made: that is, *all* people shared in art.

But some people may say: And was that to be wished for? would not this universal spreading of art stop progress in other matters, hinder the work of the world? Would it not make us unmanly? or if not that, would it not be intrusive, and push out other things necessary also for men to study?

Well, I have claimed a necessary place for art, a natural place, and it would be in the very essence of it, that it would apply its own rules of order and fitness to the general ways of life: it seems to me, therefore, that people who are over-anxious of the outward expression of beauty becoming too great a force among the other forces of life, would, if they had had the making of the external world, have been afraid of making an ear of wheat beautiful, lest it should not have been good to eat.

But indeed there seems no chance of art becoming universal, unless on the terms that it shall have little self-consciousness, and for the most part be done with little effort; so that the rough work of the world would be as little hindered by it, as the work of external nature is by the beauty of all her forms and moods: this was the case in the times that I have been speaking of: of art which was made by conscious effort, the result of the individual striving towards perfect expression of their thoughts by men very specially gifted, there was perhaps no more than there is now, except in very wonderful and short periods; though I believe that even for such men the struggle to produce beauty was not so bitter as it now is. But if there were not more great thinkers than there are now, there was a countless multitude of happy workers whose work did express, and could not choose but express, some original thought, and was consequently both interesting and beauti-ful: now there is certainly no chance of the more individual art becoming common, and either wearying us by its over-abundance, or by noisy self-assertion preventing highly cultivated men taking their due part in the other work of the world; it is too difficult to do: it will be always but the blossom of all the half-conscious work below it, the ful-filment of the shortcomings of less complete minds: but it will waste much of its power, and have much less in-fluence on men's minds, unless it be surrounded by abun-dance of that commoner work, in which all men once shared, and which, I say, will, when art has really awakened, be done so easily and constantly, that it will stand in no man's way to hinder him from doing what he will, good or evil. And as, on the one hand, I believe that art made by the people and for the people as a joy both to the maker and the user would further progress in other matters rather than hinder it, so also I firmly believe that that higher art produced only by great brains and miraculously gifted hands cannot exist without it: I believe that the present state of things in which it does exist, while popular art is, let us say, asleep or 'sick, is a transitional state, which must end at last either in utter defeat or utter victory for the arts.

For whereas all works of craftsmanship were once beautiful, unwittingly or not, they are now divided into two kinds, works of art and non-works of art: now nothing made by man's hand can be indifferent: it must be either beautiful and elevating, or ugly and degrading; and those things that are without art are so aggressively; they wound it by their existence, and they are now so much in the majority that the works of art we are obliged to set our-selves to seek for, whereas the other things are the ordinary companions of our everyday life; so that if those who cultivate art intellectually were inclined never so much to wrap themselves in their special gifts and their high cultiva-tion, and so live happily, apart from other men, and despising them, they could not do so: they are as it were living in an enemy's country; at every turn there is something lying in wait to offend and vex their nicer sense and educated eyes: they must share in the general discomfort—and I am glad of it.

So the matter stands: from the first dawn of history till quite modern times, Art, which Nature meant to solace all, fulfilled its purpose; all men shared in it: that was what made life romantic, as people call it, in those days—that and not robber-barons and inaccessible kings with their hier-archy of serving-nobles and other such rubbish: but art grew and grew, saw empires sicken and sickened with them; grew hale again, and haler, and grew so great at last, that she seemed in good truth to have conquered everything, and laid the material world under foot. Then came a change at a period of the greatest life and hope in many ways that Europe had known till then: a time of so much and such varied hope that people call it the time of the New Birth: as far as the arts are concerned I deny it that title; rather it seems to me that the great men who lived and glorified the practice of art in those days, were the fruit of the old, not the seed of the new order of things: but a stirring and hopeful time it was, and many things were newborn then which have since brought forth fruit enough: and it is strange and perplexing that from those days forward the lapse of time, which, through plenteous confusion and failure, has on the whole been steadily destroying privilege and exclusiveness in other matters, has delivered up art to be the exclusive privilege of a few, and has taken from the people their birthright; while both wronged and wrongers have been wholly unconscious of what they were doing.

Wholly unconscious—yes, but we are no longer so: there lies the sting of it, and there also the hope.

When the brightness of the so-called Renaissance faded, and it faded very suddenly, a deadly chill fell upon the arts: that New-birth mostly meant looking back to past times, wherein the men of those days thought they saw a perfection of art, which to their minds was different in kind, and not in degree only, from the ruder suggestive art of their own fathers: this perfection they were ambitious to imitate, this alone seemed to be art to them, the rest was childishness: so wonderful was their energy, their success so great, that no doubt to commonplace minds among them, though surely not to the great masters, that perfection seemed to be gained: and, perfection being gained, what are you to do?—you can go no further, you must aim at standing still—which you cannot do.

Art by no means stood still in those latter days of the Renaissance, but took the downward road with terrible swiftness, and tumbled down at the bottom of the hill, where as if bewitched it lay long in great content, believing itself to be the art of Michael Angelo,[1] while it was the art of men whom nobody remembers but those who want to sell their pictures.

Thus it fared with the more individual forms of art. As to the art of the people; in countries and places where the greater art had flourished most, it went step by step on the downward path with that: in more out-of-the-way places, England for instance, it still felt the influence of the life of its earlier and happy days, and in a way lived on a while; but its life was so feeble, and, so to say, illogical, that it could not resist any change in external circumstances, still less could it give birth to anything new; and before this century began, its last flicker had died out. Still, while it was living, in whatever dotage, it did imply something going on in those matters of daily use that we have been thinking of, and doubtless satisfied some cravings for beauty: and when it was dead, for a long time people did not know it, or what had taken its place, crept so to say into its dead body—that pretence of art, to wit, which is done with machines, though sometimes the machines are called men, and doubtless are so out of working hours: nevertheless long before it was quite dead it had fallen so low that the whole subject was usually treated with the utmost contempt by every one who had any pretence of being a sensible man, and in short the whole civilized world had forgotten that there had ever been an art *made by the people for the people as a joy for the maker and the user.*

But now it seems to me that the very suddenness of the

---

[1] Italian sculptor, painter, and architect, 1475–1564.

change ought to comfort us, to make us look upon this break in the continuity of the golden chain as an accident only, that itself cannot last: for think how many thousand years it may be since that primaeval man graved with a flint splinter on a bone the story of the mammoth he had seen, or told us of the slow uplifting of the heavily-horned heads of the reindeer that he stalked: think I say of the space of time from then till the dimming of the brightness of the Italian Renaissance! whereas from that time till popular art died unnoticed and despised among ourselves is just but two hundred years.

Strange too, that very death is contemporaneous with new-birth of something at all events; for out of all despair sprang a new time of hope lighted by the torch of the French Revolution: and things that have languished with the languishing of art, rose afresh and surely heralded its new birth: in good earnest poetry was born again, and the English Language, which under the hands of sycophantic verse-makers had been reduced to a miserable jargon, whose meaning, if it have a meaning, cannot be made out without translation, flowed clear, pure, and simple, along with the music of Blake and Coleridge: take those names, the earliest in date among ourselves, as a type of the change that has happened in literature since the time of George II.

With that literature in which romance, that is to say humanity, was re-born, there sprang up also a feeling for the romance of external nature, which is surely strong in us now, joined with a longing to know something real of the lives of those who have gone before us; of these feelings united you will find the broadest expression in the pages of Walter Scott: it is curious as showing how sometimes one art will lag behind another in a revival, that the man who wrote the exquisite and wholly unfettered naturalism of the Heart of Midlothian, for instance, thought himself continually bound to seem to feel ashamed of, and to excuse

himself for, his love of Gothic Architecture: he felt that
it was romantic, and he knew that it gave him pleasure,
but somehow he had not found out that it was art, having
been taught in many ways that nothing could be art that
was not done by a named man under academical rules.

Hopes and Fears for Art: The Beauty of Life.

THE ART OF THE PEOPLE

THERE are some of us who love Art most, and I may say
most faithfully, who see for certain that such love is rare
nowadays. We cannot help seeing, that besides a vast
number of people, who (poor souls!) are sordid and brutal
of mind and habits, and have had no chance or choice in
the matter, there are many high-minded, thoughtful, and
cultivated men who inwardly think the arts to be a foolish
accident of civilization—nay, worse perhaps, a nuisance,
a disease, a hindrance to human progress. Some of these,
doubtless, are very busy about other sides of thought. They
are, as I should put it, so *artistically* engrossed by the study
of science, politics, or what not, that they have necessarily
narrowed their minds by their hard and praiseworthy
labours. But since such men are few, this does not account
for a prevalent habit of thought that looks upon Art as at
best trifling.

What is wrong, then, with us or the arts, since what was
once accounted so glorious, is now deemed paltry?

The question is no light one; for, to put the matter in its
clearest light, I will say that the leaders of modern thought
do for the most part sincerely and single-mindedly hate and
despise the arts; and you know well that as the leaders are,
so must the people be; and that means that we who are met
together here for the furthering of Art by wide-spread
education are either deceiving ourselves and wasting our
time, since we shall one day be of the same opinion as the

best men among us, or else we represent a small minority that is right, as minorities sometimes are, while those upright men aforesaid, and the great mass of civilized men, have been blinded by untoward circumstances.

That we are of this mind—the minority that is right—is, I hope, the case. I hope we know assuredly that the arts we have met together to further are necessary to the life of man, if the progress of civilization is not to be as causeless as the turning of a wheel that makes nothing.

How, then, shall we, the minority, carry out the duty which our position thrusts upon us, of striving to grow into a majority?

If we could only explain to those thoughtful men, and the millions of whom they are the flower, what the thing is that we love, which is to us as the bread we eat, and the air we breathe, but about which they know nothing and feel nothing, save a vague instinct of repulsion, then the seed of victory might be sown. This is hard indeed to do; yet if we ponder upon a chapter of ancient or mediaeval history, it seems to me some glimmer of a chance of doing so breaks in upon us. Take for example a century of the Byzantine Empire,[1] weary yourselves with reading the names of the pedants, tyrants, and tax-gatherers to whom the terrible chain which long-dead Rome once forged, still gave the power of cheating people into thinking that they were necessary lords of the world. Turn then to the lands they governed, and read and forget a long string of the causeless murders of Northern and Saracen pirates and robbers. That is pretty much the sum of what so-called history has left us of the tale of those days—the stupid languor and the evil deeds of kings and scoundrels. Must we turn away then, and say that all was evil? How then did men live from day to day? How then did Europe grow

[1] The eastern division of the Roman Empire, and after 476 the Roman Empire itself, with its capital at Constantinople.

into intelligence and freedom? It seems there were others than those of whom history (so called) has left us the names and the deeds. These, the raw material for the treasury and the slave-market, we now call "the people", and we know that they were working all that while. Yes, and that their work was not merely slaves' work, the meal-trough before them and the whip behind them; for though history (so called) has forgotten them, yet their work has not been forgotten, but has made another history—the history of Art. There is not an ancient city in the East or the West that does not bear some token of their grief, and joy, and hope. From Ispahan[1] to Northumberland, there is no building built between the seventh and seventeenth centuries that does not show the influence of the labour of that oppressed and neglected herd of men. No one of them, indeed, rose high above his fellows. There was no Plato,[2] or Shakespeare, or Michael Angelo amongst them. Yet scattered as it was among many men, how strong their thought was, how long it abided, how far it travelled!

And so it was ever through all those days when Art was so vigorous and progressive. Who can say how little we should know of many periods, but for their art? History (so called) has remembered the kings and warriors, because they destroyed; Art has remembered the people, because they created.

I think, then, that this knowledge we have of the life of past times gives us some token of the way we should take in meeting those honest and single-hearted men who above all things desire the world's progress, but whose minds are, as it were, sick on this point of the arts. Surely you may say to them: When all is gained that you (and we) so long

---

[1] Formerly the capital of Persia. During its greatest prosperity under Shah Abbas (1586–1628) it was one of the largest cities in Asia and possessed many fine palaces and other buildings, of which the Grand Mosque still remains.

[2] The most famous Greek philosopher, 429–347 B.C.

for, what shall we do then? That great change which we are working for, each in his own way, will come like other changes, as a thief in the night, and will be with us before we know it; but let us imagine that its consummation has come suddenly and dramatically, acknowledged and hailed by all right-minded people; and what shall we do then, lest we begin once more to heap up fresh corruption for the woeful labour of ages once again? I say, as we turn away from the flagstaff where the new banner has been just run up; as we depart, our ears yet ringing with the blare of the heralds' trumpets that have proclaimed the new order of things, what shall we turn to then, what *must* we turn to then?

To what else, save to our work, our daily labour?

With what, then, shall we adorn it when we have become wholly free and reasonable? It is necessary toil, but shall it be toil only? Shall all we can do with it be to shorten the hours of that toil to the utmost, that the hours of leisure may be long beyond what men used to hope for? and what then shall we do with the leisure, if we say that all toil is irksome? Shall we sleep it all away?—Yes, and never wake up again, I should hope, in that case.

What shall we do then? what shall our necessary hours of labour bring forth?

That will be a question for all men in that day when many wrongs are righted, and when there will be no classes of degradation on whom the dirty work of the world can be shovelled; and if men's minds are still sick and loathe the arts, they will not be able to answer that question.

Once men sat under grinding tyrannies, amidst violence and fear so great, that nowadays we wonder how they lived through twenty-four hours of it, till we remember that then, as now, their daily labour was the main part of their lives, and that that daily labour was sweetened by the daily creation of Art; and shall we who are delivered from the

evils they bore, live drearier days than they did? Shall
men, who have come forth from so many tyrannies, bind
themselves to yet another one, and become the slaves of
nature, piling day upon day of hopeless, useless toil? Must
this go on worsening till it comes to this at last—that the
world shall have come into its inheritance, and with all foes
conquered and nought to bind it, shall choose to sit down
and labour for ever amidst grim ugliness? How, then, were
all our hopes cheated, what a gulf of despair should we
tumble into then!

In truth, it cannot be; yet if that sickness of repulsion
to the arts were to go on hopelessly, nought else would be,
and the extinction of the love of beauty and imagination
would prove to be the extinction of civilization. But that
sickness the world will one day throw off, yet will, I
believe, pass through many pains in so doing, some of which
will look very like the death-throes of Art, and some,
perhaps, will be grievous enough to the poor people of the
world; since hard necessity, I doubt, works many of the
world's changes, rather than the purblind striving to see,
which we call the foresight of man.

Hopes and Fears for Art: The Art of the People.

THE STUDY OF ANCIENT ART

THE remedy, I repeat, is plain if it can be applied; the
handicraftsman, left behind by the artist when the arts
sundered, must come up with him, must work side by side
with him: apart from the difference between a great master
and a scholar, apart from the differences of the natural
bent of men's minds, which would make one man an
imitative, and another an architectural or decorative artist,
there should be no difference between those employed on
strictly ornamental work; and the body of artists dealing

with this should quicken with their art all makers of things into artists also, in proportion to the necessities and uses of the things they would make.

I know what stupendous difficulties, social and economical, there are in the way of this; yet I think that they seem to be greater than they are: and of one thing I am sure, that no real living decorative art is possible if this is impossible.

It is not impossible, on the contrary it is certain to come about, if you are at heart desirous to quicken the arts; if the world will, for the sake of beauty and decency, sacrifice some of the things it is so busy over (many of which I think are not very worthy of its trouble), art will begin to grow again; as for those difficulties above mentioned, some of them I know will in any case melt away before the steady change of the relative conditions of men; the rest, reason and resolute attention to the laws of nature, which are also the laws of art, will dispose of little by little: once more, the way will not be far to seek, if the will be with us.

Yet, granted the will, and though the way lies ready to us, we must not be discouraged if the journey seem barren enough at first, nay, not even if things seem to grow worse for a while: for it is natural enough that the very evil which has forced on the beginning of reform should look uglier, while on the one hand life and wisdom are building up the new, and on the other folly and deadness are hugging the old to them.

In this, as in all other matters, lapse of time will be needed before things seem to straighten, and the courage and patience that does not despise small things lying ready to be done; and care and watchfulness, lest we begin to build the wall ere the footings are well in; and always through all things much humility that is not easily cast down by failure, that seeks to be taught, and is ready to learn.

For your teachers, they must be Nature and History: as

for the first, that you must learn of it is so obvious that I need not dwell upon that now: hereafter, when I have to speak more of matters of detail, I may have to speak of the manner in which you must learn of Nature. As to the second, I do not think that any man but one of the highest genius, could do anything in these days without much study of ancient art, and even he would be much hindered if he lacked it. If you think that this contradicts what I said about the death of that ancient art, and the necessity I implied for an art that should be characteristic of the present day, I can only say that, in these times of plenteous knowledge and meagre performance, if we do not study the ancient work directly and learn to understand it, we shall find ourselves influenced by the feeble work all round us, and shall be copying the better work through the copyists and *without* understanding it, which will by no means bring about intelligent art. Let us therefore study it wisely, be taught by it, kindled by it; all the while determining not to imitate or repeat it; to have either no art at all, or an art which we have made our own.

Yet I am almost brought to a stand-still when bidding you to study nature and the history of art, by remembering that this is London, and what it is like: how can I ask working-men passing up and down these hideous streets day by day to care about beauty? If it were politics, we must care about that; or science, you could wrap yourselves up in the study of facts, no doubt, without much caring what goes on about you—but beauty! do you not see what terrible difficulties beset art, owing to a long neglect of art —and neglect of reason, too, in this matter? It is such a heavy question by what effort, by what dead-lift, you can thrust this difficulty from you, that I must perforce set it aside for the present, and must at least hope that the study of history and its monuments will help you somewhat herein. If you can really fill your minds with memories of great works of art, and great times of art, you will, I think, be able to a certain extent to look through the aforesaid ugly surroundings, and will be moved to discontent of what is careless and brutal now, and will, I hope, at last be so much discontented with what is bad, that you will determine to bear no longer that short-sighted, reckless brutality of squalor that so disgraces our intricate civilization.

Well, at any rate, London is good for this, that it is well off for museums—which I heartily wish were to be got at seven days in the week instead of six, or at least on the only day on which an ordinarily busy man, one of the taxpayers who support them, can as a rule see them quietly —and certainly any of us who may have any natural turn for art must get more help from frequenting them than one can well say. It is true, however, that people need some preliminary instruction before they can get all the good possible to be got from the prodigious treasures of art possessed by the country in that form: there also one sees things in a piecemeal way: nor can I deny that there is something melancholy about a museum, such a tale of violence, destruction, and carelessness, as its treasured scraps tell us.

But moreover you may sometimes have an opportunity of studying ancient art in a narrower but a more intimate, a more kindly form, the monuments of our own land. Sometimes only, since we live in the middle of this world of brick and mortar, and there is little else left us amidst it, except the ghost of the great church at Westminster, ruined as its exterior is by the stupidity of the restoring architect, and insulted as its glorious interior is by the pompous undertakers' lies, by the vainglory and ignorance of the last two centuries and a half—little besides that and the matchless Hall near it: but when we can get beyond that smoky world, there, out in the country, we may still see the works of our fathers yet alive amidst the very nature they were wrought into, and of which they are so completely a part. For there indeed if anywhere, in the English country, in the days when people cared about such things, was there a full sympathy between the works of man, and the land they were made for. The land is a little land; too much shut up within the narrow seas, as it seems, to have much space for swelling into hugeness: there are no great wastes over-whelming in their dreariness, no great solitudes of forests, no terrible untrodden mountain-walls: all is measured, mingled, varied, gliding easily one thing into another: little rivers, little plains, swelling, speedily-changing uplands, all beset with handsome orderly trees; little hills, little moun-tains, netted over with the walls of sheep-walks: all is little; yet not foolish and blank, but serious rather, and abundant of meaning for such as choose to seek it: it is neither prison nor palace, but a decent home.

All which I neither praise nor blame, but say that so it is: some people praise this homeliness overmuch, as if the land were the very axle-tree of the world; so do not I, nor any unblinded by pride in themselves and all that belongs to them: others there are who scorn it and the tameness of it: not I any the more: though it would indeed be hard if there were nothing else in the world, no wonders, no terrors, no unspeakable beauties: yet when we think what a small part of the world's history, past, present, and to come, is this land we live in, and how much smaller still in the history of the arts, and yet how our forefathers clung to it, and with what care and pains they adorned it, this unromantic, uneventful-looking land of England, surely by this too our hearts may be touched, and our hope quickened.

For as was the land, such was the art of it while folk yet troubled themselves about such things; it strove little to impress people either by pomp or ingenuity: not unseldom it fell into commonplace, rarely it rose into majesty; yet was it never oppressive, never a slave's nightmare nor an insolent boast: and at its best it had an inventiveness, an individuality that grander styles have never overpassed: its best too, and that was in its very heart, was given as freely to the yeoman's house, and the humble village church, as to the lord's palace or the mighty cathedral: never coarse, though often rude enough, sweet, natural and unaffected, an art of peasants rather than of merchant-princes or courtiers, it must be a hard heart, I think, that does not love it: whether a man has been born among it like our-selves, or has come wonderingly on its simplicity from all the grandeur over-seas. A peasant art, I say, and it clung fast to the life of the people, and still lived among the cottagers and yeomen in many parts of the country while the big houses were being built "French and fine": still lived also in many a quaint pattern of loom and printing-block, and embroiderer's needle, while over-seas stupid pomp had extinguished all nature and freedom, and art was become, in France especially, the mere expression of that successful and exultant rascality, which in the flesh no long time afterwards went down into the pit for ever.

Hopes and Fears for Art: The Lesser Arts.

NEGLECT OF ART

I WILL run the risk of offending you by speaking plainly, and saying, that to me it seems over true that cultivated people in general do *not* care about the arts: nevertheless I will answer any possible challenge as to the usefulness of trying to rouse them to thought about the matter, by saying that they do not care about the arts because they do not know what they mean, or what they lose in lacking them: cultivated, that is rich, as they are, they are also under that harrow of hard necessity which is driven onward so remorselessly by the competitive commerce of the latter days; a system which is drawing near now I hope to its perfection, and therefore to its death and change: the many millions of civilization, as labour is now organized, can scarce think seriously of anything but the means of earning their daily bread; they do not know of art, it does not touch their lives at all: the few thousands of cultivated people whom Fate, not always as kind to them as she looks, has placed above the material necessity for this hard struggle, are nevertheless bound by it in spirit: the reflex of the grinding trouble of those who toil to live that they may live to toil weighs upon them also, and forbids them to look upon art as a matter of importance: they know it but as a toy, not as a serious help to life: as they know it, it can no more lift the burden from the conscience of the rich than it can from the weariness of the poor. They do not know what art means: as I have said, they think that as labour is now organized art can· go indefinitely as *it* is now organized, practised by a few for a few, adding a little interest, a little refinement to the lives of those who have come to look upon intellectual interest and spiritual refinement as their birthright.

No, no, it can never be: believe me, if it were otherwise possible that it should be an enduring condition of humanity that there must be one class utterly refined and another utterly brutal, art would bar the way and forbid the monstrosity to exist: such refinement would have to do as well as it might without the aid of Art: it may be she will die, but it cannot be that she will live the slave of the rich, and the token of the enduring slavery of the poor. If the life of the world is to be brutalized by her death, the rich must share that brutalization with the poor.

I know that there are people of good-will now, as there have been in all ages, who have conceived of art as going hand in hand with luxury, nay, as being much the same thing; but it is an idea false from the root up, and most hurtful to art, as I could demonstrate to you by many examples if I had time, lacking which I will only meet it with one, which I hope will be enough.

We are here in the richest city of the richest country of the richest age of the world: no luxury of time past can compare with our luxury; and yet if you could clear your eyes from habitual blindness you would have to confess that there is no crime against art, no ugliness, no vulgarity which is not shared with perfect fairness and equality between the modern hovels of Bethnal Green and the modern palaces of the West End: and then if you looked at the matter deeply and seriously, you would not regret it, but rejoice at it, and as you went past some notable example of the aforesaid palaces you would exult indeed as you said, "So that is all that luxury and money can do for refinement".

For the rest, if of late there has been any change for the better in the prospects of the arts; if there has been a struggle both to throw off the chains of dead and powerless tradition, and to understand the thoughts and aspirations of those among whom those traditions were once alive powerful and beneficent; if there has been abroad any spirit of resistance to the flood of sordid ugliness that modern civilization has created to make modern civilization miserable: in a word, if any of us have had the courage to be discontented that Art seems dying, and to hope for her new birth, it is because others have been discontented and hopeful in other matters than the arts; I believe most sincerely that the steady progress of those whom the stupidity of language forces me to call the lower classes in material, political, and social condition, has been our real help in all that we have been able to do or to hope, although both the helpers and the helped have been mostly unconscious of it.

It is indeed in this belief, the belief in the beneficent progress of civilization, that I venture to face you and to entreat you to strive to enter into the real meaning of the arts, which are surely the expression of reverence for nature, and the crown of nature, the life of man upon the earth.

With this intent in view I may, I think, hope to move you, I do not say to agree to all I urge upon you, yet at least to think the matter worth thinking about; and if you once do that, I believe I shall have won you. Maybe indeed that many things which I think beautiful you will deem of small account; nay, that even some things I think base and ugly will not vex your eyes or your minds: but one thing I know you will none of you like to plead guilty to—blindness to the natural beauty of the earth; and of that beauty art is the only possible guardian.

No one of you can fail to know what neglect of art has done to this great treasure of mankind: the earth which was beautiful before man lived on it, which for many ages grew in beauty as men grew in numbers and power, is now growing uglier day by day, and there the swiftest where civilization is the mightiest: this is quite certain; no one can deny it: are you contented that it should be so?

Surely there must be few of us to whom this degrading change has not been brought home personally. I think you will most of you understand me but too well when I ask you to remember the pang of dismay that comes on us when we revisit some spot of country which has been specially sympathetic to us in times past; which has refreshed us after toil, or soothed us after trouble; but where now as we turn the corner of the road or crown the hill's brow we can see first the inevitable blue slate roof, and then the blotched mud-coloured stucco, or ill-built wall of ill-made bricks of the new buildings; then as we come nearer and see the arid and pretentious little gardens, and cast-iron horrors of railings, and miseries of squalid out-houses breaking through the sweet meadows and abundant hedge-rows of our old quiet hamlet, do not our hearts sink within us, and are we not troubled with a perplexity not altogether selfish, when we think what a little bit of care-lessness it takes to destroy a world of pleasure and delight, which now whatever happens can never be recovered?

Well may we feel the perplexity and sickness of heart which some day the whole world shall feel to find its hopes disappointed, if we do not look to it; for this is not what civilization looked for: a new house added to the old vil-lage, where is the harm of that? Should it not have been a gain and not a loss; a sign of growth and prosperity which should have rejoiced the eye of an old friend? a new family come in health and hope to share the modest pleasures and labours of the place we loved; that should have been no grief, but a fresh pleasure to us.

Yes, and time was that it would have been so; the new house indeed would have taken away a little piece of the flowery green sward, a few yards of the teeming hedge-row; but a new order, a new beauty would have taken the place of the old: the very flowers of the field would have but given place to flowers fashioned by man's hand and mind: the hedge-row oak would have blossomed into fresh beauty in roof-tree and lintel and door-post: and though the new house would have looked young and trim beside the older houses and the ancient church—ancient even in those days—yet it would have a piece of history for the time to come, and its dear and dainty cream-white walls would have been a genuine link among the numberless links of that long chain whose beginnings we know not of, but on whose mighty length even the many-pillared garth of Pallas,[1] and the stately dome of the Eternal

[1] The Parthenon, the official temple of Pallas at Athens, begun about 450 B.C.

Wisdom,[1] are but single links, wondrous and resplendent though they be.

Such I say can a new house be, such it has been: for 'tis no ideal house I am thinking of: no rare marvel of art, of which but few can ever be vouchsafed to the best times and countries; no palace either, not even a manor-house, but a yeoman's steading at grandest, or even his shepherd's cottage: there they stand at this day, dozens of them yet, in some parts of England: such an one, and of the smallest, is before my eyes as I speak to you, standing by the roadside on one of the western slopes of the Cotswolds: the tops of the great trees near it can see a long way off the mountains of the Welsh border, and between a great county of hill, and waving woodland, and meadow and plain where lies hidden many a famous battle-field of our stout forefathers: there to the right a wavering patch of blue is the smoke of Worcester town, but Evesham smoke, though near, is unseen, so small it is: then a long line of haze just traceable shows where the Avon wends its way thence towards Severn, till Bredon Hill hides the sight both of it and Tewkesbury smoke: just below on either side the Broadway lie the grey houses of the village street ending with a lovely house of the fourteenth century; above, the road winds serpentine up the steep hillside, whose crest looking westward sees the glorious map I have been telling of spread before it, but eastward strains to look on Oxfordshire, and thence all waters run towards Thames: all about lie the sunny slopes, lovely of outline, flowery and sweetly grassed, dotted with the best-grown and most graceful of trees: 'tis a beautiful country-side indeed, not undignified, not unromantic, but most familiar.

And there stands the little house that was new once, a labourer's cottage built of the Cotswold limestone, and

[1] Santa Sophia, the famous metropolitan church of the Greeks at Constantinople, built by Justinian in 532, and since 1453 a mosque.

grown now, walls and roof, a lovely warm grey, though it was creamy white in its earliest day; no line of it could ever have marred the Cotswold beauty; everything about it is solid and well wrought: it is skilfully planned and well proportioned: there is a little sharp and delicate carving about its arched doorway, and every part of it is well cared for: 'tis in fact beautiful, a work of art and a piece of nature—no less: there is no man who could have done it better considering its use and its place.

Who built it then? No strange race of men, but just the mason of Broadway village: even such a man as is now running up down yonder three or four cottages of the wretched type we know too well: nor did he get an architect from London, or even Worcester, to design it: I believe 'tis but two hundred years old, and at that time, though beauty still lingered among the peasants' houses, your learned architects were building houses for the high gentry that were ugly enough, though solid and well built; nor are its materials far-fetched; from the neighbouring field came its walling-stones; and at the top of the hill they are quarrying now as good freestone as ever.

No, there was no effort or wonder about it when it was built, though its beauty makes it strange now.

And are you contented that we should lose all this; this simple, harmless beauty that was no hindrance or trouble to any man, and that added to the natural beauty of the earth instead of marring it?

Hopes and Fears for Art: The Prospects of Architecture.

THE BEAUTY OF ENGLAND

I HAVE said that education is the first remedy for the barbarism which has been bred by the hurry of civilization and competitive commerce. To know that men lived and worked mightily before you is an incentive for you to work faithfully now, that you may leave something to those who come after you.

What next is to be thought of after education? I must here admit that if you accept art and join the ranks of those who are to rise in rebellion against the Philistines, you will have a roughish time of it. "Nothing for nothing and not much for a dollar", says a Yankee somewhere, and I am sorry to say it is the rule of nature also. Those of us who have money will have to give of it to the cause, and all of us will have to give time, and thought, and trouble to it; and I must now consider a matter of the utmost importance to art and to the lives of all of us, which we can, if we please, deal with at once, but which emphatically claims of us time, thought, and money. Of all the things that is likely to give us back popular art in England, the cleaning of England is the first and the most necessary. Those who are to make beautiful things must live in a beautiful place. Some people may be inclined to say, and I have heard the argument put forward, that the very opposition between the serenity and purity of art and the turmoil and squalor of a great modern city stimulates the invention of artists, and produces special life in the art of to-day. I cannot believe it. It seems to me that at the best it but stimulates the feverish and dreamy qualities that throw some artists out of the general sympathy. But apart from that, these are men who are stuffed with memories of more romantic days and pleasanter lands, and it is on these memories they live, to my mind not altogether happily for their art; and you see it is only a very few men who could have even these doubtful advantages.

I abide by my statement that those who are to make beautiful things must live in beautiful places, but you must understand I do not mean to claim for all craftsmen a share of those gardens of the world, or of those sublime and awe-inspiring mountains and wastes that men make pilgrimages to see; that is to say, not a personal share. Most of us must be content with the tales of the poets and painters about these places, and learn to love the narrow spot that surrounds our daily life for what of beauty and sympathy there is in it.

For surely there is no square mile of earth's inhabitable surface that is not beautiful in its own way, if we men will only abstain from wilfully destroying that beauty; and it is this reasonable share in the beauty of the earth that I claim as the right of every man who will earn it by due labour; a decent house with decent surroundings for every honest and industrious family; that is the claim which I make of you in the name of art. Is it such an exorbitant claim to make of civilization? of a civilization that is too apt to boast in after-dinner speeches; too apt to thrust her blessings on far-off peoples at the cannon's mouth before she has improved the quality of those blessings so far that they are worth having at any price, even the smallest.

Well, I am afraid that claim is exorbitant. Both you as representatives of the manufacturing districts, and I as representing the metropolis, seem hitherto to have assumed that, at any rate; nor is there one family in a thousand that has established its claim to the right aforesaid. It is a pity though; for if the claim is to be considered inadmissible, then is it most certain that we have been simply filling windbags and weaving sand-ropes by all the trouble we have taken in founding schools of art, National Galleries, South Kensington Museums, and all the rest of it.

I have said education is good, is necessary, to all people; neither can you if you would withhold it; and yet to educate people with no hope, what do you expect to come of that? Perhaps you might learn what to expect in Russia.

Look you, as I sit at my work at home, which is at Hammersmith, close to the river, I often hear go past the window some of that ruffianism of which a good deal has

been said in the papers of late, and has been said before at
recurring periods. As I hear the yells and shrieks and all
the degradation cast on the glorious tongue of Shakespeare
and Milton, as I see the brutal reckless faces and figures
go past me, it rouses the recklessness and brutality in me
also, and fierce wrath takes possession of me, till I remember,
as I hope I mostly do, that it was my good luck only of
being born respectable and rich that has put me on this
side of the window among delightful books and lovely
works of art, and not on the other side, in the empty street,
the drink-steeped liquor-shops, the foul and degraded
lodgings. What words can say what all that means? Do
not think, I beg you, that I am speaking rhetorically in
saying that when I think of all this, I feel that the one
great thing I desire is that this great country should shake
off from her all foreign and colonial entanglements, and
turn that mighty force of her respectable people, the greatest
power the world has ever seen, to giving the children of
these poor folk the pleasures and the hopes of men. Is
that really impossible? is there no hope of it? If so, I
can only say that civilization is a delusion and a lie; there
is no such thing and no hope of such a thing.

But since I wish to live, and even to be happy, I cannot
believe it impossible. I know by my own feelings and
desires what these men want, what would have saved them
from this lowest depth of savagery: employment which
would foster their self-respect and win the praise and
sympathy of their fellows, and dwellings which they could
come to with pleasure, surroundings which would soothe
and elevate them; reasonable labour, reasonable rest. There
is only one thing that can give them this, and that is art.

I have no doubt that you think this statement a ridiculous exaggeration, but it is my firm conviction nevertheless,
and I can only ask you to remember that in my mind it
means the properly organized labour of all men who make

anything; that must at least be a mighty instrument in the raising of men's self-respect, in the adding of dignity to their lives. Once more, "Nothing for nothing and very little for a dollar". You can no more have art without paying for it than you can have anything else, and if you care about art, as you must when you come to know it, you will not shrink from the necessary sacrifice. After all, we are the descendants and countrymen of those who have well known how to give the lesser for the greater. What you have to sacrifice is chiefly money, that is, force, and dirt; a serious sacrifice I know; but perhaps, as I have said, we have made greater in England aforetime; nay, I am far from sure that dirt will not in the long run cost us more in hard cash even than art will.

So which shall we have, art or dirt?

What is to be done, then, if we make the better choice? The land we live in is not very big either in actual acreage or in scale of fashion, but I think it is not our natural love for it only that makes us think it as fit as any land for the peaceful dwellings of serious men. Our fathers have shown us that, if it could otherwise be doubted. I say, without fear of contradiction, that no dwelling of men has ever been sweeter or pleasanter than an ancient English house; but our fathers treated our lovely land well, and we have treated it ill. Time was when it was beautiful from end to end, and now you have to pick your way carefully to avoid coming across blotches of hideousness which are a disgrace, I will not say to civilization, but to human nature. I have seen no statistics of the size of these blotches in relation to the unspoiled, or partially spoiled, country, but in some places they run together so as to cover a whole county, or even several counties, while they increase at a fearful rate, fearful in good earnest and literally. Now, while this goes on unchecked, nay, unlamented, it is really idle to talk about art. While we are doing this or letting it be done, we are really covertly rejecting art, and it would be honester and better for us if we did so openly. If we accept art we must atone for what we have done and pay the cost of it. We must turn this land from the grimy back-yard of a workshop into a garden. If that seems difficult, or rather impossible, to some of you, I cannot help it; I only know that it is necessary.

As to its being impossible, I do not believe it. The men of this generation even have accomplished matters that but a very little while ago would have been thought impossible. They conquered their difficulties because their faces were set in that direction; and what was done once can be done again. Why even the money and the science that we expend in devices for killing and maiming our enemies present and future would make a good nest-egg towards the promotion of decency of life if we could make up our minds to that tremendous sacrifice.

Lectures on Art and Industry: Art and the Beauty of the Earth.

THE MODERN CITY

Furthermore, the repression of the instinct for beauty which has destroyed the Decorative and injured the Intellectual arts has not stopped there in the injury it has done us. I can myself sympathize with a feeling which I suppose is still not rare, a craving to escape sometimes to mere Nature, not only from ugliness and squalor, not only from a condition of superabundance of art, but even from a condition of art severe and well ordered, even, say, from such surroundings as the lovely simplicity of Periclean Athens.[1] I can deeply sympathize with a weary man finding his account in interest in mere life and communion with external nature, the face of the country, the wind and weather, and the course of the day, and the lives of animals,

[1] See note to p. 77.

wild and domestic; and man's daily dealings with all this for his daily bread, and rest, and innocent beast-like pleasure. But the interest in the mere animal life of man has become impossible to be indulged in in its fulness by most civilized people. Yet civilization, it seems to me, owes us some compensation for the loss of this romance, which now only hangs like a dream about the country life of busy lands. To keep the air pure and the rivers clean, to take some pains to keep the meadows and tillage as pleasant as reasonable use will allow them to be; to allow peaceable citizens freedom to wander where they will, so they do no hurt to garden or cornfield; nay, even to leave here and there some piece of waste or mountain sacredly free from fence or tillage as a memory of man's ruder struggles with nature in his earlier days: is it too much to ask civilization to be so far thoughtful of man's pleasure and rest, and to help so far as this her children to whom she has most often set such heavy tasks of grinding labour? Surely not an unreasonable asking. But not a whit of it shall we get under the present system of society. That loss of the instinct for beauty which has involved us in the loss of popular art is also busy in depriving us of the only compensation possible for that loss, by surely and not slowly destroying the beauty of the very face of the earth. Not only are London and our other great commercial cities mere masses of sordidness, filth, and squalor, embroidered with patches of pompous and vulgar hideousness, no less revolting to the eye and the mind when one knows what it means: not only have whole counties of England, and the heavens that hang over them, disappeared beneath a crust of unutterable grime, but the disease, which, to a visitor coming from the times of art, reason, and order, would seem to be a love of dirt and ugliness for its own sake, spreads all over the country, and every little market-town seizes the opportunity to imitate, as far as it can, the majesty of the hell of London and Manchester. Need I speak to you of the wretched suburbs that sprawl all round our fairest and most ancient cities? Must I speak to you of the degradation that has so speedily befallen this city,[1] still the most beautiful of them all; a city which, with its surroundings, would, if we had had a grain of common sense, have been treated like a most precious jewel, whose beauty was to be preserved at any cost? I say at any cost, for it was a possession which did not belong to us, but which we were trustees of for all posterity. I am old enough to know how we have treated that jewel; as if it were any common stone kicking about on the highway, good enough to throw at a dog. When I remember the contrast between the Oxford of to-day and the Oxford which I first saw thirty years ago, I wonder I can face the misery (there is no other word for it) of visiting it, even to have the honour of addressing you to-night. But furthermore, not only are the cities a disgrace to us, and the smaller towns a laughing-stock; not only are the dwellings of man grown inexpressibly base and ugly, but the very cowsheds and cart-stables, nay, the merest piece of necessary farm-engineering, are tarred with the same brush. Even if a tree is cut down or blown down, a worse one, if any, is planted in its stead, and, in short, our civilization is passing like a blight, daily growing heavier and more poisonous, over the whole face of the country, so that every change is sure to be a change for the worse in its outward aspect. So then it comes to this, that not only are the minds of great artists narrowed and their sympathies frozen by their isolation, not only has co-operative art come to a standstill, but the very food on which both the greater and the lesser art subsist is being destroyed; the well of art is poisoned at its spring.

Lectures on Socialism: Art under Plutocracy.

[1] This lecture was delivered at University College, Oxford, 14th November, 1883.

ARCHITECTURE

W HAT else can we do to help to educate ourselves and others in the path of art, to be on the road to attaining an *Art made by the people and for the people as a joy to the maker and the user?*

Why, having got to understand something of what art was, having got to look upon its ancient monuments as friends that can tell us something of times bygone, and whose faces we do not wish to alter, even though they be worn by time and grief: having got to spend money and trouble upon matters of decency, great and little; having made it clear that we really do care about nature even in the suburbs of a big town—having got so far, we shall begin to think of the houses in which we live.

For I must tell you that unless you are resolved to have good and rational architecture, it is, once again, useless your thinking about art at all.

I have spoken of the popular arts, but they might all be summed up in that one word Architecture; they are all parts of that great whole, and the art of house-building begins it all: if we did not know how to dye or to weave; if we had neither gold, nor silver, nor silk; and no pigments to paint with, but half-a-dozen ochres and umbers, we might yet frame a worthy art that would lead to everything, if we had but timber, stone, and lime, and a few cutting tools to make these common things not only shelter us from wind and weather, but also express the thoughts and aspirations that stir in us.

Architecture would lead us to all the arts, as it did with earlier men: but if we despise it and take no note of how we are housed, the other arts will have a hard time of it indeed.

Now I do not think the greatest of optimists would deny that, taking us one and all, we are at present housed in a perfectly shameful way, and since the greatest part of us have to live in houses already built for us, it must be admitted that it is rather hard to know what to do, beyond waiting till they tumble about our ears.

Only we must not lay the fault upon the builders, as some people seem inclined to do: they are our very humble servants, and will build what we ask for; remember, that rich men are not obliged to live in ugly houses, and yet you see they do; which the builders may be well excused for taking as a sign of what is wanted.

Well, the point is, we must do what we can, and make people understand what we want them to do for us, by letting them see what we do for ourselves.

Hitherto, judging us by that standard, the builders may well say, that we want the pretence of a thing rather than the thing itself; that we want a show of petty luxury if we are unrich, a show of insulting stupidity if we are rich: and they are quite clear that as a rule we want to get something that shall look as if it cost twice as much as it really did.

You cannot have Architecture on those terms: simplicity and solidity are the very first requisites of it: just think if it is not so: How we please ourselves with an old building by thinking of all the generations of men that have passed through it! do we not remember how it has received their joy, and borne their sorrow, and not even their folly has left sourness upon it? it still looks as kind to us as it did to them. And the converse of this we ought to feel when we look at a newly-built house if it were as it should be: we should feel a pleasure in thinking how he who had built it had left a piece of his soul behind him to greet the new-comers one after another long and long after he was gone:—but what sentiment can an ordinary modern house move in us, or what thought—save a hope that we may speedily forget its base ugliness?

Hopes and Fears for Art: The Beauty of Life.

Though many of us love architecture dearly, and believe that it helps the healthiness both of body and soul to live among beautiful things, we of the big towns are mostly compelled to live in houses which have become a by-word of contempt for their ugliness and inconvenience. The stream of civilization is against us, and we cannot battle against it.

Once more, those devoted men who have upheld the standard of truth and beauty amongst us, and whose pictures, painted amidst difficulties that none but a painter can know, show qualities of mind unsurpassed in any age—these great men have but a narrow circle that can understand their works, and are utterly unknown to the great mass of the people: civilization is so much against them, that they cannot move the people.

Therefore, looking at all this, I cannot think that all is well with the root of the tree we are cultivating. Indeed, I believe that if other things were but to stand still in the world, this improvement before mentioned would lead to a kind of art which, in that impossible case, would be in a way stable, would perhaps stand still also. This would be an art cultivated professedly by a few, and for a few, who would consider it necessary—a duty, if they could admit duties—to despise the common herd, to hold themselves aloof from all that the world has been struggling for from the first, to guard carefully every approach to their palace of art. It would be a pity to waste many words on the prospect of such a school of art as this, which does in a way, theoretically at least, exist at present, and has for its watchword a piece of slang that does not mean the harmless thing it seems to mean—art for art's sake. Its fore-doomed end must be, that art at last will seem too delicate a thing for even the hands of the initiated to touch; and the initiated must at last sit still and do nothing—to the grief of no one.

Well, certainly, if I thought you were come here to further such an art as this I could not have stood up and called you *friends*; though such a feeble folk as I have told you of one could scarce care to call foes.

Yet, as I say, such men exist, and I have troubled you with speaking of them, because I know that those honest and intelligent people, who are eager for human progress, and yet lack part of the human senses and are anti-artistic, suppose that such men are artists, and that this is what art means, and what it does for people, and that such a narrow, cowardly life is what we, fellow-handicraftsmen, aim at. I see this taken for granted continually, even by many who, to say truth, ought to know better, and I long to put the slur from off us; to make people understand that we, least of all men, wish to widen the gulf between the classes, nay, worse still, to make new classes of elevation, and new classes of degradation—new lords and new slaves; that we, least of all men, want to cultivate the "plant called man" in different ways—here stingily, there wastefully: I wish people to understand that the art we are striving for is a good thing which all can share, which will elevate all; in good sooth, if all people do not soon share it there will soon be none to share; if all are not elevated by it, mankind will lose the elevation it has gained. Nor is such an art as we long for a vain dream; such an art once was in times that were worse than these, when there was less courage, kindness, and truth in the world than there is now; such an art there will be hereafter, when there will be more courage, kindness, and truth than there is now in the world.

Let us look backward in history once more for a short while, and then steadily forward till my words are done: I began by saying that part of the common and necessary advice given to Art students was to study antiquity; and no doubt many of you, like me, have done so; have wandered, for instance, through the galleries of the admirable museum of South Kensington, and, like me, have been filled with wonder and gratitude at the beauty which has been born from the brain of man. Now, consider, I pray you, what these wonderful works are, and how they were made; and indeed, it is neither in extravagance nor without due meaning that I use the word "wonderful" in speaking of them. Well, these things are just the common household goods of those past days, and that is one reason why they are so few and so carefully treasured. They were common things in their own day, used without fear of breaking or spoiling—no rarities then—and yet we have called them "wonderful".

And how were they made? Did a great artist draw the designs for them—a man of cultivation, highly paid, daintily fed, carefully housed, wrapped up in cotton wool, in short, when he was not at work? By no means. Wonderful as these works are, they were made by "common fellows", as the phrase goes, in the common course of their daily labour. Such were the men we honour in honouring those works. And their labour—do you think it was irksome to them? Those of you who are artists know very well that it was not; that it could not be. Many a grin of pleasure, I'll be bound—and you will not contradict me—went to the carrying through of those mazes of mysterious beauty, to the invention of those strange beasts and birds and flowers that we ourselves have chuckled over at South Kensington. While they were at work, at least, these men were not unhappy, and I suppose they worked most days, and the most part of the day, as we do.

Or those treasures of architecture that we study so carefully nowadays—what are they? how were they made? There are great minsters among them, indeed, and palaces of kings and lords, but not many; and, noble and awe-inspiring as these may be, they differ only in size from the little grey church that still so often makes the commonplace English landscape beautiful, and the little grey house that still, in some parts of the country at least, makes an English village a thing apart, to be seen and pondered on by all who love romance and beauty. These form the mass of our architectural treasures, the houses that everyday people lived in, the unregarded churches in which they worshipped.

And, once more, who was it that designed and ornamented them? The great architect, carefully kept for the purpose, and guarded from the common troubles of common men? By no means. Sometimes, perhaps, it was the monk, the ploughman's brother; oftenest his other brother, the village carpenter, smith, mason, what not—"a common fellow", whose common everyday labour fashioned works that are to-day the wonder and despair of many a hard-working "cultivated" architect. And did he loathe his work? No, it is impossible. I have seen, as we most of us have, work done by such men in some out-of-the-way hamlet—where to-day even few strangers ever come, and whose people seldom go five miles from their own doors; in such places, I say, I have seen work so delicate, so careful, and so inventive, that nothing in its way could go further. And I will assert, without fear of contradiction, that no human ingenuity can produce work such as this without pleasure being a third party to the brain that conceived and the hand that fashioned it. Nor are such works rare. The throne of the great Plantagenet,[1] or the great Valois,[2] was no more daintily carved than the seat of the village mass-john, or the chest of the yeoman's good-wife.

So, you see, there was much going on to make life endurable in those times. Not every day, you may be sure,

[1] The line of English kings from 1154 to 1399, founded by Henry II and ending with Richard II.
[2] A French dynasty, a branch of the Capetian family, which provided the French kings from 1328 to 1589.

was a day of slaughter and tumult, though the histories read almost as if it were so; but every day the hammer chinked on the anvil, and the chisel played about the oak beam, and never without some beauty and invention being born of it, and consequently some human happiness.

That last word brings me to the very kernel and heart of what I have come here to say to you, and I pray you to think of it most seriously—not as to my words, but as to a thought which is stirring in the world, and will one day grow into something.

That thing which I understand by real art is the expression by man of his pleasure in labour. I do not believe he can be happy in his labour without expressing that happiness; and especially is this so when he is at work at anything in which he specially excels. A most kind gift is this of nature, since all men, nay, it seems all things too, must labour; so that not only does the dog take pleasure in hunting, and the horse in running, and the bird in flying, but so natural does the idea seem to us, that we imagine to ourselves that the earth and the very elements rejoice in doing their appointed work; and the poets have told us of the spring meadows smiling, of the exultation of the fire, of the countless laughter of the sea.

Nor until these latter days has man ever rejected this universal gift, but always, when he has not been too much perplexed, too much bound by disease or beaten down by trouble, has striven to make his work at least happy. Pain he has too often found in his pleasure, and weariness in his rest, to trust to these. What matter if his happiness lie with what must be always with him—his work?

And, once more, shall we, who have gained so much, forego this gain, the earliest, most natural gain of mankind? If we have to a great extent done so, as I verily fear we have, what strange fog-lights must have misled us; or rather let me say, how hard pressed we must have been in the battle with the evils we have overcome, to have forgotten the greatest of all evils. I cannot call it less than that. If a man has work to do which he despises, which does not satisfy his natural and rightful desire for pleasure, the greater part of his life must pass unhappily and without self-respect. Consider, I beg of you, what that means, and what ruin must come of it in the end.

Hopes and Fears for Art: The Art of the People.

I think one may divide the work with which Architecture is conversant into three classes: first there is the purely mechanical: those who do this are machines only, and the less they think of what they are doing the better for the purpose, supposing they are properly drilled: the purpose of this work, to speak plainly, is not the making of wares of any kind, but what on the one hand is called employment, on the other what is called money-making: that is to say, in other words, the multiplication of the species of the mechanical workman, and the increase of the riches of the man who sets him to work, called in our modern jargon by a strange perversion of language, a manufacturer:* Let us call this kind of work Mechanical Toil.

The second kind is more or less mechanical as the case may be; but it can always be done better or worse: if it is to be well done, it claims attention from the workman, and he must leave on it signs of his individuality: there will be more or less of art in it, over which the workman has at least some control; and he will work on it partly to earn his bread in not too toilsome or disgusting a way, but in a way which makes even his work-hours pass pleasantly to him, and partly to make wares, which when made will be a distinct gain to the world; things that will be praised and delighted in. This work I would call Intelligent Work.

* Or, to put it plainer still, the unlimited breeding of mechanical workmen as *mechanical workmen*, not as *men*.

The third kind of work has but little if anything mechanical about it; it is altogether individual; that is to say, that what any man does by means of it could never have been done by any other man. Properly speaking, this work is all pleasure: true, there are pains and perplexities and weariness in it, but they are like the troubles of a beautiful life; the dark places that make the bright ones brighter: they are the romance of the work and do but elevate the workman, not depress him: I would call this Imaginative Work.

Now I can fancy that at first sight it may seem to you as if there were more difference between this last and Intelligent Work, than between Intelligent Work and Mechanical Toil: but 'tis not so. The difference between these two is the difference between light and darkness, between Ormuzd and Ahriman:[1] whereas the difference between Intelligent work and what for want of a better word I am calling Imaginative work, is a matter of degree only; and in times when art is abundant and noble there is no break in the chain from the humblest of the lower to the greatest of the higher class; from the poor weaver who chuckles as the bright colour comes round again, to the great painter anxious and doubtful if he can give to the world the whole of his thought or only nine-tenths of it, they are all artists— that is men; while the mechanical workman, who does not note the difference between bright and dull in his colours, but only knows them by numbers, is, while he is at his work, no man, but a machine. Indeed when Intelligent work coexists with Imaginative, there is no hard and fast line between them; in the very best and happiest times of art, there is scarce any Intelligent work which is not

---

[1] In the dual system of Zoroaster, the founder of the ancient Persian religion, Ormuzd (Ormazd), The Good Spirit, is in eternal conflict with Ahriman, The Spiritual Enemy, and the good kingdom will eventually be established by the triumph of Ormuzd.

Imaginative also; and there is but little of effort or doubt, or sign of unexpressed desires even in the highest of the Imaginative work: the blessing of Equality elevates the lesser, and calms the greater, art.

Now further, Mechanical Toil is bred of that hurry and thoughtlessness of civilization of which, as aforesaid, the middle classes of this country have been such powerful furtherers: on the face of it it is hostile to civilization, a curse that civilization has made for itself and can no longer think of abolishing or controlling: such it seems, I say; but since it bears with it change and tremendous change, it may well be that there is something more than mere loss in it: it will full surely destroy art as we know art, unless art new-born destroy it: yet belike at the worst it will destroy other things beside which are the poison of art, and in the long run itself also, and thus make way for the new art, of whose form we know nothing.

Intelligent work is the child of struggling, hopeful, progressive civilization: and its office is to add fresh interest to simple and uneventful lives, to soothe discontent with innocent pleasure fertile of deeds gainful to mankind; to bless the many toiling millions with hope daily recurring, and which it will by no means disappoint.

Imaginative work is the very blossom of civilization triumphant and hopeful; it would fain lead men to aspire towards perfection: each hope that it fulfils gives birth to yet another hope: it bears in its bosom the worth and the meaning of life and the counsel to strive to understand everything; to fear nothing and to hate nothing: in a word, 'tis the symbol and sacrament of the Courage of the World.

Hopes and Fears for Art: The Prospects of Architecture.

MACHINERY

I do not think that anything will take the place of art; not that I doubt the ingenuity of man, which seems to be boundless in the direction of making himself unhappy, but because I believe the springs of art in the human mind to be deathless, and also because it seems to me easy to see the causes of the present obliteration of the arts.

For we civilized people have not given them up consciously, or of our free will; we have been *forced* to give them up. Perhaps I can illustrate that by the detail of the application of machinery to the production of things in which artistic form of some sort is possible. Why does a reasonable man use a machine? Surely to save his labour. There are some things which a machine can do as well as a man's hand, *plus* a tool, can do them. He need not, for instance, grind his corn in a hand-quern; a little trickle of water, a wheel, and a few simple contrivances will do it all perfectly well, and leave him free to smoke his pipe and think, or to carve the handle of his knife. That, so far, is unmixed gain in the use of a machine—always, mind you, supposing equality of condition among men; no art is lost, leisure or time for more pleasurable work is gained. Perhaps a perfectly reasonable and free man would stop there in his dealings with machinery; but such reason and freedom are too much to expect, so let us follow our machine-inventor a step farther. He has to weave plain cloth, and finds doing so dullish on the one hand, and on the other that a power-loom will weave the cloth nearly as well as a hand-loom: so, in order to gain more leisure or time for more pleasurable work, he uses a power-loom, and foregoes the small advantage of the little extra art in the cloth. But so doing, as far as the art is concerned, he has not got a pure gain; he has made a bargain between art and labour, and got a makeshift as a consequence. I do not say that he may not be right in so doing, but that he has lost as well as gained. Now, this is as far as a man who values art and is reasonable would go in the matter of machinery *as long as he was free*—that is, was not *forced* to work for another man's profit; so long as he was living in a society *that had accepted equality of condition.* Carry the machine used for art a step farther, and he becomes an unreasonable man, if he values art and is free. To avoid misunderstanding, I must say that I am thinking of the modern machine, which is as it were alive, and to which the man is auxiliary, and not of the old machine, the improved tool, which is auxiliary to the man, and only works as long as his hand is thinking; though I will remark, that even this elementary form of machine has to be dropped when we come to the higher and more intricate forms of art. Well, as to the machine proper used for art, when it gets to the stage above dealing with a necessary production that has accidentally some beauty about it, a reasonable man with a feeling for art will only use it when he is *forced* to. If he thinks he would like ornament, for instance, and knows that the machine cannot do it properly, and does not care to spend the time to do it properly, why should he do it at all? He will not diminish his leisure for the sake of making something he does not want unless some man or band of men force him to it; so he will either go without the ornament, or sacrifice some of his leisure to have it genuine. That will be a sign that he wants it very much, and that it will be worth his trouble: in which case, again, his labour on it will not be mere trouble, but will interest and please him by satisfying the needs of his mood of energy.

This, I say, is how a reasonable man would act if he were free from man's compulsion; not being free, he acts very differently. He has long passed the stage at which machines are only used for doing work repulsive to an average man, or for doing what could be as well done by a machine as a man, and he instinctively expects a machine to be invented whenever any product of industry becomes sought after. He is the slave to machinery; the new machine *must* be invented, and when invented he *must*—I will not say use it; but be used by it, whether he likes it or not.

Signs of Change: The Aims of Art.

THE NECESSITIES OF LIFE

W H A T is it that I need, therefore, which my surrounding circumstances can give me—my dealings with my fellow-men—setting aside inevitable accidents which co-operation and forethought cannot control, if there be such?

Well, first of all I claim good health; and I say that a vast proportion of people in civilization scarcely even know what that means. To feel mere life a pleasure; to enjoy the moving one's limbs and exercising one's bodily powers; to play, as it were, with sun and wind and rain; to rejoice in satisfying the due bodily appetites of a human animal without fear of degradation or sense of wrong-doing: yes, and therewithal to be well-formed, straight-limbed, strongly knit, expressive of countenance—to be, in a word, beautiful —that also I claim. If we cannot have this claim satisfied, we are but poor creatures after all; and I claim it in the teeth of those terrible doctrines of asceticism, which, born of the despair of the oppressed and degraded, have been for so many ages used as instruments for the continuance of that oppression and degradation.

And I believe that this claim for a healthy body for all of us carries with it all other due claims: for who knows where the seeds of disease which even rich people suffer from were first sown: from the luxury of an ancestor, perhaps; yet often, I suspect, from his poverty. And for the poor: a distinguished physicist has said that the poor suffer always from one disease—hunger; and at least I know this, that if a man is overworked in any degree he cannot enjoy the sort of health I am speaking of; nor can he if he is continually chained to one dull round of mechanical work, with no hope at the other end of it; nor if he lives in continual sordid anxiety for his livelihood, nor if he is ill-housed, nor if he is deprived of all enjoyment of the natural beauty of the world, nor if he has no amusement to quicken the flow of his spirits from time to time: all these things, which touch more or less directly on his bodily condition, are born of the claim I make to live in good health; indeed, I suspect that these good conditions must have been in force for several generations before a population in general will be really healthy, as I have hinted above; but also I doubt not that in the course of time they would, joined to other conditions, of which more hereafter, gradually breed such a population, living in enjoyment of animal life at least, happy therefore, and beautiful according to the beauty of their race. On this point I may note that the very variations in the races of men are caused by the conditions under which they live, and though in these rougher parts of the world we lack some of the advantages of climate and surroundings, yet, if we were working for livelihood and not for profit, we might easily neutralize many of the disadvantages of our climate, at least enough to give due scope to the full development of our race.

Now the next thing I claim is education. And you must not say that every English child is educated now; that sort of education will not answer my claim, though I cheerfully admit it is something: something, and yet after all only class education. What I claim is liberal education; opportunity, that is, to have my share of whatever knowledge there is in the world according to my capacity or bent of mind, historical or scientific; and also to have my share of skill of hand which is about in the world, either in the industrial handicrafts or in the fine arts; picture-painting, sculpture, music, acting, or the like: I claim to be taught, if I can be taught, more than one craft to exercise for the benefit of the community. You may think this a large claim, but I am clear it is not too large a claim if the community is to have any gain out of my special capacities, if we are not all to be beaten down to a dull level of mediocrity as we are now, all but the very strongest and toughest of us.

But also I know that this claim for education involves one for public advantages in the shape of public libraries, schools, and the like, such as no private person, not even the richest, could command: but these I claim very confidently, being sure that no reasonable community could bear to be without such helps to a decent life.

Again, the claim for education involves a claim for abundant leisure, which once more I make with confidence; because when once we have shaken off the slavery of profit, labour would be organized so unwastefully that no heavy burden would be laid on the individual citizens; every one of whom as a matter of course would have to pay his toll of some obviously useful work. At present you must note that all the amazing machinery which we have invented has served only to increase the amount of profit-bearing wares; in other words, to increase the amount of profit pouched by individuals for their own advantage, part of which profit they use as capital for the production of more profit, with ever the same waste attached to it; and part as private riches or means for luxurious living, which again is sheer waste—is in fact to be looked on as a kind of bonfire on which rich men burn up the product of the labour they have fleeced from the workers beyond what they themselves can use. So I say that, in spite of our inventions, no worker works under the present system an

hour the less on account of those labour-saving machines,
so-called. But under a happier state of things they would
be used simply for saving labour, with the result of a vast
amount of leisure gained for the community to be added
to that gained by the avoidance of the waste of useless
luxury, and the abolition of the service of commercial
war.

And I may say that as to that leisure, as I should in no
case do any harm to any one with it, so I should often do
some direct good to the community with it, by practising
arts or occupations for my hands or brain which would give
pleasure to many of the citizens; in other words, a great
deal of the best work done would be done in the leisure
time of men relieved from any anxiety as to their livelihood,
and eager to exercise their special talent, as all men, nay,
all animals are.

Now, again, this leisure would enable me to please myself and expand my mind by travelling if I had a mind to it:
because, say, for instance, that I were a shoemaker; if due
social order were established, it by no means follows that
I should always be obliged to make shoes in one place; a
due amount of easily conceivable arrangement would enable
me to make shoes in Rome, say, for three months, and to
come back with new ideas of building, gathered from the
sight of the works of past ages, amongst other things which
would perhaps be of service in London.

But now, in order that my leisure might not degenerate
into idleness and aimlessness, I must set up a claim for due
work to do. Nothing to my mind is more important than
this demand, and I must ask your leave to say something
about it. I have mentioned that I should probably use my
leisure for doing a good deal of what is now called work;
but it is clear that if I am a member of a Socialist Community I must do my due share of rougher work than this
—my due share of what my capacity enables me to do,

that is; no fitting of me to a Procrustean bed;[1] but even
that share of work necessary to the existence of the simplest
social life must, in the first place, whatever else it is, be
reasonable work; that is, it must be such work as a good
citizen can see the necessity for; as a member of the community, I must have agreed to do it.

To take two strong instances of the contrary, I won't
submit to be dressed up in red and marched off to shoot at
my French or German or Arab friend in a quarrel that I
don't understand; I will rebel sooner than do that.

Nor will I submit to waste my time and energies in
making some trifling toy which I know only a fool can
desire; I will rebel sooner than do that.

However, you may be sure that in a state of social order
I shall have no need to rebel against any such pieces of
unreason; only I am forced to speak from the way we live
to the way we might live.

Again, if the necessary reasonable work be of a mechanical kind, I must be helped to do it by a machine, not
to cheapen my labour, but so that as little time as possible
may be spent upon it, and that I may be able to think of
other things while I am tending the machine. And if the
work be specially rough or exhausting, you will, I am sure,
agree with me in saying that I must take turns in doing it
with other people; I mean I mustn't, for instance, be
expected to spend my working hours always at the bottom
of a coal-pit. I think such work as that ought to be largely
volunteer work, and done, as I say, in spells. And what
I say of very rough work I say also of nasty work. On
the other hand, I should think very little of the manhood
of a stout and healthy man who did not feel a pleasure in
doing rough work; always supposing him to work under

---

[1] Procrustes was a legendary Attic robber who tortured his prisoners
upon a bed: those who were too short he stretched to fit it, and those
who were too tall had their limbs cut to the proper length.

the conditions I have been speaking of—namely, feeling that it was useful (and consequently honoured), and that it was not continuous or hopeless, and that he was really doing it of his own free will.

The last claim I make for my work is that the places I worked in, factories or workshops, should be pleasant, just as the fields where our most necessary work is done are pleasant. Believe me there is nothing in the world to prevent this being done, save the necessity of making profits on all wares; in other words, the wares are cheapened at the expense of people being forced to work in crowded, unwholesome, squalid, noisy dens: that is to say, they are cheapened at the expense of the workman's life.

Well, so much for my claims as to my *necessary* work, my tribute to the community. I believe people would find, as they advanced in their capacity for carrying on social order, that life so lived was much less expensive than we now can have any idea of, and that, after a little, people would rather be anxious to seek work than to avoid it; that our working hours would rather be merry parties of men and maids, young men and old enjoying themselves over their work, than the grumpy weariness it mostly is now. Then would come the time for the new birth of art, so much talked of, so long deferred; people could not help showing their mirth and pleasure in their work, and would be always wishing to express it in a tangible and more or less enduring form, and the workshop would once more be a school of art, whose influence no one could escape from.

Again, again, that word art leads me to my last claim, which is that the material surroundings of my life should be pleasant, generous, and beautiful; that I know is a large claim, but this I will say about it, that if it cannot be satisfied, if every civilized community cannot provide such surroundings for all its members, I do not want the world to go on; it is a mere misery that man has ever existed.

I do not think it possible under the present circumstances to speak too strongly on this point. I feel sure that the time will come when people will find it difficult to believe that a rich community such as ours, having such command over external Nature, could have submitted to live such a mean, shabby, dirty life as we do.

Signs of Change: How we live and how we might live.

MEANS OF IMPROVEMENT

THE first step towards making labour attractive is to get the means of making labour fruitful, the Capital, including the land, machinery, factories, etc., into the hands of the community, to be used for the good of all alike, so that we might all work at "supplying" the real "demands" of each and all—that is to say, work for livelihood, instead of working to supply the demand of the profit market—instead of working for profit—i.e., the power of compelling other men to work against their will.

When this first step has been taken and men begin to understand that Nature wills all men either to work or starve, and when they are no longer such fools as to allow some the alternative of stealing, when this happy day is come, we shall then be relieved from the tax of waste, and consequently shall find that we have, as aforesaid, a mass of labour-power available, which will enable us to live as we please within reasonable limits. We shall no longer be hurried and driven by the fear of starvation, which at present presses no less on the greater part of men in civilized communities than it does on mere savages. The first and most obvious necessities will be so easily provided for in a community in which there is no waste of labour, that we shall have time to look round and consider what we really do want, that can be obtained without overtaxing our energies; for the often-expressed fear of mere idleness falling upon us when the force supplied by the present hierarchy of compulsion is withdrawn, is a fear which is but generated by the burden of excessive and repulsive labour, which we most of us have to bear at present.

I say once more that, in my belief, the first thing which we shall think so necessary as to be worth sacrificing some idle time for, will be the attractiveness of labour. No very heavy sacrifice will be required for attaining this object, but some *will* be required. For we may hope that men who have just waded through a period of strife and revolution will be the last to put up long with a life of mere utilitarianism, though Socialists are sometimes accused by ignorant persons of aiming at such a life. On the other hand, the ornamental part of modern life is already rotten to the core, and must be utterly swept away before the new order of things is realized. There is nothing of it—there is nothing which could come of it that could satisfy the aspirations of men set free from the tyranny of commercialism.

We must begin to build up the ornamental part of life —its pleasures, bodily and mental, scientific and artistic, social and individual—on the basis of work undertaken willingly and cheerfully, with the consciousness of benefiting ourselves and our neighbours by it. Such absolutely necessary work as we should have to do would in the first place take up but a small part of each day, and so far would not be burdensome; but it would be a task of daily recurrence, and therefore would spoil our day's pleasure unless it were made at least endurable while it lasted. In other words, all labour, even the commonest, must be made attractive.

How can this be done?—is the question the answer to which will take up the rest of this paper. In giving some hints on this question, I know that, while all Socialists will agree with many of the suggestions made, some of them may seem to some strange and venturesome. These must be considered as being given without any intention of dogmatizing, and as merely expressing my own personal opinion.

From all that has been said already it follows that labour, to be attractive, must be directed towards some obviously useful end, unless in cases where it is undertaken voluntarily by each individual as a pastime. This element of obvious usefulness is all the more to be counted on in sweetening tasks otherwise irksome, since social morality, the responsibility of man towards the life of man, will, in the new order of things, take the place of theological morality, or the responsibility of man to some abstract idea. Next, the day's work will be short. This need not be insisted on. It is clear that with work unwasted it *can* be short. It is clear also that much work which is now a torment, would be easily endurable if it were much shortened.

Variety of work is the next point, and a most important one. To compel a man to do day after day the same task, without any hope of escape or change, means nothing short of turning his life into a prison-torment. Nothing but the tyranny of profit-grinding makes this necessary. A man might easily learn and practise at least three crafts, varying sedentary occupation with outdoor—occupation calling for the exercise of strong bodily energy for work in which the mind had more to do. There are few men, for instance, who would not wish to spend part of their lives in the most necessary and pleasantest of all work—cultivating the earth. One thing which will make this variety of employment possible will be the form that education will take in a socially ordered community. At present all education is directed towards the end of fitting people to take their places in the hierarchy of commerce—these as masters, those as workmen. The education of the masters is more ornamental than that of the workmen, but it is commercial still; and even at the ancient universities learning is but little regarded, unless it can in the long run be made *to pay*. Due education is a totally different thing from this, and concerns itself in finding out what different people are fit for, and helping them along the road which they are inclined to take. In a duly ordered society, therefore, young people would be taught such handicrafts as they had a turn for as a part of their education, the discipline of their minds and bodies; and adults would also have opportunities of learning in the same schools, for the development of individual capacities would be of all things chiefly aimed at by education, instead, as now, the subordination of all capacities to the great end of "money-making" for oneself—or one's master. The amount of talent, and even genius, which the present system crushes, and which would be drawn out by such a system, would make our daily work easy and interesting.

Under this head of variety I will note one product of industry which has suffered so much from commercialism that it can scarcely be said to exist, and is, indeed, so foreign from our epoch that I fear there are some who will find it difficult to understand what I have to say on the subject, which I nevertheless must say, since it is really a most important one. I mean that side of art which is, or ought to be, done by the ordinary workman while he is about his ordinary work, and which has got to be called, very properly, Popular Art. This art, I repeat, no longer exists now, having been killed by commercialism. But from the beginning of man's contest with Nature till the rise of the present capitalistic system, it was alive, and generally flourished. While it lasted, everything that was made by man was adorned by man, just as everything made by Nature is adorned by her. The craftsman, as he fashioned the thing he had under his hand, ornamented it so naturally and so entirely without conscious effort, that it is often difficult to distinguish where the mere utilitarian part of his work ended and the ornamental began. Now the origin of this art was the necessity that the workman felt for variety in his work, and though the beauty produced by this desire was a great gift to the world, yet the obtaining variety and pleasure in the work by the workman was a matter of more importance still, for it stamped all labour with the impress of pleasure. All this has now quite disappeared from the work of civilization. If you wish to have ornament, you must pay specially for it, and the workman is compelled to produce ornament, as he is to produce other wares. He is compelled to pretend happiness in his work, so that the beauty produced by man's hand, which was once a solace to his labour, has now become an extra burden to him, and ornament is now but one of the follies of useless toil, and perhaps not the least irksome of its fetters.

Besides the short duration of labour, its conscious use-fulness, and the variety which should go with it, there is another thing needed to make it attractive, and that is pleasant surroundings. The misery and squalor which we people of civilization bear with so much complacency as a necessary part of the manufacturing system, is just as neces-sary to the community at large as a proportionate amount of filth would be in the house of a private rich man. If such a man were to allow the cinders to be raked all over his drawing-room, and a privy to be established in each corner of his dining-room, if he habitually made a dust and refuse heap of his once beautiful garden, never washed his sheets or changed his tablecloth, and made his family sleep five in a bed, he would surely find himself in the claws of a commission *de lunatico*. But such acts of miserly folly are just what our present society is doing daily under the compulsion of a supposed necessity, which is nothing short of madness. I beg you to bring your commission of lunacy against civilization without more delay.

For all our crowded towns and bewildering factories are simply the outcome of the profit system. Capitalistic manufacture, capitalistic land-owning, and capitalistic exchange force men into big cities in order to manipulate them in the interests of capital; the same tyranny contracts the due space of the factory so much that (for instance) the interior of a great weaving-shed is almost as ridiculous a spectacle as it is a horrible one. There is no other necessity for all this, save the necessity for grinding profits out of men's lives, and of producing cheap goods for the use (and subjection) of the slaves who grind. All labour is not yet driven into factories; often where it is there is no necessity for it, save again the profit-tyranny. People engaged in all such labour need by no means be compelled to pig together in close city quarters. There is no reason why they should not follow their occupations in quiet country homes, in industrial colleges, in small towns, or, in short, where they find it happiest for them to live.

As to that part of labour which must be associated on a large scale, this very factory system, under a reasonable order of things (though to my mind there might still be drawbacks to it), would at least offer opportunities for a full and eager social life surrounded by many pleasures. The factories might be centres of intellectual activity also, and work in them might well be varied very much: the tending of the necessary machinery might to each individual be but a short part of the day's work. The other work might vary from raising food from the surrounding country to the study and practice of art and science. It is a matter of course that people engaged in such work, and being the masters of their own lives, would not allow any hurry or want of foresight to force them into enduring dirt, disorder, or want of room. Science duly applied would enable them to get rid of refuse, to minimize, if not wholly to destroy, all the inconveniences which at present attend the use of elaborate machinery, such as smoke, stench, and noise; nor would they endure that the buildings in which they worked or lived should be ugly blots on the fair face of the earth. Beginning by making their factories, buildings, and sheds decent and convenient like their homes, they would infallibly go on to make them not merely negatively good, inoffensive merely, but even beautiful, so that the glorious art of architecture, now for some time slain by commercial greed, would be born again and flourish.

So, you see, I claim that work in a duly ordered community should be made attractive by the consciousness of usefulness, by its being carried on with intelligent interest, by variety, and by its being exercised amidst pleasurable surroundings. But I have also claimed, as we all do, that the day's work should not be wearisomely long. It may be said, "How can you make this last claim square with the others? If the work is to be so refined, will not the goods made be very expensive?"

I do admit, as I have said before, that some sacrifice will be necessary in order to make labour attractive. I mean that, if we *could* be contented in a free community to work in the same hurried, dirty, disorderly, heartless way as we do now, we might shorten our day's labour very much more than I suppose we shall do, taking all kinds of labour into account. But if we did, it would mean that our new-won freedom of condition would leave us listless and wretched, if not anxious, as we are now, which I hold is simply impossible. We should be contented to make the sacrifices necessary for raising our condition to the standard called out for as desirable by the whole community. Nor only so. We should, individually, be emulous to sacrifice quite freely still more of our time and our ease towards the raising of the standard of life. Persons, either by themselves or associated for such purposes, would freely, and for the love of the work and for its results—stimulated by the hope of the pleasure of creation—produce those ornaments of life for the service of all, which they are now bribed to produce (or pretend to produce) for the service of a few rich men. The experiment of a civilized community living wholly without art or literature has not yet been tried. The past degradation and corruption of civilization may force this denial of pleasure upon the society which will arise from its ashes. If that must be, we will accept the passing phase of utilitarianism as a foundation for the art which is to be. If the cripple and the starveling disappear from our streets, if the earth nourish us all alike, if the sun shine for all of us alike, if to one and all of us the glorious drama of the earth—day and night, summer and winter—can be presented as a thing to understand and love, we can afford to wait awhile till we are purified from the shame of the past corruption, and till art arises again amongst people freed from the terror of the slave and the shame of the robber.

Meantime, in any case, the refinement, thoughtfulness, and deliberation of labour must indeed be paid for, but not by compulsion to labour long hours. Our epoch has invented machines which would have appeared wild dreams to the men of past ages, and of those machines we have as yet *made no use*.

They are called "labour-saving" machines—a commonly used phrase which implies what we expect of them; but we do not get what we expect. What they really do is to reduce the skilled labourer to the ranks of the unskilled, to increase the number of the "reserve army of labour"—that is, to increase the precariousness of life among the workers and to intensify the labour of those who serve the machines (as slaves their masters). All this they do by the way, while they pile up the profits of the employers of labour, or force them to expend those profits in bitter commercial war with each other. In a true society these miracles of ingenuity would be for the first time used for minimizing the amount of time spent in unattractive labour, which by their means might be so reduced as to be but a very light burden on each individual. All the more as these machines would most certainly be very much improved when it was no longer a question as to whether their improvement would "pay" the individual, but rather whether it would benefit the community.

So much for the ordinary use of machinery, which would probably, after a time, be somewhat restricted when men found out that there was no need for anxiety as to mere subsistence, and learned to take an interest and pleasure in handiwork which, done deliberately and thoughtfully, could be made more attractive than machine work.

Again, as people freed from the daily terror of starvation find out what they really wanted, being no longer compelled by anything but their own needs, they would refuse to produce the mere inanities which are now called luxuries, or the poison and trash now called cheap wares. No one would make plush breeches when there were no flunkies to wear them, nor would anybody waste his time over making oleo-margarine when no one was *compelled* to abstain from real butter. Adulteration laws are only needed in a society of thieves—and in such a society they are a dead letter.

Socialists are often asked how work of the rougher and more repulsive kind could be carried out in the new condition of things. To attempt to answer such questions fully or authoritatively would be attempting the impossibility of constructing a scheme of a new society out of the materials of the old, before we knew which of those materials would disappear and which endure through the evolution which is leading us to the great change. Yet it is not difficult to conceive of some arrangement whereby those who did the roughest work should work for the shortest spells. And again, what is said above of the variety of work applies specially here. Once more I say, that for a man to be the whole of his life hopelessly engaged in performing one repulsive and never-ending task, is an arrangement fit enough for the hell imagined by theologians, but scarcely fit for any other form of society. Lastly, if this rougher work were of any special kind, we may suppose that special volunteers would be called on to perform it, who would surely be forthcoming, unless men in a state of freedom should lose the sparks of manliness which they possessed as slaves.

And yet if there be any work which cannot be made other than repulsive, either by the shortness of its duration or the intermittency of its recurrence, or by the sense of special and peculiar usefulness (and therefore honour) in the mind of the man who performs it freely—if there be any work which cannot be but a torment to the worker, what then? Well, then, let us see if the heavens will fall on us if we leave it undone, for it were better that they should. The produce of such work cannot be worth the price of it.

Signs of Change: Useful Work v. *Useless Toil.*

THE DECORATIVE ARTS

I HAVE not undertaken to talk to you of Architecture, Sculpture, and Painting, in the narrower sense of those words, since, most unhappily as I think, these master-arts, these arts more specially of the intellect, are at the present day divorced from decoration in its narrower sense. Our subject is that great body of art, by means of which men have at all times more or less striven to beautify the familiar matters of everyday life: a wide subject, a great industry; both a great part of the history of the world, and a most helpful instrument to the study of that history.

A very great industry indeed, comprising the crafts of house-building, painting, joinery and carpentry, smiths' work, pottery and glass-making, weaving, and many others: a body of art most important to the public in general, but still more so to us handicraftsmen; since there is scarce anything that they use, and that we fashion, but it has always been thought to be unfinished till it has had some touch or other of decoration about it. True it is that in many or most cases we have got so used to this ornament, that we look upon it as if it had grown of itself, and note it no more than the mosses on the dry sticks with which we light our fires. So much the worse! for there *is* the decoration, or some pretence of it, and it has, or ought to have, a use and a meaning. For, and this is at the root of the whole matter, everything made by man's hands has a form, which must be either beautiful or ugly; beautiful if it is in accord with Nature, and helps her; ugly if it is discordant with Nature, and thwarts her; it cannot be indifferent: we, for our parts, are busy or sluggish, eager or unhappy, and our eyes are apt to get dulled to this eventfulness of form in those things which we are always looking at. Now it is one of the chief uses of decoration, the chief part of its alliance with Nature, that it has to sharpen our dulled senses in this matter: for this end are those wonders of intricate patterns interwoven, those strange forms invented, which men have so long delighted in: forms and intricacies that do not necessarily imitate Nature, but in which the hand of the craftsman is guided to work in the way that she does, till the web, the cup, or the knife, look as natural, nay as lovely, as the green field, the river bank, or the mountain flint.

To give people pleasure in the things they must perforce *use*, that is one great office of decoration; to give people pleasure in the things they must perforce *make*, that is the other use of it.

Nevertheless there *is* dull work to be done, and a weary business it is setting men about such work, and seeing them through it, and I would rather do the work twice over with my own hands than have such a job: but now only let the arts which we are talking of beautify our labour, and be widely spread, intelligent, well understood both by the maker and the user, let them grow in one word *popular*, and there will be pretty much an end of dull work and its wearing slavery; and no man will any longer have an excuse for talking about the curse of labour, no man will any longer have an excuse for evading the blessing of labour. I believe there is nothing that will aid the world's progress so much as the attainment of this; I protest there is nothing in the world that I desire so much as this, wrapped up, as I am sure it is, with changes political and social, that in one way or another we all desire.

These arts, I have said, are part of a great system invented for the expression of a man's delight in beauty: all peoples and times have used them; they have been the joy of free nations, and the solace of oppressed nations; religion has used and elevated them, has abused and degraded them; they are connected with all history, and are clear teachers of it; and, best of all, they are the sweeteners of human labour, both to the handicraftsman, whose life is spent in working in them, and to people in general who are influenced by the sight of them at every turn of the day's work: they make our toil happy, our rest fruitful.

Time was when the mystery and wonder of handicrafts were well acknowledged by the world, when imagination and fancy mingled with all things made by man; and in those days all handicraftsmen were *artists*, as we should now call them. But the thought of man became more intricate, more difficult to express; art grew a heavier thing to deal with, and its labour was more divided among great men, lesser men, and little men; till that art, which was once scarce more than a rest of body and soul, as the hand cast the shuttle or swung the hammer, became to some men so serious a labour, that their working lives have been one long tragedy of hope and fear, joy and trouble. This was the growth of art: like all growth, it was good and fruitful for awhile; like all fruitful growth, it grew into decay; like all decay of what was once fruitful, it will grow into something new.

Into decay; for as the arts sundered into the greater and the lesser, contempt on one side, carelessness on the other arose, both begotten of ignorance of that *philosophy* of the Decorative Arts, a hint of which I have tried just now to put before you. The artist came out from the handicrafts-men, and left them without hope of elevation, while he himself was left without the help of intelligent, industrious sympathy. Both have suffered; the artist no less than the workman. It is with art as it fares with a company of soldiers before a redoubt, when the captain runs forward full of hope and energy, but looks not behind him to see if his men are following, and they hang back, not knowing why they are brought there to die. The captain's life is spent for nothing, and his men are sullen prisoners in the redoubt of Unhappiness and Brutality.

I must in plain words say of the Decorative Arts, of all the arts, that it is not so much that we are inferior in them to all who have gone before us, but rather that they are in a state of anarchy and disorganisation, which makes a sweeping change necessary and certain.

So that again I ask my question, All that good fruit which the arts should bear, will you have it? will you cast it from you? Shall that sweeping change that must come, be the change of loss or of gain?

We who believe in the continuous life of the world, surely we are bound to hope that the change will bring us gain and not loss, and to strive to bring that gain about.

Yet how the world may answer my question, who can say? A man in his short life can see but a little way ahead, and even in mine wonderful and unexpected things have come to pass. I must needs say that therein lies my hope rather than in all I see going on round about us. Without disputing that if the imaginative arts perish, some new thing, at present unguessed of, *may* be put forward to supply their loss in men's lives, I cannot feel happy in that prospect, nor can I believe that mankind will endure such a loss for ever: but in the meantime the present state of the arts and their dealings with modern life and progress seem to me to point, in appearance at least, to this immediate future; that the world, which has for a long time busied itself about other matters than the arts, and has carelessly let them sink lower and lower, till many not uncultivated men, ignorant of what they once were, and hopeless of what they might yet be, look upon them with mere contempt; that the world, I say, thus busied and hurried, will one day wipe the slate, and be clean rid in her impatience of the whole matter with all its tangle and trouble.

And then—what then?

Even now amid the squalor of London it is hard to imagine what it will be. Architecture, Sculpture, Painting, with the crowd of lesser arts that belong to them, these, together with Music and Poetry, will be dead and forgotten, will no longer excite or amuse people in the least: for, once more, we must not deceive ourselves; the death of one art means the death of all; the only difference in their fate will be that the luckiest will be eaten the last—the luckiest, or the unluckiest: in all that has to do with beauty the invention and ingenuity of man will have come to a dead stop; and all the while Nature will go on with her eternal recurrence of lovely change—spring, summer, autumn, and winter; sunshine, rain, and snow; storm and fair weather; dawn, noon, and sunset; day and night—ever bearing witness against man that he has deliberately chosen ugliness instead of beauty, and to live where he is strongest amidst squalor or blank emptiness.

Hopes and Fears for Art: The Lesser Arts.

ART AND MORALS

N o w there is one art of which the old architect of Edward the Third's time was thinking—he who founded New College at Oxford,[1] I mean—when he took this for his motto: "Manners maketh man": he meant by manners the art of morals, the art of living worthily, and like a man. I must needs claim this art also as dealing with my subject.

There is a great deal of sham work in the world, hurtful to the buyer, more hurtful to the seller, if he only knew it, most hurtful to the maker: how good a foundation it would be towards getting good Decorative Art, that is ornamental workmanship, if we craftsmen were to resolve to turn out nothing but excellent workmanship in all things, instead of having, as we too often have now, a very low average standard of work, which we often fall below.

I do not blame either one class or another in this matter, I blame all: to set aside our own class of handicraftsmen, of whose shortcomings you and I know so much that we need talk no more about it, I know that the public in general are set on having things cheap, being so ignorant that they do not know when they get them nasty also; so ignorant that they neither know nor care whether they give a man his due: I know that the manufacturers (so called) are so set on carrying out competition to its utmost, competition of cheapness, not of excellence, that they meet the bargain-hunters half way, and cheerfully furnish them

[1] William of Wykeham (1324–1404), Bishop of Winchester, founded New College, Oxford, in 1380, and Winchester College in 1388.

with nasty wares at the cheap rate they are asked for, by means of what can be called by no prettier name than fraud. England has of late been too much busied with the counting-house and not enough with the workshop: with the result that the counting-house at the present moment is rather barren of orders.

I say all classes are to blame in this matter, but also I say that the remedy lies with the handicraftsmen, who are not ignorant of these things like the public, and who have no call to be greedy and isolated like the manufacturers or middlemen; the duty and honour of educating the public lies with them, and they have in them the seeds of order and organization which make that duty the easier.

When will they see to this and help to make men of us all by insisting on this most weighty piece of manners: so that we may adorn life with the pleasure of cheerfully *buying* goods at their due price; with the pleasure of *selling* goods that we could be proud of both for fair price and fair workmanship; with the pleasure of working soundly and without haste at *making* goods that we could be proud of?— much the greatest pleasure of the three is that last, such a pleasure as, I think, the world has none like it.

You must not say that this piece of manners lies out of my subject: it is essentially a part of it and most important: for I am bidding you learn to be artists, if art is not to come to an end amongst us: and what is an artist but a workman who is determined that, whatever else happens, his work shall be excellent? or, to put it in another way: the decoration of workmanship, what is it but the expression of man's pleasure in successful labour? But what pleasure can there be in *bad* work, in *un*successful labour; why should we decorate *that*? and how can we bear to be always unsuccessful in our labour?

As greed of unfair gain, wanting to be paid for what we have not earned, cumbers our path with this tangle of bad work, of sham work, so the heaped-up money which this greed has brought us (for greed will have its way, like all other strong passions), this money, I say, gathered into heaps little and big, with all the false distinction which so unhappily it yet commands amongst us, has raised up against the arts a barrier of the love of luxury and show, which is of all obvious hindrances the worst to overpass: the highest and most cultivated classes are not free from the vulgarity of it, the lower are not free from its pretence. I beg you to remember both as a remedy against this, and as explaining exactly what I mean, that nothing can be a work of art which is not useful; that is to say, which does not minister to the body when well under command of the mind, or which does not amuse, soothe, or elevate the mind in a healthy state. What tons upon tons of unutterable rubbish pretending to be works of art in some degree would this maxim clear out of our London houses, if it were understood and acted upon! To my mind it is only here and there (out of the kitchen) that you can find in a well-to-do house things that are of any use at all: as a rule all the decoration (so called) that has got there is there for the sake of show, not because anybody likes it. I repeat, this stupidity goes through all classes of society: the silk curtains in my Lord's drawing-room are no more a matter of art to him than the powder in his footman's hair; the kitchen in a country farmhouse is most commonly a pleasant and homelike place, the parlour dreary and useless.

Simplicity of life, begetting simplicity of taste, that is, a love for sweet and lofty things, is of all matters most necessary for the birth of the new and better art we crave for; simplicity everywhere, in the palace as well as in the cottage. *Hopes and Fears for Art: The Lesser Arts.*

I cannot forget that, in my mind, it is not possible to dissociate art from morality, politics, and religion. Truth in these great matters of principle is of one, and it is only in formal treatises that it can be split up diversely. I must also ask you to remember how I have already said, that though my mouth alone speaks, it speaks, however feebly and disjointedly, the thoughts of many men better than myself. And further, though when things are tending to the best, we shall still, as aforesaid, need our best men to lead us quite right; yet even now surely, when it is far from that, the least of us can do some yeoman's service to the cause, and live and die not without honour.

So I will say that I believe there are two virtues much needed in modern life, if it is ever to become sweet; and I am quite sure that they are absolutely necessary in the sowing the seed of an *art which is to be made by the people and for the people, as a happiness to the maker and the user.* These virtues are honesty, and simplicity of life. To make my meaning clearer I will name the opposing vice of the second of these—luxury to wit. Also I mean by honesty, the careful and eager giving his due to every man, the determination not to gain by any man's loss, which in my experience is not a common virtue.

But note how the practice of either of these virtues will make the other easier to us. For if our wants are few, we shall have but little chance of being driven by our wants into injustice; and if we are fixed in the principle of giving every man his due, how can our self-respect bear that we should give too much to ourselves?

And in art, and in that preparation for it without which no art that is stable or worthy can be, the raising, namely, of those classes which have heretofore been degraded, the practice of these virtues would make a new world of it. For if you are rich, your simplicity of life will both go towards smoothing over the dreadful contrast between waste and want, which is the great horror of civilized countries, and will also give an example and standard of dignified life to those classes which you desire to raise, who, as it is indeed, being like enough to rich people, are given both to envy and to imitate the idleness and waste that the possession of much money produces.

Nay, and apart from the morality of the matter, which I am forced to speak to you of, let me tell you that though simplicity in art may be costly as well as uncostly, at least it is not wasteful, and nothing is more destructive to art han the want of it. I have never been in any rich man's house which would not have looked the better for having a bonfire made outside of it of nine-tenths of all that it held. Indeed, our sacrifice on the side of luxury will, it seems to me, be little or nothing: for, as far as I can make out, what people usually mean by it, is either a gathering of possessions which are sheer vexations to the owner, or a chain of pompous circumstance, which checks and annoys the rich man at every step. Yes, luxury cannot exist without slavery of some kind or other, and its abolition will be blessed, like the abolition of other slaveries, by the freeing both of the slaves and of their masters.

Lastly, if, besides attaining to simplicity of life, we attain also to the love of justice, then will all things be ready for the new springtime of the arts. For those of us that are employers of labour, how can we bear to give any man less money than he can decently live on, less leisure than his education and self-respect demand? or those of us who are workmen, how can we bear to fail in the contract we have undertaken, or to make it necessary for a foreman to go up and down spying out our mean tricks and evasions? or we the shopkeepers—can we endure to lie about our wares, that we may shuffle off our losses on to some one else's shoulders? or we the public—how can we bear to pay a price for a piece of goods which will help to trouble one man, to ruin another, and starve a third? Or, still more, I think, how can we bear to use, how can we enjoy something which has been a pain and a grief for the maker to make?

Hopes and Fears for Art: The Art of the People.

THE BEST ART

Now, before we go further, we may as well ask ourselves what reason or right this so-called ornamental art has to existence? We might answer the question shortly by saying that it seems clear that mankind has hitherto determined to have it even at the cost of a good deal of labour and trouble: an answer good enough to satisfy our consciences that we are not necessarily wasting our time in meeting here to consider it; but we may furthermore try to get at the reasons that have forced men in the mass always to expect to have what to some of them doubtless seems an absurd superfluity of life.

I do not know a better way of getting at these reasons than for each of us to suppose himself to be in the room in which he will have to pass a good part of his life, the said room being quite bare of ornament, and to be there that he may consider what he can do to make the bare walls pleasant and helpful to him; I say the walls, because, after all, the widest use of pattern-designing is the clothing of the walls of a room, hall, church, or what building you will. Doubtless there will be some, in these days at least, who will say, "'Tis most helpful to me to let the bare walls alone". So also there would be some who, when asked with what manner of books they will furnish their room, would answer, "With none". But I think you will agree with me in thinking that both these sets of people would be in an unhealthy state of mind, and probably of body also; in which case we need not trouble ourselves about their whims, since it is with healthy and sane people only that art has dealings.

Again, a healthy and sane person being asked with what kind of art he would clothe his walls, might well answer, "With the best art", and so end the question. Yet, out on it! so complex is human life, that even this seemingly most reasonable answer may turn out to be little better than an evasion.

For I suppose the best art to be the pictured representation of men's imaginings; what they have thought has happened to the world before their time, or what they deem they have seen with the eyes of the body or the soul: and the imaginings thus represented are always beautiful indeed, but oftenest stirring to men's passions and aspirations, and not seldom sorrowful or even terrible.

Stories that tell of men's aspirations for more than material life can give them, their struggles for the future welfare of their race, their unselfish love, their unrequited service: things like this are the subjects for the best art; in such subjects there is hope surely, yet the aspect of them is likely to be sorrowful enough: defeat the seed of victory, and death the seed of life, will be shown on the face of most of them.

Take note, too, that in the best art all these solemn and awful things are expressed clearly and without any vagueness, with such life and power that they impress the beholder so deeply that he is brought face to face with the very scenes, and lives among them for a time; so raising his life above the daily tangle of small things that wearies him, to the level of the heroism which they represent.

This is the best art; and who can deny that it is good for us all that it should be at hand to stir our emotions: yet its very greatness makes it a thing to be handled carefully, for we cannot always be having our emotions deeply stirred: that wearies us body and soul; and man, an animal that longs for rest like other animals, defends himself against the weariness by hardening his heart, and refusing to be

moved every hour of the day by tragic emotions; nay, even
by beauty that claims his attention over-much.

Such callousness is bad, both for the arts and our own
selves; and therefore it is not so good to have the best art
for ever under our eyes, though it is abundantly good that
we should be able to get at it from time to time.

Meantime, I cannot allow that it is good for any hour of
the day to be wholly stripped of life and beauty; therefore
we must provide ourselves with lesser (I will not say worse)
art with which to surround our common workaday or
restful times; and for those times, I think, it will be enough
for us to clothe our daily and domestic walls with ornament
that reminds us of the outward face of the earth, of the
innocent love of animals, or of man passing his days
between work and rest as he does. I say, with ornament
that reminds us of these things, and sets our minds and
memories at work easily creating them; because scientific
representation of them would again involve us in the
problems of hard fact and the troubles of life, and so once
more destroy our rest for us.

If this lesser art will really be enough to content us, it is
a good thing; for as to the higher art there never can be
very much of it going on, since but few people can be found
to do it; also few can find money enough to possess themselves of any portion of it, and, if they could, it would be a
piece of preposterous selfishness to shut it up from other
people's eyes; while of the secondary art there ought to be
abundance for all men, so much that you need but call in
the neighbours, and not all the world, to see your pretty
new wall when it is finished.

But this kind of art must be suggestive rather than
imitative; because, in order to have plenty of it, it must be
a kind of work that is not too difficult for ordinary men
with imaginations capable of development; men from whom
you cannot expect miracles of skill, and from whose hands

you must not ask too much, lest you lose what their intelligence has to give you, by over-wearying them. Withal, the
representation of this lower kind of life is pretty sure to
become soulless and tiresome unless it have a soul given
to it by the efforts of men forced by the limits of order and
the necessities of art to think of these things for themselves,
and so to give you some part of the infinite variety which
abides in the mind of man.

Of course you understand that it is impossible to imitate
nature literally; the utmost realism of the most realistic
painter falls a long way short of that; and as to the work
which must be done by ordinary men not unskilled or dull
to beauty, the attempt to attain to realism would be sure
to result in obscuring their intelligence, and in starving
you of all the beauty which you desire in your hearts,
but which you have not learned to express by means of
art.

Let us go back to our wall again, and think of it. If you
are to put nothing on it but what strives to be a literal
imitation of nature, all you can do is to have a few cut
flowers or bits of boughs nailed to it, with perhaps a blue-
bottle fly or a butterfly here and there. Well, I don't deny
that this may make good decoration now and then, but if
all decoration had to take that form I think weariness of it
would drive you to a white-washed wall; and at the best it
is a very limited view to take of nature.

Is it not better to be reminded, however simply, of the
close vine-trellis that keeps out the sun by the Nile side; or
of the wild-woods and their streams, with the dogs panting
beside them; or of the swallows sweeping above the garden
boughs toward the house-eaves where their nestlings are,
while the sun breaks through the clouds on them; or of
the many-flowered summer meadows of Picardy? Is not
all this better than having to count day after day a few
sham-real boughs and flowers, casting sham-real shadows

on your walls with little hint of anything beyond Covent Garden in them?

You may be sure that any decoration is futile, and has fallen into at least the first stage of degradation, when it does not remind you of something beyond itself, of something of which it is but a visible symbol.

Now, to sum up, what we want to clothe our walls with is (1) something that it is possible for us to get; (2) something that is beautiful; (3) something which will not drive us either into unrest or into callousness; (4) something which reminds us of life beyond itself, and which has the impress of human imagination strong on it; and (5) something which can be done by a great many people without too much difficulty and with pleasure.

Lectures on Art and Industry: Some Hints on Pattern-Designing.

GARDENS

Before we go inside our house, nay, before we look at its outside, we may consider its garden, chiefly with reference to town gardening; which, indeed, I, in common, I suppose, with most others who have tried it, have found uphill work enough—all the more as in our part of the world few indeed have any mercy upon the one thing necessary for decent life in a town, its trees; till we have come to this, that one trembles at the very sound of an axe as one sits at one's work at home. However, uphill work or not, the town garden must not be neglected if we are to be in earnest in making the best of it.

Now I am bound to say town gardeners generally do rather the reverse of that: our suburban gardeners in London, for instance, oftenest wind about their little bit of gravel walk and grass plot in ridiculous imitation of an ugly big garden of the landscape-gardening style, and then

with a strange perversity fill up the spaces with the most
formal plants they can get; whereas the merest common
sense should have taught them to lay out their morsel of
ground in the simplest way, to fence it as orderly as might
be, one part from the other (if it be big enough for that)
and the whole from the road, and then to fill up the
flower-growing space with things that are free and interesting in their growth, leaving Nature to do the desired
complexity, which she will certainly not fail to do if we
do not desert her for the florist, who, I must say, has made
it harder work than it should be to get the best of flowers.

It is scarcely a digression to note his way of dealing with
flowers, which, moreover, gives us an apt illustration of
that change without thought of beauty, change for the
sake of change, which has played such a great part in the
degradation of art in all times. So I ask you to note the
way he has treated the rose, for instance: the rose has been
grown double from I don't know when; the double rose
was a gain to the world, a new beauty was given us by it,
and nothing taken away, since the wild rose grows in every
hedge. Yet even then one might be excused for thinking
that the wild rose was scarce improved on, for nothing can
be more beautiful in general growth or in detail than a
wayside bush of it, nor can any scent be as sweet and pure
as its scent. Nevertheless the garden-rose had a new beauty
of abundant form, while its leaves had not lost the wonderfully delicate texture of the wild one. The full colour it
had gained, from the blush-rose to the damask, was pure
and true amidst all its added force, and though its scent
had certainly lost some of the sweetness of the eglantine,
it was fresh still, as well as so abundantly rich. Well, all
that lasted till quite our own day, when the florist fell
upon the rose—men who could never have enough—they
strove for size and got it, a fine specimen of a florist's rose
being about as big as a moderate Savoy cabbage. They

tried for strong scent and got it—till a florist's rose has
not unseldom a suspicion of the scent of the aforesaid
cabbage—not at its best. They tried for strong colour and
got it, strong and bad—like a conqueror. But all this while
they missed the very essence of the rose's being; they
thought there was nothing in it but redundance and luxury;
they exaggerated these into coarseness, while they threw
away the exquisite subtilty of form, delicacy of texture,
and sweetness of colour, which, blent with the richness
which the true garden-rose shares with many other flowers,
yet makes it the queen of them all—the flower of flowers.
Indeed, the worst of this is that these sham roses are
driving the real ones out of existence. If we do not look
to it our descendants will know nothing of the cabbage-
rose, the loveliest in form of all, or the blush-rose with its
dark green stems and unequalled colour, or the yellow-
centred rose of the East, which carries the richness of scent
to the very furthest point it can go without losing freshness:
they will know nothing of all these, and I fear they will
reproach the poets of past time for having done according
to their wont, and exaggerated grossly the beauties of the
rose.

Well, as a Londoner perhaps I have said too much of
roses, since we can scarcely grow them among suburban
smoke, but what I have said of them applies to other
flowers, of which I will say this much more. Be very shy
of double flowers; choose the old columbine where the
clustering doves are unmistakable and distinct, not the
double one, where they run into mere tatters. Choose (if
you can get it) the old china-aster with the yellow centre,
that goes so well with the purple-brown stems and curiously
coloured florets, instead of the lumps that look like cut
paper, of which we are now so proud. Don't be swindled
out of that wonder of beauty, a single snowdrop; there is
no gain and plenty of loss in the double one. More loss

still in the double sunflower, which is a coarse-coloured and dull plant, whereas the single one, though a late comer to our gardens, is by no means to be despised, since it will grow anywhere, and is both interesting and beautiful, with its sharply chiselled yellow florets relieved by the quaintly patterned sad-coloured centre clogged with honey and beset with bees and butterflies.

So much for over-artificiality in flowers. A word or two about the misplacing of them. Don't have ferns in your garden. The hart's tongue in the clefts of the rock, the queer things that grow within reach of the spray of the waterfall, these are right in their places. Still more the brake on the woodside, whether in late autumn, when its withered haulm helps out the well-remembered woodland scent, or in spring, when it is thrusting its volutes through last year's waste. But all this is nothing to a garden, and is not to be got out of it; and if you try it you will take away from it all possible romance, the romance of a garden.

The same thing may be said about many plants which are curiosities only, which Nature meant to be grotesque, not beautiful, and which are generally the growth of hot countries where things sprout over-quick and rank. Take note that the strangest of these come from the jungle and the tropical waste, from places where man is not at home, but is an intruder, an enemy. Go to a botanical garden and look at them, and think of those strange places to your heart's content. But don't set them to starve in your smoke-drenched scrap of ground amongst the bricks, for they will be no ornament to it.

As to colour in gardens. Flowers in masses are mighty strong colour, and if not used with a great deal of caution are very destructive to pleasure in gardening. On the whole, I think the best and safest plan is to mix up your flowers, and rather eschew great masses of colour—in combination I mean. But there are some flowers (inventions of men, *i.e.* florists) which are bad colour altogether, and not to be used at all. Scarlet geraniums, for instance, or the yellow calceolaria, which indeed are not uncommonly grown together profusely, in order, I suppose, to show that even flowers can be thoroughly ugly.

Another thing also much too commonly seen is an aberration of the human mind, which otherwise I should have been ashamed to warn you of. It is technically called carpet-gardening. Need I explain it further? I had rather not, for when I think of it even when I am quite alone I blush with shame at the thought.

I am afraid it is specially necessary in these days when making the best of it is a hard job, and when the ordinary iron hurdles are so common and so destructive of any kind of beauty in a garden, to say when you fence anything in a garden use a live hedge, or stones set flatwise (as they do in some parts of the Cotswold country), or timber, or wattle, or, in short, anything but iron.*

And now to sum up as to a garden. Large or small, it should look both orderly and rich. It should be well fenced from the outside world. It should by no means imitate either the wilfulness or the wildness of Nature, but should look like a thing never to be seen except near a house. It should, in fact, look like part of the house. It follows from this that no private pleasure-garden should be very big, and a public garden should be divided and made to look like so many flower-closes in a meadow, or a wood, or amidst the pavement.

It will be a key to right thinking about gardens if you consider in what kind of places a garden is most desired. In a very beautiful country, especially if it be mountainous,

---

* I know that well-designed hammered iron trellises and gates have been used happily enough, though chiefly in rather grandiose gardens, and so they might be again—one of these days—but I fear not yet awhile.

we can do without it well enough; whereas in a flat and dull country we crave after it, and there it is often the very making of the homestead. While in great towns, gardens, both private and public, are positive necessities if the citizens are to live reasonable and healthy lives in body and mind. *Hopes and Fears for Art: Making the Best of It.*

FURNITURE

Believe me, if we want art to begin at home, as it must, we must clear our houses of troublesome superfluities that are for ever in our way: conventional comforts that are no real comforts, and do but make work for servants and doctors: if you want a golden rule that will fit everybody, this is it:

Have nothing in your houses that you do not know to be useful, or believe to be beautiful.

And if we apply that rule strictly, we shall in the first place show the builders and such-like servants of the public what we really want, we shall create a demand for real art, as the phrase goes; and in the second place, we shall surely have more money to pay for decent houses.

Perhaps it will not try your patience too much if I lay before you my idea of the fittings necessary to the sitting-room of a healthy person: a room, I mean, which he would not have to cook in much, or sleep in generally, or in which he would not have to do any very litter-making manual work.

First a book-case with a great many books in it: next a table that will keep steady when you write or work at it: then several chairs that you can move, and a bench that you can sit or lie upon: next a cupboard with drawers: next, unless either the book-case or the cupboard be very beautiful with painting or carving, you will want pictures or engravings, such as you can afford, only not stopgaps, but real works of art on the wall; or else the wall itself must be ornamented with some beautiful and restful pattern: we shall also want a vase or two to put flowers in, which latter you must have sometimes, especially if you live in a town. Then there will be the fireplace of course, which in our climate is bound to be the chief object in the room.

That is all we shall want, especially if the floor be good; if it be not, as, by the way, in a modern house it is pretty certain not to be, I admit that a small carpet which can be bundled out of the room in two minutes will be useful, and we must also take care that it is beautiful, or it will annoy us terribly.

Now unless we are musical, and need a piano (in which case, as far as beauty is concerned, we are in a bad way), that is quite all we want: and we can add very little to these necessaries without troubling ourselves and hindering our work, our thought, and our rest.

If these things were done at the least cost for which they could be done well and solidly, they ought not to cost much; and they are so few, that those that could afford to have them at all, could afford to spend some trouble to get them fitting and beautiful: and all those who care about art ought to take great trouble to do so, and to take care that there be no sham art amongst them, nothing that it has degraded a man to make or sell. And I feel sure, that if all who care about art were to take this pains, it would make a great impression upon the public.

This simplicity you may make as costly as you please or can, on the other hand: you may hang your walls with tapestry instead of whitewash or paper; or you may cover them with mosaic, or have them frescoed by a great painter: all this is not luxury, if it be done for beauty's sake, and not for show: it does not break our golden rule: *Have*

nothing in your houses which you do not know to be useful or
believe to be beautiful.

Hopes and Fears for Art: The Beauty of Life.

As for movable furniture, even if time did not fail us,
'tis a large subject—or a very small one—so I will but say,
don't have too much of it; have none for mere finery's
sake, or to satisfy the claims of custom—these are flat
truisms, are they not? But really it seems as if some people
had never thought of them, for 'tis almost the universal
custom to stuff up some rooms so that you can scarcely
move in them, and to leave others deadly bare; whereas
all rooms ought to look as if they were lived in, and to
have, so to say, a friendly welcome ready for the in-
comer.

A dining-room ought not to look as if one went into it
as one goes into a dentist's parlour—for an operation, and
came out of it when the operation was over—the tooth
out, or the dinner in. A drawing-room ought to look as
if some kind of work could be done in it less toilsome than
being bored. A library certainly ought to have books in it,
not boots only, as in Thackeray's country snob's house,[1]
but so ought each and every room in the house more or less;
also, though all rooms should look tidy, and even very tidy,
they ought not to look too tidy.

Furthermore, no room of the richest man should look
grand enough to make a simple man shrink in it, or
luxurious enough to make a thoughtful man feel ashamed
in it; it will not do so if Art be at home there, for she has
no foes so deadly as insolence and waste. Indeed, I fear
that at present the decoration of rich men's houses is mostly
wrought out at the bidding of grandeur and luxury, and
that art has been mostly cowed or shamed out of them; nor

[1] Thackeray, *The Book of Snobs*, chap. xxvi.

when I come to think of it will I lament it overmuch.
Art was not born in the palace; rather she fell sick there,
and it will take more bracing air than that of rich men's
houses to heal her again. If she is ever to be strong enough
to help mankind once more, she must gather strength in
simple places; the refuge from wind and weather to which
the goodman comes home from field or hill-side; the well-
tidied space into which the craftsman draws from the litter
of loom, and smithy, and bench; the scholar's island in the
sea of books; the artist's clearing in the canvas-grove: it is
from these places that Art must come if she is ever again
to be enthroned in that other kind of building, which I
think, under some name or other, whether you call it
Church or Hall of Reason, or what not, will always be
needed; the building in which people meet to forget their
own transient personal and family troubles in aspirations
for their fellows and the days to come, and which to a
certain extent make up to town-dwellers for their loss of
field, and river, and mountain.

Hopes and Fears for Art: Making the Best of It.

Simplicity is the one thing needful in furnishing, of that
I am certain; I mean first as to quantity, and secondly as to
kind and manner of design. The arrangement of our houses
ought surely to express the kind of life we lead, or desire to
lead; and to my mind, if there is anything to be said in
favour of that to-day somewhat well-abused English middle
class, it is that, amidst all the narrowness that is more or
less justly charged against it, it has a kind of orderly intelligence which is not without some value. Such as it is,
such its houses ought to be if it takes any pains about them,
as I think it should: they should look like part of the life of
decent citizens prepared to give good commonplace reasons
for what they do. For us to set to work to imitate the

minor vices of the Borgias,[1] or the degraded and nightmare
whims of the *blasé* and bankrupt French aristocracy of
Louis the Fifteenth's time,[2] seems to me merely ridiculous.
So I say our furniture should be good citizen's furniture,
solid and well made in workmanship, and in design should
have nothing about it that is not easily defensible, no
monstrosities or extravagances, not even of beauty, lest we
weary of it. As to matters of construction, it should not
have to depend on the special skill of a very picked workman, or the super-excellence of his glue, but be made on
the proper principles of the art of joinery: also I think
that, except for very movable things like chairs, it should
not be so very light as to be nearly imponderable; it should
be made of timber rather than walking-sticks. Moreover,
I must needs think of furniture as of two kinds: one part
of it being chairs, dining and working tables, and the like,
the necessary work-a-day furniture in short, which should
be of course both well made and well proportioned, but
simple to the last degree; nay, if it were rough I should
like it the better, not the worse; with work-a-day furniture
like this we should among other blessings avoid the terror
which now too often goes with the tolerably regularly
recurring accidents of the week.

But besides this kind of furniture, there is the other kind
of what I should call state-furniture, which I think is
proper even for a citizen; I mean sideboards, cabinets, and
the like, which we have quite as much for beauty's sake
as for use; we need not spare ornament on these, but may
make them as elegant and elaborate as we can with carving,

[1] An Italian family of Spanish origin which acquired great
eminence from 1455 to 1550. Two of the best known members of
the family, Cesare Borgia (1478–1507), duke of Romagna, and
Lucrezia Borgia (1480–1519), his sister, were accused of unscrupulous
ambition and gross crimes.
[2] The reign of Louis XV, king of France, 1715–74, was charac-
terized by the corruptness of the court and government.

inlaying, or painting; these are the blossoms of the art of furniture, as picture tapestry is of the art of weaving: but these also should not be scattered about the house at haphazard, but should be used architecturally to dignify important chambers and important places in them. And once more, whatever you have in your rooms think first of the walls, for they are that which makes your house and home; and if you don't make some sacrifice in their favour, you will find your chambers have a kind of makeshift, lodging-house look about them, however rich and handsome your movables may be.

Lectures on Art and Industry: The Lesser Arts of Life.

POTTERY

L ET us begin with pottery, the most ancient and universal, as it is perhaps (setting aside house-building) the most important of the lesser arts, and one, too, the consideration of which recommends itself to us from a more or less historical point of view, because, owing to the indestructibility of its surface, it is one of the few domestic arts of which any specimens are left to us of the ancient and classical times. Now all nations, however barbarous, have made pottery, sometimes of shapes obviously graceful, sometimes with a mingling of wild grotesquery amid gracefulness; but none have ever failed to make it on true principles, none have made shapes ugly or base till quite modern times. I should say that the making of ugly pottery was one of the most remarkable inventions of our civilization. All nations with any turn for art have speedily discovered what capabilities for producing beautiful form lie in the making of an earthen pot of the commonest kind, and what opportunities it offers for the reception of swift and unlaborious, but rich ornament; and how nothing hinders that ornament from taking the form of representation of history and legend. In favour of this art the classical nations relaxed the artistic severity that insisted otherwhere on perfection of figure-drawing in architectural work; and we may partly guess what an astonishing number of capable and ready draughtsmen there must have been in the good times of Greek art from the great mass of first-rate painting on pottery, garnered from the tombs mostly, and still preserved in our museums after all these centuries of violence and neglect.

Side by side with the scientific and accomplished work of the Greeks, and begun much earlier than the earliest of it, was being practised another form of the art in Egypt and the Euphrates valley; it was less perfect in the highest qualities of design, but was more elaborate in technique, which elaboration no doubt was forced into existence by a craving for variety and depth of colour and richness of decoration, which did not press heavily on the peoples of the classical civilization, who, masters of form as they were, troubled themselves but little about the refinements of colour. This art has another interest for us in the fact that from it sprang all the great school of pottery which has flourished in the East, apart from the special and peculiar work of China. Though the fictile art of that country is a development of so much later date than what we have just been considering, let us make a note of it here as the third kind of potter's work, which no doubt had its origin in the exploitation of local material joined to the peculiar turn of the Chinese workmanship for finesse of manual skill and for boundless patience.

Northern Europe during the Middle Ages, including our own country, could no more do without a native art of pottery than any other simple peoples; but the work done by them being very rough, and serving for the commonest domestic purposes (always with the exception of certain

tile-work), had not the chance of preservation which superstition gave to the Greek pottery, and very little of it is
left; that little shows us that our Gothic forefathers shared
the pleasure in the potter's wheel and the capabilities of clay
for quaint and pleasant form and fanciful invention which
has been common to most times and places, and this rough
craft even lived on as a village art till almost the days of our
grandfathers, turning out worthy work enough, done in a
very unconscious and simple fashion on the old and true
principles of art, side by side with the whims and inanities
which mere fashion had imposed on so-called educated
people.

Every one of these forms of art, with many another
which I have no time to speak of, was good in itself; the
general principles of them may be expressed somewhat as
follows. First. Your vessel must be of a convenient shape
for its purpose. Second. Its shape must show to the greatest
advantage the plastic and easily-worked nature of clay; the
lines of its contour must flow easily; but you must be on
the look-out to check the weakness and languidness that
comes from striving after over-elegance. Third. All the
surface must show the hand of the potter, and not be
finished with a baser tool. Fourth. Smoothness and high
finish of surface, though a quality not to be despised, is
to be sought after as a means for gaining some special
elegance of ornament, and not as an end for its own sake.
Fifth. The commoner the material the rougher the ornament, but by no means the scantier; on the contrary, a pot
of fine materials may be more slightly ornamented, both
because all the parts of the ornamentation will be minuter,
and also because it will in general be considered more
carefully. Sixth. As in the making of the pot, so in its
surface ornament, the hand of the workman must be always
visible in it; it must glorify the necessary tools and necessary
pigment: swift and decided execution is necessary to it;

whatever delicacy there may be in it must be won in the
teeth of the difficulties that will result from this; and
because of these difficulties the delicacy will be more
exquisite and delightful than in easier arts where, so to
say, the execution can wait for more laborious patience.
These, I say, seem to me the principles that guided the
potter's art in the days when it was progressive: it began
to cease to be so in civilized countries somewhat late in
that period of blight which was introduced by the so-called
Renaissance. Excuse a word or two more of well-known
history in explanation. Our own pottery of Northern
Europe, made doubtless without any reference to classical
models, was very rude, as I have said; it was fashioned
of natural clay, glazed when necessary transparently with
salt or lead, and the ornament on it was done with another
light-coloured clay, sometimes coloured further with metallic oxides under the glaze. During the fourteenth and
fifteenth centuries the more finished work, which had its
origin, as before mentioned, in Egypt and the Euphrates
valley, was introduced into Southern Europe through
Moorish or rather Arab Spain, and other points of contact
between Europe and the East. This ware, known now as
Majolica, was of an earthen body covered with opaque
white glaze, ornamented with colours formed of oxides,
some of which were by a curious process reduced into a
metallic state, giving thereby strange and beautiful lustrous
colours. This art quickly spread through Italy, and for a
short time was practised there with very great success, but
was not much taken up by the nations of Northern Europe,
who for the most part went on making the old lead or salt
glazed earthenware; the latter, known as Grès de Cologne,
still exists as a rough manufacture in the border lands of
France and Germany, though I should think it is not
destined to live much longer otherwise than as a galvanized
modern antique.

When Italy was still turning out fine works in the Majolica wares much of the glory of the Renaissance was yet shining; but the last flicker of that glory had died out by the time that another form of Eastern art invaded our European pottery. Doubtless the folly of the time would have found another instrument for destroying whatever of genuine art was left among our potters if it had not had the work of China ready to hand, but it came to pass that this was the instrument that finally made nonsense of the whole craft among us. True it is that a very great proportion of the Chinese work imported consisted of genuine works of art of their kind, though mostly much inferior to the work of Persia, Damascus, or Granada;[1] but the fact is, it was not the art in it that captivated our forefathers, but its grosser and more material qualities. The whiteness of the paste, the hardness of the glaze, the neatness of the painting, and the consequent delicacy, or luxuriousness rather, of the ware, were the qualities that the eighteenth-century potters strove so hard to imitate. They were indeed valuable qualities in the hands of a Chinaman, deft as he was of execution, fertile of design, fanciful though not imaginative, in short, a born maker of pretty toys: but such daintinesses were of little avail to a good workman of our race; eager, impatient, imaginative, with something of melancholy or moroseness even in his sport, his very jokes two-edged and fierce, he had other work to do, if his employers but knew it, than the making of toys. Well, but in the time we have before us the workman was but thought of as a convenient machine, and this machine, driven by the haphazard whims of the time, produced at Meissen, at Sèvres, at Chelsea, at Derby, and in Staffordshire,[2] a most woeful set of works of art, of which perhaps

[1] Damascus, formerly the capital of Syria, and Granada, the capital of the medieval Moorish kingdom in Spain, were both famous for the beauty of their arts.

[2] Meissen, near Dresden in Saxony; Sèvres near Paris; Chelsea,

those of Sèvres were the most repulsively hideous, those
of Meissen (at their worst) the most barbarous, and those
made in England the stupidest, though it may be the least
ugly.

Now this is very briefly the history of the art of pottery
down to our own times, when styleless anarchy prevails;
a state of things not so hopeless as in the last century,
because it shows a certain uneasiness as to whether we are
right or wrong, which may be a sign of life. Meanwhile,
as to matters of art, the craft which turns out such tons of
commercial wares, every piece of which ought to be a
work of art, produces almost literally nothing. On this
dismal side of things I will not dwell, but will ask you to
consider with me what can be done to remedy it; a question
which I know exercises much many excellent and public-
spirited men who are at the head of pottery works. Well,
in the first place, it is clear that the initiative cannot be
wholly taken by these men; we, all of us I mean who care
about the arts, must help them by asking for the right thing,
and making them quite clear what it is we ask for. To my
mind it should be something like this, which is but another
way of putting those principles of the art which I spoke
of before. First. No vessel should be fashioned by being
pressed into a mould that can be made by throwing on the
wheel, or otherwise by hand. Second. All vessels should
be finished on the wheel, not turned in a lathe, as is now
the custom. How can you expect to have good workmen
when they know that whatever surface their hands may
put on the work will be taken off by a machine? Third.
It follows, as a corollary to the last point, that we must
not demand excessive neatness in pottery, and this more
especially in cheap wares. Workmanlike finish is necessary,
but finish to be workmanlike must always be in proportion

Derby, and the Potteries in Staffordshire, are all famous centres of
the porcelain and pottery industry.

to the kind of work. What we get in pottery at present is mechanical finish, not workmanlike, and is as easy to do as the other is hard: one is a matter of a manager's system, the other comes of constant thought and trouble on the part of the men, who by that time are artists, as we call them. Fourth. As to the surface decoration on pottery, it is clear it must never be printed; for the rest, it would take more than an hour to go even very briefly into the matter of painting on pottery; but one rule we have for a guide, and whatever we do if we abide by it, we are quite sure to go wrong if we reject it: and it is common to all the lesser arts. Think of your material. Don't paint any-thing on pottery save what can be painted only on pottery; if you do, it is clear that, however good a draughtsman you may be, you do not care about that special art. You can't suppose that the Greek wall-painting was anything like their painting on pottery; there is plenty of evidence to show that it was not. Or take another example from the Persian art; it is easy for those conversant with it to tell from an outline tracing of a design whether it was done for pottery-painting or for other work. Fifth. Finally, when you have asked for these qualities from the potters, and even in a very friendly way boycotted them a little till you get them, you will of course be prepared to pay a great deal more for your pottery than you do now, even for the rough work you may have to take. I'm sure that won't hurt you; we shall only have less and break less, and our incomes will still be the same.

Lectures on Art and Industry: The Lesser Arts of Life.

ART FOR ALL

U n l e s s something or other is done to give all men some pleasure for the eyes and rest for the mind in the aspect of their own and their neighbours' houses, until the contrast

is less disgraceful between the fields where beasts live and
the streets where men live, I suppose that the practice of
the arts must be mainly kept in the hands of a few highly
cultivated men, who can go often to beautiful places, whose
education enables them, in the contemplation of the past
glories of the world, to shut out from their view the everyday squalors that the most of men move in. Sirs, I believe
that art has such sympathy with cheerful freedom, open-
heartedness and reality, so much she sickens under selfishness and luxury, that she will not live thus isolated and
exclusive. I will go further than this and say that on such
terms I do not wish her to live. I protest that it would be
a shame to an honest artist to enjoy what he had huddled
up to himself of such art, as it would be for a rich man to
sit and eat dainty food amongst starving soldiers in a beleaguered fort.

I do not want art for a few, any more than education
for a few, or freedom for a few.

No, rather than art should live this poor thin life among
a few exceptional men, despising those beneath them for an
ignorance for which they themselves are responsible, for a
brutality that they will not struggle with,—rather than
this, I would that the world should indeed sweep away all
art for awhile, as I said before I thought it possible she
might do; rather than the wheat should rot in the miser's
granary, I would that the earth had it, that it might yet
have a chance to quicken in the dark.

I have a sort of faith, though, that this clearing away
of all art will not happen, that men will get wiser, as well
as more learned; that many of the intricacies of life, on
which we now pride ourselves more than enough, partly
because they are new, partly because they have come with
the gain of better things, will be cast aside as having
played their part, and being useful no longer. I hope that
we shall have leisure from war—war commercial, as well

as war of the bullet and the bayonet; leisure from the knowledge that darkens counsel; leisure above all from the greed of money, and the craving for that overwhelming distinction that money now brings: I believe that as we have even now partly achieved LIBERTY, so we shall one day achieve EQUALITY, which, and which only, means FRATERNITY, and so have leisure from poverty and all its griping, sordid cares.

Then having leisure from all these things, amidst renewed simplicity of life we shall have leisure to think about our work, that faithful daily companion, which no man any longer will venture to call the Curse of labour: for surely then we shall be happy in it, each in his place, no man grudging at another; no one bidden to be any man's *servant*, every one scorning to be any man's *master*: men will then assuredly be happy in their work, and that happiness will assuredly bring forth decorative, noble, *popular* art.

That art will make our streets as beautiful as the woods, as elevating as the mountain-sides: it will be a pleasure and a rest, and not a weight upon the spirits to come from the open country into a town; every man's house will be fair and decent, soothing to his mind and helpful to his work: all the works of man that we live amongst and handle will be in harmony with nature, will be reasonable and beautiful: yet all will be simple and inspiriting, not childish nor enervating; for as nothing of beauty and splendour that man's mind and hand may compass shall be wanting from our public buildings, so in no private dwelling will there be any signs of waste, pomp, or insolence, and every man will have his share of the *best*.

Hopes and Fears for Art: The Lesser Arts.

UTOPIAN ENGLAND

THE GUEST HOUSE

I LINGERED a little behind the others to have a stare at this house, which stood on the site of my old dwelling.

It was a longish building with its gable ends turned away from the road, and long traceried windows coming rather low down set in the wall that faced us. It was very handsomely built of red brick with a lead roof; and high up above the windows there ran a frieze of figure subjects in baked clay, very well executed, and designed with a force and directness which I have never noticed in modern work before. The subjects I recognized at once, and indeed was very particularly familiar with them.

However, all this I took in in a minute; for we were presently within doors, and standing in a hall with a floor of marble mosaic and an open timber roof. There were no windows on the side opposite to the river, but arches below leading into chambers, one of which showed a glimpse of a garden beyond, and above them a long space of wall gaily painted (in fresco, I thought) with similar subjects to those of the frieze outside; everything about the place was handsome and generously solid as to material; and though it was not very large (somewhat smaller than Crosby Hall[1] perhaps), one felt in it that exhilarating sense of space and freedom which satisfactory architecture always gives to an unanxious man who is in the habit of using his eyes.

[1] Great Hall of Crosby Place, Bishopsgate, London, E.C., the best example in London of fifteenth century English domestic architecture. It was built by Sir John Crosby in 1466, and is associated with Richard III, Sir Thomas More, and the East India Company. It was re-erected at Chelsea near the corner of Cheyne Walk and Danvers Street in 1910.

In this pleasant place, which of course I knew to be the hall of the Guest House, three young women were flitting to and fro. As they were the first of the sex I had seen on this eventful morning, I naturally looked at them very attentively, and found them at least as good as the gardens, the architecture, and the male men. As to their dress, which of course I took note of, I should say that they were decently veiled with drapery, and not bundled up with millinery; that they were clothed like women, not up-holstered like arm-chairs, as most women of our time are. In short, their dress was somewhat between that of the ancient classical costume and the simpler forms of the fourteenth century garments, though it was clearly not an imitation of either: the materials were light and gay to suit the season. As to the women themselves, it was pleasant indeed to see them, they were so kind and happy-looking in expression of face, so shapely and well-knit of body, and thoroughly healthy-looking and strong. All were at least comely, and one of them very handsome and regular of feature. They came up to us at once merrily and without the least affectation of shyness, and all three shook hands with me as if I were a friend newly come back from a long journey: though I could not help noticing that they looked askance at my garments; for I had on my clothes of last night, and at the best was never a dressy person.

A word or two from Robert the weaver, and they bustled about on our behoof, and presently came and took us by the hands and led us to a table in the pleasantest corner of the hall, where our breakfast was spread for us; and, as we sat down, one of them hurried out by the chambers aforesaid, and came back again in a little while with a great bunch of roses, very different in size and quality to what Hammersmith had been wont to grow, but very like the produce of an old country garden. She hurried back thence into the buttery, and came back once more with a delicately made glass, into which she put the flowers and set them down in the midst of our table. One of the others, who had run off also, then came back with a big cabbage-leaf filled with strawberries, some of them barely ripe, and said as she set them on the table, "There, now; I thought of that before I got up this morning; but looking at the stranger here getting into your boat, Dick, put it out of my head; so that I was not before *all* the blackbirds: however, there are a few about as good as you will get them anywhere in Hammersmith this morning".

Robert patted her on the head in a friendly manner; and we fell to on our breakfast, which was simple enough, but most delicately cooked, and set on the table with much daintiness. The bread was particularly good, and was of several different kinds, from the big, rather close, dark-coloured, sweet-tasting farmhouse loaf, which was most to my liking, to the thin pipe-stems of wheaten crust, such as I have eaten in Turin.

As I was putting the first mouthfuls into my mouth, my eye caught a carved and gilded inscription on the panelling, behind what we should have called the High Table in an Oxford college hall, and a familiar name in it forced me to read it through. Thus it ran:

> "*Guests and neighbours, on the site of this Guest-hall once stood the lecture-room of the Hammersmith Socialists.*[1] *Drink a glass to the memory! May 1962.*"

It is difficult to tell you how I felt as I read these words, and I suppose my face showed how much I was moved, for both my friends looked curiously at me, and there was silence between us for a little while.

"Here, Boffin", he cried out, after a pause; "here we are, if you must have it!"

---

[1] See Introduction, p. xviii.

I looked over my shoulder, and saw something flash and gleam in the sunlight that lay across the hall; so I turned round, and at my ease saw a splendid figure slowly sauntering over the pavement; a man whose surcoat was embroidered most copiously as well as elegantly, so that the sun flashed back from him as if he had been clad in golden armour. The man himself was tall, dark-haired, and exceedingly handsome, and though his face was no less kindly in expression than that of the others, he moved with that somewhat haughty mien which great beauty is apt to give to both men and women. He came and sat down at our table with a smiling face, stretching out his long legs and hanging his arm over the chair in the slowly graceful way which tall and well-built people may use without affectation. He was a man in the prime of life, but looked as happy as a child who has just got a new toy. He bowed gracefully to me and said:

"I see clearly that you are the guest, of whom Annie has just told me, who have come from some distant country that does not know of us, or our ways of life. So I daresay you would not mind answering me a few questions; for you see—"

Here Dick broke in: "No, please, Boffin! let it alone for the present. Of course you want the guest to be happy and comfortable; and how can that be if he has to trouble himself with answering all sorts of questions while he is still confused with the new customs and people about him? No, no: I am going to take him where he can ask questions himself, and have them answered; that is, to my great-grandfather in Bloomsbury: and I am sure you can't have anything to say against that. So instead of bothering, you had much better go out to James Allen's and get a carriage for me, as I shall drive him up myself; and please tell Jim to let me have the old grey, for I can drive a wherry much better than a carriage. Jump up, old fellow, and don't be disappointed; our guest will keep himself for you and your stories".

I stared at Dick; for I wondered at his speaking to such a dignified-looking personage so familiarly, not to say curtly; for I thought that this Mr Boffin, in spite of his well-known name out of Dickens, must be at the least a senator of these strange people. However, he got up and said, "All right, old oar-wearer, whatever you like; this is not one of my busy days; and though" (with a condescending bow to me) "my pleasure of a talk with this learned guest is put off, I admit that he ought to see your worthy kinsman as soon as possible. Besides, perhaps he will be the better able to answer *my* questions after his own have been answered".

And therewith he turned and swung himself out of the hall.

When he was well gone, I said: "Is it wrong to ask what Mr Boffin is? whose name, by the way, reminds me of many pleasant hours passed in reading Dickens".[1]

Dick laughed. "Yes, yes," said he, "as it does us. I see you take the allusion. Of course his real name is not Boffin, but Henry Johnson; we only call him Boffin as a joke, partly because he is a dustman, and partly because he will dress so showily, and get as much gold on him as a baron of the Middle Ages. As why should he not if he likes? only we are his special friends, you know, so of course we jest with him."

I held my tongue for some time after that; but Dick went on:

"He is a capital fellow, and you can't help liking him; but he has a weakness: he will spend his time in writing reactionary novels, and is very proud of getting the local

[1] Dickens, *Our Mutual Friend*. Nicodemus Boffin inherits the large estate of his master Mr Harmon, a dust contractor, and is thenceforward known as the Golden Dustman.

colour right, as he calls it; and as he thinks you come from some forgotten corner of the earth, where people are un-happy, and consequently interesting to a story-teller, he thinks he might get some information out of you. O, he will be quite straightforward with you, for that matter. Only for your own comfort beware of him!"

"Well, Dick," said the weaver, doggedly, "I think his novels are very good."

"Of course you do", said Dick; "birds of a feather flock together; mathematics and antiquarian novels stand on much the same footing. But here he comes again."

And in effect the Golden Dustman hailed us from the hall-door; so we all got up and went into the porch, before which, with a strong grey horse in the shafts, stood a carriage ready for us which I could not help noticing. It was light and handy, but had none of that sickening vulgarity which I had known as inseparable from the car-riages of our time, especially the "elegant" ones, but was as graceful and pleasant in line as a Wessex waggon. We got in, Dick and I. The girls, who had come into the porch to see us off, waved their hands to us; the weaver nodded kindly; the dustman bowed as gracefully as a troubadour; Dick shook the reins, and we were off.

News from Nowhere, chap. iii.

HAMMERSMITH MARKET

WE turned away from the river at once, and were soon in the main road that runs through Hammersmith. But I should have had no guess as to where I was, if I had not started from the waterside; for King Street was gone, and the highway ran through wide sunny meadows and garden-like tillage. The Creek, which we crossed at once, had been rescued from its culvert, and as we went over its pretty bridge we saw its waters, yet swollen by the tide, covered with gay boats of different sizes. There were houses about, some on the road, some amongst the fields with pleasant lanes leading down to them, and each surrounded by a teeming garden. They were all pretty in design, and as solid as might be, but countryfied in appearance, like yeomen's dwellings; some of them of red brick like those by the river, but more of timber and plaster, which were by the necessity of their construction so like mediaeval houses of the same materials that I fairly felt as if I were alive in the fourteenth century; a sensation helped out by the costume of the people that we met or passed, in whose dress there was nothing "modern". Almost everybody was gaily dressed, but especially the women, who were so well-looking, or even so handsome, that I could scarcely refrain my tongue from calling my companion's attention to the fact. Some faces I saw that were thoughtful, and in these I noticed great nobility of expression, but none that had a glimmer of unhappiness, and the greater part (we came upon a good many people) were frankly and openly joyous.

I thought I knew the Broadway by the lie of the roads that still met there. On the north side of the road was a range of buildings and courts, low, but very handsomely built and ornamented, and in that way forming a great contrast to the unpretentiousness of the houses round about; while above this lower building rose the steep lead-covered roof and the buttresses and higher part of the wall of a great hall, of a splendid and exuberant style of architecture, of which one can say little more than that it seemed to me to embrace the best qualities of the Gothic of northern Europe with those of the Saracenic and Byzantine, though there was no copying of any one of these styles. On the other, the south side, of the road was an octagonal building with a high roof, not unlike the Baptistry at Florence[1] in

[1] The famous baptistry at Florence, remodelled by Arnolfo di Cambio in the thirteenth century. It is octagonal in shape, and is noted for its three magnificent double gates in bronze.

outline, except that it was surrounded by a lean-to that clearly made an arcade or cloisters to it: it also was most delicately ornamented.

This whole mass of architecture which we had come upon so suddenly from amidst the pleasant fields was not only exquisitely beautiful in itself, but it bore upon it the expression of such generosity and abundance of life that I was exhilarated to a pitch that I had never yet reached. I fairly chuckled for pleasure. My friend seemed to understand it, and sat looking on me with a pleased and affectionate interest. We had pulled up amongst a crowd of carts, wherein sat handsome healthy-looking people, men, women, and children very gaily dressed, and which were clearly market carts, as they were full of very tempting-looking country produce.

I said, "I need not ask if this is a market, for I see clearly that it is; but what market is it that it is so splendid? And what is the glorious hall there, and what is the building on the south side?"

"O," said he, "it is just our Hammersmith market; and I am glad you like it so much, for we are really proud of it. Of course the hall inside is our winter Mote-House; for in summer we mostly meet in the fields down by the river opposite Barn Elms. The building on our right hand is our theatre: I hope you like it."

"I should be a fool if I didn't", said I.

He blushed a little as he said: "I am glad of that, too, because I had a hand in it; I made the great doors, which are of damascened bronze. We will look at them later in the day, perhaps: but we ought to be getting on now. As to the market, this is not one of our busy days; so we shall do better with it another time, because you will see more people".

I thanked him, and said: "Are these the regular country people? What very pretty girls there are amongst them!"

As I spoke, my eye caught the face of a beautiful woman, tall, dark-haired, and white-skinned, dressed in a pretty light-green dress in honour of the season and the hot day, who smiled kindly on me, and more kindly still, I thought, on Dick; so I stopped a minute, but presently went on:

"I ask because I do not see any of the country-looking people I should have expected to see at a market—I mean selling things there".

"I don't understand", said he, "what kind of people you would expect to see; nor quite what you mean by 'country' people. These are the neighbours, and that like they run in the Thames valley. There are parts of these islands which are rougher and rainier than we are here, and there people are rougher in their dress; and they themselves are tougher and more hard-bitten than we are to look at. But some people like their looks better than ours; they say they have more character in them—that's the word. Well, it's a matter of taste.—Anyhow, the cross between us and them generally turns out well", added he, thoughtfully.

I heard him, though my eyes were turned away from him, for that pretty girl was just disappearing through the gate with her big basket of early peas, and I felt that disappointed kind of feeling which overtakes one when one has seen an interesting or lovely face in the streets which one is never likely to see again; and I was silent a little. At last I said: "What I mean is, that I haven't seen any poor people about—not one".

He knit his brows, looked puzzled, and said: "No, naturally; if anybody is poorly, he is likely to be within doors, or at best crawling about the garden: but I don't know of any one sick at present. Why should you expect to see poorly people on the road?"

"No, no," I said; "I don't mean sick people. I mean poor people, you know; rough people."

"No," said he, smiling merrily, "I really do not know.

The fact is, you must come along quick to my great-grandfather, who will understand you better than I do. Come on, Greylocks!" Therewith he shook the reins, and we jogged along merrily eastward.

News from Nowhere, chap. iv.

EDUCATION

Romantic as this Kensington wood was, however, it was not lonely. We came on many groups both coming and going, or wandering in the edges of the wood. Amongst these were many children from six or eight years old up to sixteen or seventeen. They seemed to me to be especially fine specimens of their race, and were clearly enjoying themselves to the utmost; some of them were hanging about little tents pitched on the greensward, and by some of these fires were burning, with pots hanging over them gipsy fashion. Dick explained to me that there were scattered houses in the forest, and indeed we caught a glimpse of one or two. He said they were mostly quite small, such as used to be called cottages when there were slaves in the land, but they were pleasant enough and fitting for the wood.

"They must be pretty well stocked with children", said I, pointing to the many youngsters about the way.

"O," said he, "these children do not all come from the near houses, the woodland houses, but from the countryside generally. They often make up parties, and come to play in the woods for weeks together in summer-time, living in tents, as you see. We rather encourage them to it; they learn to do things for themselves, and get to notice the wild creatures; and, you see, the less they stew inside houses the better for them. Indeed, I must tell you that many grown people will go to live in the forests through the summer;

though they for the most part go to the bigger ones, like Windsor, or the Forest of Dean, or the northern wastes. Apart from the other pleasures of it, it gives them a little rough work, which I am sorry to say is getting somewhat scarce for these last fifty years."

He broke off, and then said, "I tell you all this, because I see that if I talk I must be answering questions, which you are thinking, even if you are not speaking them out; but my kinsman will tell you more about it".

I saw that I was likely to get out of my depth again, and so merely for the sake of tiding over an awkwardness and to say something, I said:

"Well, the youngsters here will be all the fresher for school when the summer gets over and they have to go back again".

"School?" he said; "yes, what do you mean by that word? I don't see how it can have anything to do with children. We talk, indeed, of a school of herring, and a school of painting, and in the former sense we might talk of a school of children—but otherwise", said he, laughing, "I must own myself beaten."

Hang it! thought I, I can't open my mouth without digging up some new complexity. I wouldn't try to set my friend right in his etymology; and I thought I had best say nothing about the boy-farms which I had been used to call schools, as I saw pretty clearly that they had disappeared; and so I said after a little fumbling, "I was using the word in the sense of a system of education".

"Education?" said he, meditatively, "I know enough Latin to know that the word must come from *educere*, to lead out; and I have heard it used; but I have never met anybody who could give me a clear explanation of what it means."

You may imagine how my new friends fell in my esteem when I heard this frank avowal; and I said, rather contemptuously, "Well, education means a system of teaching young people".

"Why not old people also?" said he with a twinkle in his eye. "But", he went on, "I can assure you our children learn, whether they go through a 'system of teaching' or not. Why, you will not find one of these children about here, boy or girl, who cannot swim; and every one of them has been used to tumbling about the little forest ponies—there's one of them now! They all of them know how to cook; the bigger lads can mow; many can thatch and do odd jobs at carpentering; or they know how to keep shop. I can tell you they know plenty of things."

"Yes, but their mental education, the teaching of their minds", said I, kindly translating my phrase.

"Guest," said he, "perhaps you have not learned to do these things I have been speaking about; and if that's the case, don't you run away with the idea that it doesn't take some skill to do them, and doesn't give plenty of work for one's mind: you would change your opinion if you saw a Dorsetshire lad thatching, for instance. But, however, I understand you to be speaking of book-learning; and as to that, it is a simple affair. Most children, seeing books lying about, manage to read by the time they are four years old; though I am told it has not always been so. As to writing, we do not encourage them to scrawl too early (though scrawl a little they will), because it gets them into a habit of ugly writing; and what's the use of a lot of ugly writing being done, when rough printing can be done so easily. You understand that handsome writing we like, and many people will write their books out when they make them, or get them written; I mean books of which only a few copies are needed—poems, and such like, you know. However, I am wandering from my lambs; but you must excuse me, for I am interested in this matter of writing, being myself a fair-writer."

"Well," said I, "about the children; when they know how to read and write, don't they learn something else—languages, for instance?"

"Of course," he said; "sometimes even before they can read, they can talk French, which is the nearest language talked on the other side of the water; and they soon get to know German also, which is talked by a huge number of communes and colleges on the mainland. These are the principal languages we speak in these islands, along with English or Welsh, or Irish, which is another form of Welsh; and children pick them up very quickly, because their elders all know them; and besides our guests from over sea often bring their children with them, and the little ones get together, and rub their speech into one another."

"And the older languages?" said I.

"O, yes," said he, "they mostly learn Latin and Greek along with the modern ones, when they do anything more than merely pick up the latter."

"And history?" said I; "how do you teach history?"

"Well," said he, "when a person can read, of course he reads what he likes to; and he can easily get someone to tell him what are the best books to read on such or such a subject, or to explain what he doesn't understand in the books when he is reading them."

"Well," said I, "what else do they learn? I suppose they don't all learn history?"

"No, no," said he; "some don't care about it; in fact, I don't think many do. I have heard my great-grandfather say that it is mostly in periods of turmoil and strife and confusion that people care much about history; and you know", said my friend, with an amiable smile, "we are not like that now. No; many people study facts about the make of things and the matters of cause and effect, so that knowledge increases on us, if that be good; and some, as you heard about friend Bob yonder, will spend time over mathematics. 'Tis no use forcing people's tastes."

Said I: "But you don't mean that children learn all these things?"

Said he: "That depends on what you mean by children; and also you must remember how much they differ. As a rule, they don't do much reading, except for a few story-books, till they are about fifteen years old; we don't encourage early bookishness: though you will find some children who *will* take to books very early; which perhaps is not good for them; but it's no use thwarting them; and very often it doesn't last long with them, and they find their level before they are twenty years old. You see, children are mostly given to imitating their elders, and when they see most people about them engaged in genuinely amusing work, like house-building and street-paving, and gardening, and the like, that is what they want to be doing; so I don't think we need fear having too many book-learned men".

News from Nowhere, chap. v.

SHOPPING IN PICCADILLY

WE came suddenly out of the woodland into a short street of handsomely built houses, which my companion named to me at once as Piccadilly: the lower part of these I should have called shops, if it had not been that, as far as I could see, the people were ignorant of the arts of buying and selling. Wares were displayed in their finely designed fronts, as if to tempt people in, and people stood and looked at them, or went in and came out with parcels under their arms, just like the real thing. On each side of the street ran an elegant arcade to protect foot-passengers, as in some of the old Italian cities. About half-way down, a huge

building of the kind I was now prepared to expect told
me that this also was a centre of some kind, and had its
special public buildings.

Said Dick: "Here, you see, is another market on a
different plan from most others: the upper stories of these
houses are used for guest-houses; for people from all about
the country are apt to drift up hither from time to time,
as folk are very thick upon the ground, which you will
see evidence of presently, and there are people who are
fond of crowds, though I can't say that I am".

By this time we were within the shop or booth, which
had a counter, and shelves on the walls, all very neat,
though without any pretence of showiness, but otherwise
not very different to what I had been used to. Within were
a couple of children—a brown-skinned boy of about twelve,
who sat reading a book, and a pretty little girl of about a
year older, who was sitting also reading behind the counter;
they were obviously brother and sister.

"Good morning, little neighbours", said Dick. "My
friend here wants tobacco and a pipe; can you help
him?"

"O yes, certainly", said the girl with a sort of demure
alertness which was somewhat amusing. The boy looked
up, and fell to staring at my outlandish attire, but presently
reddened and turned his head, as if he knew that he was
not behaving prettily.

"Dear neighbour," said the girl, with the most solemn
countenance of a child playing at keeping shop, "what
tobacco is it you would like?"

"Latakia",[1] quoth I, feeling as if I were assisting at a
child's game, and wondering whether I should get anything but make-believe.

But the girl took a dainty little basket from a shelf

[1] Ladikiyeh, a tobacco exported from Ladikieh, or Latakia, in
Syria, Asiatic Turkey.

beside her, went to a jar, and took out a lot of tobacco and put the filled basket down on the counter before me, where I could both smell and see that it was excellent Latakia.

"But you haven't weighed it," said I, "and—and how much am I to take?"

"Why," she said, "I advise you to cram your bag, because you may be going where you can't get Latakia. Where is your bag?"

I fumbled about, and at last pulled out my piece of cotton print which does duty with me for a tobacco pouch. But the girl looked at it with some disdain, and said:

"Dear neighbour, I can give you something much better than that cotton rag". And she tripped up the shop and came back presently, and as she passed the boy whispered something in his ear, and he nodded and got up and went out. The girl held up in her finger and thumb a red morocco bag, gaily embroidered, and said, "There, I have chosen one for you, and you are to have it: it is pretty, and will hold a lot".

Therewith she fell to cramming it with the tobacco, and laid it down by me and said, "Now for the pipe: that also you must let me choose for you; there are three pretty ones just come in".

She disappeared again, and came back with a big-bowled pipe in her hand, carved out of some hard wood very elaborately, and mounted in gold sprinkled with little gems. It was, in short, as pretty and gay a toy as I had ever seen; something like the best kind of Japanese work, but better.

"Dear me!" said I, when I set eyes on it, "this is altogether too grand for me, or for anybody but the Emperor of the World. Besides, I shall lose it: I always lose my pipes."

The child seemed rather dashed, and said, "Don't you like it, neighbour?"

"O yes," I said, "of course I like it."

"Well, then, take it," said she, "and don't trouble about losing it. What will it matter if you do? Somebody is sure to find it, and he will use it, and you can get another."

I took it out of her hand to look at it, and while I did so, forgot my caution, and said "But however am I to pay for such a thing as this?"

Dick laid his hand on my shoulder as I spoke, and turning I met his eyes with a comical expression in them, which warned me against another exhibition of extinct commercial morality; so I reddened and held my tongue, while the girl simply looked at me with the deepest gravity, as if I were a foreigner blundering in my speech, for she clearly didn't understand me a bit.

"Thank you so very much", I said at last, effusively, as I put the pipe in my pocket, not without a qualm of doubt as to whether I shouldn't find myself before a magistrate presently.

"O, you are so very welcome", said the little lass, with an affectation of grown-up manners at their best which was very quaint. "It is such a pleasure to serve dear old gentlemen like you; specially when one can see at once that you have come from far over sea."

"Yes, my dear," quoth I, "I have been a great traveller."

As I told this lie from pure politeness, in came the lad again, with a tray in his hands, on which I saw a long flask and two beautiful glasses. "Neighbours," said the girl (who did all the talking, her brother being very shy, clearly) "please to drink a glass to us before you go, since we do not have guests like this every day."

Therewith the boy put the tray on the counter and solemnly poured out a straw-coloured wine into the long bowls. Nothing loth, I drank, for I was thirsty with the hot day; and thinks I, I am yet in the world, and the grapes of the Rhine have not yet lost their flavour; for if ever I

drank good Steinberg,[1] I drank it that morning; and I
made a mental note to ask Dick how they managed to
make fine wine when there were no longer labourers compelled to drink rot-gut instead of the fine wine which they
themselves made.

"Don't you drink a glass to us, dear little neighbours?"
said I.

"I don't drink wine", said the lass; "I like lemonade
better: but I wish your health!"

"And I like ginger-beer better", said the little lad.

Well, well, thought I, neither have children's tastes
changed much. And therewith we gave them good day
and went out of the booth.

News from Nowhere, chap. vi.

GOVERNMENT

"Well," I said, "about those 'arrangements' which
you spoke of as taking the place of government, could you
give me any account of them?"

"Neighbour," he said, "although we have simplified
our lives a great deal from what they were, and have got
rid of many conventionalities and many sham wants, which
used to give our forefathers much trouble, yet our life is
too complex for me to tell you in detail by means of words
how it is arranged; you must find that out by living amongst
us. It is true that I can better tell you what we don't do,
than what we do do."

"Well?" said I.

"This is the way to put it", said he: "We have been
living for a hundred and fifty years, at least, more or less
in our present manner, and a tradition or habit of life has
been growing on us; and that habit has become a habit

[1] Hock, from Steinberg, near Wiesbaden on the Rhine.

of acting on the whole for the best. It is easy for us to live without robbing each other. It would be possible for us to contend with and rob each other, but it would be harder for us than refraining from strife and robbery. That is in short the foundation of our life and our happiness."

"Whereas in the old days", said I, "it was very hard to live without strife and robbery. That's what you mean, isn't it, by giving me the negative side of your good conditions?"

"Yes," he said, "it was so hard, that those who habitually acted fairly to their neighbours were celebrated as saints and heroes, and were looked up to with the greatest reverence."

"While they were alive?" said I.

"No," said he, "after they were dead."

"But as to these days", I said; "you don't mean to tell me that no one ever transgresses this habit of good fellowship?"

"Certainly not," said Hammond, "but when the transgressions occur, everybody, transgressors and all, know them for what they are; the errors of friends, not the habitual actions of persons driven into enmity against society."

"I see", said I; "you mean that you have no 'criminal' classes."

"How could we have them," said he, "since there is no rich class to breed enemies against the state by means of the injustice of the state?"

Said I: "I thought that I understood from something that fell from you a little while ago that you had abolished civil law. Is that so, literally?"

"It abolished itself, my friend", said he. "As I said before, the civil law-courts were upheld for the defence of private property; for nobody ever pretended that it was possible to make people act fairly to each other by means of brute force. Well, private property being abolished, all the laws and all the legal 'crimes' which it had manufactured of course came to an end. Thou shalt not steal, had to be translated into, Thou shalt work in order to live happily. Is there any need to enforce that commandment by violence?"

"Well," said I, "that is understood, and I agree with it; but how about the crimes of violence? would not their occurrence (and you admit that they occur) make criminal law necessary?"

Said he: "In your sense of the word, we have no criminal law either. Let us look at the matter closer, and see whence crimes of violence spring. By far the greater part of these in past days were the result of the laws of private property, which forbade the satisfaction of their natural desires to all but a privileged few, and of the general visible coercion which came of those laws. All *that* cause of violent crime is gone. Another cognate cause of crimes of violence was the family tyranny, which was the subject of so many novels and stories of the past, and which once more was the result of private property. Of course that is all ended, since families are held together by no bond of coercion, legal or social, but by mutual liking and affection, and everybody is free to come or go as he or she pleases. Furthermore, our standards of honour and public estimation are very different from the old ones; success in besting our neighbours is a road to renown now closed, let us hope for ever. Each man is free to exercise his special faculty to the utmost, and every one encourages him in so doing. So that we have got rid of the scowling envy, coupled by the poets with hatred, and surely with good reason; heaps of unhappiness and ill-blood were caused by it, which with irritable and passionate men—i.e., energetic and active men—often led to violence".

I laughed, and said: "So that you now withdraw your

admission, and say that there is no violence amongst you?"

"No", said he, "I withdraw nothing; as I told you, such things will happen. Hot blood will err sometimes. A man may strike another, and the stricken strike back again, and the result be a homicide, to put it at the worst. But what then? Shall we the neighbours make it worse still? Shall we think so poorly of each other as to suppose that the slain man calls on us to revenge him, when we *know* that if he had been maimed, he would, when in cold blood and able to weigh all the circumstances, have forgiven his maimer? Or will the death of the slayer bring the slain man to life again and cure the unhappiness his loss has caused?"

"Yes," I said, "but consider, must not the safety of society be safeguarded by some punishment?"

"There, neighbour!" said the old man, with some exultation. "You have hit the mark. That *punishment* of which men used to talk so wisely and act so foolishly, what was it but the expression of their fear? And they had need to fear, since *they*—i.e., the rulers of society—were dwelling like an armed band in a hostile country. But we who live amongst our friends need neither fear nor punish. Surely if we, in dread of an occasional rare homicide, an occasional rough blow, were solemnly and legally to commit homicide and violence, we could only be a society of ferocious cowards. Don't you think so, neighbour?"

"Yes, I do, when I come to think of it from that side", said I.

"Yet you must understand", said the old man, "that when any violence is committed, we expect the transgressor to make any atonement possible to him, and he himself expects it. But again, think if the destruction or serious injury of a man momentarily overcome by wrath or folly can be any atonement to the commonwealth? Surely it can only be an additional injury to it."

Said I: "But suppose the man has a habit of violence,— kills a man a year, for instance?"

"Such a thing is unknown", said he. "In a society where there is no punishment to evade, no law to triumph over, remorse will certainly follow transgression."

"And lesser outbreaks of violence," said I, "how do you deal with them? for hitherto we have been talking of great tragedies, I suppose?"

Said Hammond: "If the ill-doer is not sick or mad (in which case he must be restrained till his sickness or madness is cured) it is clear that grief and humiliation must follow the ill-deed; and society in general will make that pretty clear to the ill-doer if he should chance to be dull to it; and again, some kind of atonement will follow,—at the least, an open acknowledgement of the grief and humiliation. Is it so hard to say, I ask your pardon, neighbour?— Well, sometimes it is hard—and let it be".

"You think that enough?" said I.

"Yes," said he, "and moreover it is all that we *can* do. If in addition we torture the man, we turn his grief into anger, and the humiliation he would otherwise feel for *his* wrongdoing is swallowed up by a hope of revenge for *our* wrongdoing to him. He has paid the legal penalty, and can 'go and sin again' with comfort. Shall we commit such a folly, then? Remember Jesus had got the legal penalty remitted before he said 'Go and sin no more'. Let alone that in a society of equals you will not find any one to play the part of torturer or jailer, though many to act as nurse or doctor."

"So", said I, "you consider crime a mere spasmodic disease, which requires no body of criminal law to deal with it?"

"Pretty much so", said he; "and since, as I have told you, we are a healthy people generally, so we are not likely to be much troubled with *this* disease."

"Well, you have no civil law, and no criminal law. But have you no laws of the market, so to say—no regulation for the exchange of wares? for you must exchange, even if you have no property."

Said he: "We have no obvious individual exchange, as you saw this morning when you went a-shopping; but of course there are regulations of the markets, varying according to the circumstances and guided by general custom. But as these are matters of general assent, which nobody dreams of objecting to, so also we have made no provision for enforcing them: therefore I don't call them laws. In law, whether it be criminal or civil, execution always follows judgment, and someone must suffer. When you see the judge on his bench, you see through him, as clearly as if he were made of glass, the policeman to emprison, and the soldier to slay some actual living person. Such follies would make an agreeable market, wouldn't they?"

"Certainly", said I, "that means turning the market into a mere battle-field, in which many people must suffer as much as in the battle-field of bullet and bayonet. And from what I have seen I should suppose that your marketing, great and little, is carried on in a way that makes it a pleasant occupation."

"You are right, neighbour", said he. "Although there are so many, indeed by far the greater number amongst us, who would be unhappy if they were not engaged in actually making things, and things which turn out beautiful under their hands,—there are many, like the housekeepers I was speaking of, whose delight is in administration and organization, to use long-tailed words; I mean people who like keeping things together, avoiding waste, seeing that nothing sticks fast uselessly. Such people are thoroughly happy in their business, all the more as they are dealing with actual facts, and not merely passing counters round to see what share they shall have in the privileged taxation

of useful people, which was the business of the commercial
folk in past days."

News from Nowhere, chap. xii.

ART AND INDUSTRY

"THE wares which we make are made because they are
needed: men make for their neighbours' use as if they were
making for themselves, not for a vague market of which
they know nothing, and over which they have no control:
as there is no buying and selling, it would be mere insanity
to make goods on the chance of their being wanted; for
there is no longer anyone who can be *compelled* to buy
them. So that whatever is made is good, and thoroughly
fit for its purpose. Nothing *can* be made except for genuine
use; therefore no inferior goods are made. Moreover, as
aforesaid, we have now found out what we want, so we
make no more than we want; and as we are not driven
to make a vast quantity of useless things, we have time and
resources enough to consider our pleasure in making them.
All work which would be irksome to do by hand is done
by immensely improved machinery; and in all work which
it is a pleasure to do by hand machinery is done without.
There is no difficulty in finding work which suits the
special turn of mind of everybody; so that no man is sacri-
ficed to the wants of another. From time to time, when
we have found out that some piece of work was too dis-
agreeable or troublesome, we have given it up and done
altogether without the thing produced by it. Now, surely
you can see that under these circumstances all the work
that we do is an exercise of the mind and body more or
less pleasant to be done: so that instead of avoiding work
everybody seeks it: and, since people have got defter in
doing the work generation after generation, it has become
so easy to do, that it seems as if there were less done,

though probably more is produced. I suppose this explains
that fear, which I hinted at just now, of a possible scarcity
in work, which perhaps you have already noticed, and which
is a feeling on the increase, and has been for a score of
years."

"But do you think", said I, "that there is any fear of
a work-famine amongst you?"

"No, I do not," said he, "and I will tell why; it
is each man's business to make his own work pleasanter
and pleasanter, which of course tends towards raising the
standard of excellence, as no man enjoys turning out work
which is not a credit to him, and also to greater deliberation
in turning it out; and there is such a vast number of things
which can be treated as works of art, that this alone gives
employment to a host of deft people. Again, if art be
inexhaustible, so is science also; and though it is no longer
the only innocent occupation which is thought worth an
intelligent man spending his time upon, as it once was,
yet there are, and I suppose will be, many people who are
excited by its conquest of difficulties, and care for it more
than for anything else. Again, as more and more of pleasure
is imported into work, I think we shall take up kinds of
work which produce desirable wares, but which we gave
up because we could not carry them on pleasantly. Moreover, I think that it is only in parts of Europe which are
more advanced than the rest of the world that you will
hear this talk of the fear of a work-famine. Those lands
which were once the colonies of Great Britain, for instance, and especially America—that part of it, above all,
which was once the United States—are now and will be
for a long while a great resource to us. For these lands,
and, I say, especially the northern parts of America, suffered so terribly from the full force of the last days of
civilization, and became such horrible places to live in, that
they are now very backward in all that makes life pleasant.

Indeed, one may say that for nearly a hundred years the people of the northern parts of America have been engaged in gradually making a dwelling-place out of a stinking dust-heap; and there is still a great deal to do, especially as the country is so big."

News from Nowhere, chap. xv.

THE CHANGE IN INDUSTRY

We stopped at Wallingford for our mid-day meal; of course, all signs of squalor and poverty had disappeared from the streets of the ancient town, and many ugly houses had been taken down and many pretty new ones built, but I thought it curious, that the town still looked like the old place I remembered so well; for indeed it looked like that ought to have looked.

At dinner we fell in with an old, but very bright and intelligent man, who seemed in a country way to be another edition of old Hammond.[1] He had an extraordinary detailed knowledge of the ancient history of the countryside from the time of Alfred to the days of the Parliamentary Wars, many events of which, as you may know, were enacted round about Wallingford. But, what was more interesting to us, he had detailed record of the period of the change to the present state of things, and told us a great deal about it, and especially of that exodus of the people from the town to the country, and the gradual recovery by the town-bred people on one side, and the country-bred people on the other, of those arts of life which they had each lost; which loss, as he told us, had at one time gone so far that not only was it impossible to find a carpenter or a smith in a village or small country town, but that people in such places had even forgotten how to bake bread, and that at Wallingford, for instance, the bread

[1] The old man at the British Museum with whom the writer discusses the affairs of the new era.

came down with the newspapers by an early train from London, worked in some way, the explanation of which I could not understand. He told us also that the towns-people who came into the country used to pick up the agricultural arts by carefully watching the way in which the machines worked, gathering an idea of handicraft from machinery; because at that time almost everything in and about the fields was done by elaborate machines used quite unintelligently by the labourers. On the other hand, the old men amongst the labourers managed to teach the younger ones gradually a little artizanship, such as the use of the saw and the plane, the work of the smithy, and so forth; for once more, by that time it was as much as—or rather, more than—a man could do to fix an ash pole to a rake by handiwork; so that it would take a machine worth a thousand pounds, a group of workmen, and half a day's travelling, to do five shillings' worth of work. He showed us, among other things, an account of a certain village council who were working hard at all this business; and the record of their intense earnestness in getting to the bottom of some matter which in time past would have been thought quite trivial, as, for example, the due proportions of alkali and oil for soap-making for the village wash, or the exact heat of the water into which a leg of mutton should be plunged for boiling—all this joined to the utter absence of anything like party feeling, which even in a village assembly would certainly have made its appearance in an earlier epoch, was very amusing, and at the same time instructive.

This old man, whose name was Henry Morsom, took us, after our meal and a rest, into a biggish hall which con-tained a large collection of articles of manufacture and art from the last days of the machine period to that day; and he went over them with us, and explained them with great care. They also were very interesting, showing the transition from the makeshift work of the machines (which was at about its worst a little after the Civil War before told of[1]) into the first years of the new handicraft period. Of course, there was much overlapping of the periods: and at first the new handwork came in very slowly.

"You must remember", said the old antiquary, "that the handicraft was not the result of what used to be called material necessity: on the contrary, by that time the machines had been so much improved that almost all necessary work might have been done by them: and indeed many people at that time, and before it, used to think that machinery would entirely supersede handicraft; which certainly, on the face of it, seemed more than likely. But there was another opinion, far less logical, prevalent amongst the rich people before the days of freedom, which did not die out at once after that epoch had begun. This opinion, which from all I can learn seemed as natural then, as it seems absurd now, was, that while the ordinary daily work of the world would be done entirely by automatic machinery, the energies of the more intelligent part of mankind would be set free to follow the higher forms of the arts, as well as science and the study of history. It was strange, was it not, that they should thus ignore that aspiration after complete equality which we now recognize as the bond of all happy human society?"

I did not answer, but thought the more. Dick looked thoughtful, and said:

"Strange, neighbour? Well, I don't know. I have often heard my old kinsman say the one aim of all people before our time was to avoid work, or at least they thought it was; so of course the work which their daily life *forced* them to do, seemed more like work than that which they *seemed* to choose for themselves."

[1] The civil war in the middle of the twentieth century, which was supposed to have brought about the change to the new era.

"True enough", said Morsom. "Anyhow, they soon began to find out their mistake, and that only slaves and slave-holders could live solely by setting machines going."

Clara broke in here, flushing a little as she spoke: "Was not their mistake once more bred of the life of slavery that they had been living?—a life which was always looking upon everything, except mankind, animate and inanimate —'nature', as people used to call it—as one thing, and mankind as another. It was natural to people thinking in this way, that they should try to make 'nature' their slave, since they thought 'nature' was something outside them".

"Surely", said Morsom; "and they were puzzled as to what to do, till they found the feeling against a mechanical life, which had begun before the Great Change amongst people who had leisure to think of such things, was spreading insensibly; till at last under the guise of pleasure that was not supposed to be work, work that was pleasure began to push out the mechanical toil, which they had once hoped at the best to reduce to narrow limits indeed, but never to get rid of; and which, moreover, they found they could not limit as they had hoped to do."

"When did this new revolution gather head?" said I.

"In the half-century that followed the Great Change", said Morsom, "it began to be noteworthy; machine after machine was quietly dropped under the excuse that the machines could not produce works of art, and that works of art were more and more called for. Look here," he said, "here are some of the works of that time—rough and unskilful in handiwork, but solid and showing some sense of pleasure in the making."

"They are very curious", said I, taking up a piece of pottery from amongst the specimens which the antiquary was showing us; "not a bit like the work of either savages or barbarians, and yet with what would once have been called a hatred of civilization impressed upon them."

"Yes," said Morsom, "you must not look for delicacy there: in that period you could only have got that from a man who was practically a slave. But now, you see," said he, leading me on a little, "we have learned the trick of handicraft, and have added the utmost refinement of workmanship to the freedom of fancy and imagination."

I looked, and wondered indeed at the deftness and abundance of beauty of the work of men who had at last learned to accept life itself as a pleasure, and the satisfaction of the common needs of mankind and the preparation for them, as work fit for the best of the race. I mused silently; but at last I said:

"What is to come after this?"

The old man laughed. "I don't know", said he; "we will meet it when it comes."

News from Nowhere, chap. xxvii.

THE TOWNS

AFTER a pause, I said: "Your big towns, now; how about them? London, which—which I have read about as the modern Babylon of civilization,[1] seems to have disappeared".

"Well, well," said old Hammond, "perhaps after all it is more like ancient Babylon now than the 'modern Babylon' of the nineteenth century was. But let that pass. After all, there is a good deal of population in places between here and Hammersmith; nor have you seen the most populous part of the town yet."

"Tell me, then," said I, "how is it towards the east?"

Said he: "Time was when if you mounted a good horse

[1] Babylon, one of the oldest cities of Mesopotamia and capital of the kingdom of Babylon, reached the height of its magnificence under Nebuchadnezzar (605–562 B.C.), but it decayed rapidly after the conquest of Cyrus in 538 B.C.

and rode straight away from my door here at a round trot
for an hour and a half, you would still be in the thick of
London, and the greater part of that would be 'slums', as
they were called; that is to say, places of torture for innocent men and women; or worse, stews for rearing and
breeding men and women in such degradation that that
torture should seem to them mere ordinary and natural
life".

"I know, I know", I said, rather impatiently. "That
was what was; tell me something of what is. Is any of
that left?"

"Not an inch", said he; "but some memory of it abides
with us, and I am glad of it. Once a year, on May-day,
we hold a solemn feast in those easterly communes of
London to commemorate The Clearing of Misery, as it is
called. On that day we have music and dancing, and merry
games and happy feasting on the site of some of the worst
of the old slums, the traditional memory of which we have
kept. On that occasion the custom is for the prettiest girls
to sing some of the old revolutionary songs, and those
which were the groans of the discontent, once so hopeless,
on the very spots where those terrible crimes of class-
murder were committed day by day for so many years. To
a man like me, who have studied the past so diligently,
it is a curious and touching sight to see some beautiful girl,
daintily clad, and crowned with flowers from the neighbouring meadows, standing amongst the happy people, on
some mound where of old time stood the wretched apology
for a house, a den in which men and women lived packed
amongst the filth like pilchards in a cask; lived in such a
way that they could only have endured it, as I said just
now, by being degraded out of humanity—to hear the
terrible words of threatening and lamentation coming from
her sweet and beautiful lips, and she unconscious of their
real meaning: to hear her, for instance, singing Hood's

Song of the Shirt, and to think that all the time she does not understand what it is all about—a tragedy grown inconceivable to her and her listeners. Think of that, if you can, and of how glorious life is grown!"

"Indeed," said I, "it is difficult for me to think of it."

And I sat watching how his eyes glittered, and how the fresh life seemed to glow in his face, and I wondered how at his age he should think of the happiness of the world, or indeed anything but his coming dinner.

"Tell me in detail," said I, "what lies east of Bloomsbury now?"

Said he: "There are but few houses between this and the outer part of the old city; but in the city we have a thickly-dwelling population. Our forefathers, in the first clearing of the slums, were not in a hurry to pull down the houses in what was called at the end of the nineteenth century the business quarter of the town, and what later got to be known as the Swindling Kens. You see, these houses, though they stood hideously thick on the ground, were roomy and fairly solid in building, and clean, because they were not used for living in, but as mere gambling booths; so the poor people from the cleared slums took them for lodgings and dwelt there, till the folk of those days had time to think of something better for them; so the buildings were pulled down so gradually that people got used to living thicker on the ground there than in most places; therefore it remains the most populous part of London, or perhaps of all these islands. But it is very pleasant there, partly because of the splendour of the architecture, which goes further than what you will see elsewhere. However, this crowding, if it may be called so, does not go further than a street called Aldgate, a name which perhaps you may have heard of. Beyond that the houses are scattered wide about the meadows there, which are very beautiful, especially when you get on to the lovely river Lea[1] (where old Isaak Walton[2] used to fish, you know) about the places called Stratford[3] and Old Ford, names which of course you will not have heard of, though the Romans were busy there once upon a time".

Not heard of them! thought I to myself. How strange! that I who had seen the very last remnant of the pleasantness of the meadows by the Lea destroyed, should have heard them spoken of with pleasantness come back to them in full measure.

Hammond went on: "When you get down to the Thames side you come on the Docks, which are works of the nineteenth century, and are still in use, although not so thronged as they once were, since we discourage centralization all we can, and we have long ago dropped the pretension to be the market of the world. About these Docks are a good few houses, which, however, are not inhabited by many people permanently; I mean, those who use them come and go a good deal, the place being too low and marshy for pleasant dwelling. Past the Docks eastward and landward it is all flat pasture, once marsh, except for a few gardens, and there are very few permanent dwellings there: scarcely anything but a few sheds, and cots for the men who come to look after the great herds of cattle pasturing there. But however, what with the beasts and the men, and the scattered red-tiled roofs and the big hayricks, it does not make a bad holiday to get a quiet pony and ride about there on a sunny afternoon of autumn, and look over the river and the craft passing up and down, and on to Shooters' Hill[4] and the Kentish uplands, and then

[1] The river Lea joins the Thames about four miles east of London.

[2] English writer and angler, 1593–1683; author of *The Compleat Angler*.

[3] Not the Stratford in Warwickshire, but a suburb five miles E.N.E. of London, in Essex, on the river Lea.

[4] A prominent hill in Kent, eight miles south-east of London.

turn round to the wide green sea of the Essex marshland, with the great domed line of the sky, and the sun shining down in one flood of peaceful light over the long distance. There is a place called Canning's Town, and further out, Silvertown, where the pleasant meadows are at their pleasantest: doubtless they were once slums, and wretched enough".[1]

The names grated on my ear, but I could not explain why to him. So I said: "And south of the river, what is it like?"

He said: "You would find it much the same as the land about Hammersmith. North, again, the land runs up high, and there is an agreeable and well-built town called Hampstead, which fitly ends London on that side. It looks down on the north-western end of the forest you passed through".

I smiled. "So much for what was once London", said I. "Now tell me about the other towns of the country."

He said: "As to the big murky places which were once, as we know, the centres of manufacture, they have, like the brick and mortar desert of London, disappeared; only, since they were centres of nothing but 'manufacture', and served no purpose but that of the gambling market, they have left less signs of their existence than London. Of course, the great change in the use of mechanical force made this an easy matter, and some approach to their break-up as centres would probably have taken place, even if we had not changed our habits so much: but they being such as they were, no sacrifice would have seemed too great a price to pay for getting rid of the 'manufacturing districts', as they used to be called. For the rest, whatever coal or mineral we need is brought to grass and sent whither it is needed with as little as possible of dirt, confusion, and

---

[1] Canning's Town and Silvertown are two suburbs, east of London, which contain the Victoria and Royal Albert Docks.

the distressing of quiet people's lives. One is tempted to believe from what one has read of the condition of those districts in the nineteenth century, that those who had them under their power worried, befouled, and degraded men out of malice prepense: but it was not so; like the mis-education of which we were talking just now, it came of their dreadful poverty. They were obliged to put up with everything, and even pretend that they liked it; whereas we can now deal with things reasonably, and refuse to be saddled with what we do not want".

I said: "We have heard about London and the manu-facturing districts and the ordinary towns: how about the villages?"

Said Hammond: "You must know that toward the end of the nineteenth century the villages were almost destroyed, unless where they became mere adjuncts to the manu-facturing districts, or formed a sort of minor manufacturing district themselves. Houses were allowed to fall into decay and actual ruin; trees were cut down for the sake of the few shillings which the poor sticks would fetch; the building became inexpressibly mean and hideous. Labour was scarce; but wages fell nevertheless. All the small country arts of life which once added to the little pleasures of country people were lost. The country produce which passed through the hands of the husbandmen never got so far as their mouths. Incredible shabbiness and niggardly pinching reigned over the fields and acres which, in spite of the rude and careless husbandry of the times, were so kind and bountiful. Had you any inkling of all this?"

"I have heard that it was so," said I; "but what fol-lowed?"

"The change," said Hammond, "which in these matters took place very early in our epoch, was most strangely rapid. People flocked into the country villages, and, so to say, flung themselves upon the freed land like a wild beast upon his prey; and in a very little time the villages of England were more populous than they had been since the fourteenth century, and were still growing fast. Of course, this invasion of the country was awkward to deal with, and would have created much misery, if the folk had still been under the bondage of class monopoly. But as it was, things soon righted themselves. People found out what they were fit for, and gave up attempting to push themselves into occupations in which they must needs fail. The town invaded the country; but the invaders, like the warlike invaders of early days, yielded to 'the influence of their surroundings, and became country people; and in their turn, as they became more numerous than the townsmen, influenced them also; so that the difference between town and country grew less and less; and it was indeed this world of the country vivified by the thought and briskness of town-bred folk which has produced that happy and leisurely but eager life of which you have had a first taste. Again I say, many blunders were made, but we have had time to set them right. Much was left for the men of my earlier life to deal with. The crude ideas of the first half of the twentieth century, when men were still oppressed by the fear of poverty, and did not look enough to the present pleasure of ordinary daily life, spoilt a great deal of what the commercial age had left us of external beauty: and I admit that it was but slowly that men recovered from the injuries they had inflicted on themselves even after they became free. But slowly as the recovery came, it *did* come; and the more you see of us, the clearer it will be to you that we are happy. That we live amidst beauty without any fear of becoming effeminate; that we have plenty to do, and on the whole enjoy doing it. What more can we ask of life?"

He paused, as if he were seeking for words with which to express his thought. Then he said:

"This is how we stand. England was once a country of clearings amongst the woods and wastes, with a few towns interspersed, which were fortresses for the feudal army, markets for the folk, gathering places for the craftsmen. It then became a country of huge and foul workshops and fouler gambling-dens, surrounded by an ill-kept, poverty-stricken farm, pillaged by the masters of the workshops. It is now a garden, where nothing is wasted and nothing is spoilt, with the necessary dwellings, sheds, and workshops scattered up and down the country, all trim and neat and pretty. For, indeed, we should be too much ashamed of ourselves if we allowed the making of goods, even on a large scale, to carry with it the appearance, even, of desolation and misery. Why, my friend, those housewives we were talking of just now would teach us better than that".

Said I: "This side of your change is certainly for the better. But though I shall soon see some of these villages, tell me in a word or two what they are like, just to prepare me".

"Perhaps", said he, "you have seen a tolerable picture of these villages as they were before the end of the nineteenth century. Such things exist."

"I have seen several of such pictures", said I.

"Well," said Hammond, "our villages are something like the best of such places, with the church or mote-house of the neighbours for their chief building. Only note that there are no tokens of poverty about them: no tumbledown picturesque; which, to tell you the truth, the artist usually availed himself of to veil his incapacity for drawing architecture. Such things do not please us, even when they indicate no misery. Like the mediaevals, we like everything trim and clean, and orderly and bright; as people always do when they have any sense of architectural power; because then they know that they can have what they want, and they won't stand any nonsense from Nature in their dealings with her."

"Besides the villages, are there any scattered country houses?" said I.

"Yes, plenty", said Hammond; "in fact, except in the wastes and forests and amongst the sand-hills (like Hindhead in Surrey), it is not easy to be out of sight of a house; and where the houses are thinly scattered they run large, and are more like the old colleges than ordinary houses as they used to be. That is done for the sake of society, for a good many people can dwell in such houses, as the country dwellers are not necessarily husbandmen; though they almost all help in such work at times. The life that goes on in these big dwellings in the country is very pleasant, especially as some of the most studious men of our time live in them, and altogether there is a great variety of mind and mood to be found in them which brightens and quickens the society there."

News from Nowhere, chap. x.

HAMPTON COURT

At last we came to a reach of the river where on the left hand a very pretty little village with some old houses in it came down to the edge of the water, over which was a ferry; and beyond these houses the elm-beset meadows ended in a fringe of tall willows, while on the right hand went the tow-path and a clear space before a row of trees, which rose up behind huge and ancient, the ornaments of a great park: but these drew back still further from the river at the end of the reach to make way for a little town of quaint and pretty houses, some new, some old, dominated by the long walls and sharp gables of a great red-brick pile of building, partly of the latest Gothic, partly of the court-

style of Dutch William,[1] but so blended together by the
bright sun and beautiful surroundings, including the bright
blue river, which it looked down upon, that even amidst
the beautiful buildings of that new happy time it had a
strange charm about it. A great wave of fragrance, amidst
which the lime-tree blossom was clearly to be distinguished,
came down to us from its unseen gardens, as Clara sat up
in her place, and said:

"O Dick, dear, couldn't we stop at Hampton Court[2]
for to-day, and take the guest about the park a little, and
show him those sweet old buildings? Somehow, I suppose
because you have lived so near it, you have seldom taken
me to Hampton Court".

Dick rested on his oars a little, and said: "Well, well,
Clara, you are lazy to-day. I didn't feel like stopping short
of Shepperton[3] for the night; suppose we just go and have
our dinner at the Court, and go on again about five
o'clock?"

"Well," she said, "so be it; but I should like the guest
to have spent an hour or two in the Park."

"The Park!" said Dick; "why, the whole Thames-
side is a park this time of the year; and for my part, I had
rather lie under an elm-tree on the borders of a wheat-field,
with the bees humming about me and the corn-crake
crying from furrow to furrow, than in any park in England.
Besides—"

"Besides," said she, "you want to get on to your dearly-
loved upper Thames, and show your prowess down the
heavy swathes of the mowing grass."

[1] William III (1650–1702), stadholder of the United Netherlands
and king of England, 1689–1702.
[2] A royal palace on the Thames, twelve miles from London,
built by Cardinal Wolsey and used by many English kings from
Henry VIII. Many additions were made by Sir Christopher Wren
in the reign of William III.
[3] On the Thames in Middlesex, nineteen miles S.W. of London.

She looked at him fondly, and I could tell that she was seeing him in her mind's eye showing his splendid form at its best amidst the rhymed strokes of the scythes; and she looked down at her own pretty feet with a half sigh, as though she were contrasting her slight woman's beauty with his man's beauty; as women will when they are really in love, and are not spoiled with conventional sentiment.

As for Dick, he looked at her admiringly a while, and then said at last: "Well, Clara, I do wish we were there! But, hilloa! we are getting back way". And he set to work sculling again, and in two minutes we were all standing on the gravelly strand below the bridge, which, as you may imagine, was no longer the old hideous iron abortion, but a handsome piece of very solid oak framing.

We went into the Court and straight into the great hall, so well remembered, where there were tables spread for dinner, and everything arranged much as in Hammersmith Guest Hall. Dinner over, we sauntered through the ancient rooms, where the pictures and tapestry were still preserved, and nothing was much changed, except that the people whom we met there had an indefinable kind of look of being at home and at ease, which communicated itself to me, so that I felt that the beautiful old place was mine in the best sense of the word; and my pleasure of past days seemed to add itself to that of to-day, and filled my whole soul with content.

Dick (who, in spite of Clara's gibe, knew the place very well) told me that the beautiful old Tudor rooms, which I remembered had been the dwellings of the lesser fry of Court flunkies,[1] were now much used by people coming and going; for, beautiful as architecture had now become, and although the whole face of the country had quite recovered its beauty, there was still a sort of tradition of

[1] Part of the palace is now assigned by the state to officials and persons of good family in reduced circumstances.

pleasure and beauty which clung to that group of buildings, and people thought going to Hampton Court a necessary summer outing, as they did in the days when London was so grimy and miserable. We went into some of the rooms looking into the old garden, and were well received by the people in them, who got speedily into talk with us, and looked with politely half-concealed wonder at my strange face. Besides these birds of passage, and a few regular dwellers in the place, we saw out in the meadows near the garden, down "the Long Water", as it used to be called, many gay tents with men, women, and children round about them. As it seemed, this pleasure-loving people were fond of tent-life, with all its inconveniences, which, indeed, they turned into pleasure also.

We left this old friend by the time appointed, and I made some feeble show of taking the sculls; but Dick repulsed me, not much to my grief, I must say, as I found I had quite enough to do between the enjoyment of the beautiful time and my own lazily blended thoughts.

As to Dick, it was quite right to let him pull, for he was as strong as a horse, and had the greatest delight in bodily exercise, whatever it was. We really had some difficulty in getting him to stop when it was getting rather more than dusk, and the moon was brightening just as we were off Runnymede.[1] We landed there, and were looking about for a place whereon to pitch our tents (for we had brought two with us), when an old man came up to us, bade us good evening, and asked if we were housed for that night; and finding that we were not, bade us home to his house. Nothing loth, we went with him, and Clara took his hand in a coaxing way which I noticed she used with old men; and as we went on our way, made some commonplace

[1] A meadow on the right bank of the Thames, near Egham in Surrey, twenty-one miles west of London. Magna Carta was signed here by King John in 1215.

remark about the beauty of the day. The old man stopped short, and looked at her and said: "You really like it, then?"

"Yes," she said, looking very much astonished, "don't you?"

"Well," said he, "perhaps I do. I did, at any rate, when I was younger; but now I think I should like it cooler."

She said nothing, and went on, the night growing about as dark as it would be; till just at the rise of the hill we came to a hedge with a gate in it, which the old man unlatched and led us into a garden, at the end of which we could see a little house, one of whose little windows was already yellow with candle-light. We could see even under the doubtful light of the moon and the last of the western glow that the garden was stuffed full of flowers; and the fragrance it gave out in the gathering coolness was so wonderfully sweet, that it seemed the very heart of the delight of the June dusk; so that we three stopped instinctively, and Clara gave forth a little sweet "O", like a bird beginning to sing.

"What's the matter?" said the old man, a little testily, and pulling at her hand. "There's no dog; or have you trodden on a thorn and hurt your foot?"

"No, no, neighbour," she said; "but how sweet, how sweet it is!"

News from Nowhere, chap. xxii.

THE UPPER THAMES

Presently at a place where the river flowed round a headland of the meadows, we stopped a while for rest and victuals, and settled ourselves on a beautiful bank which almost reached the dignity of a hill-side: the wide meadows spread before us, and already the scythe was busy amidst the hay. One change I noticed amidst the quiet beauty of the fields—to wit, that they were planted with trees here and there, often fruit-trees, and that there was none of the niggardly begrudging of space to a handsome tree which I remembered too well; and though the willows were often polled (or shrowded, as they call it in that country-side), this was done with some regard to beauty: I mean that there was no polling of rows on rows so as to destroy the pleasantness of half a mile of country, but a thoughtful sequence in the cutting, that prevented a sudden bareness anywhere. To be short, the fields were everywhere treated as a garden made for the pleasure as well as the livelihood of all, as old Hammond told me was the case.

On this bank or bent of the hill, then, we had our mid-day meal; somewhat early for dinner, if that mattered, but we had been stirring early: the slender stream of the Thames winding below us between the garden of a country I have been telling of; a furlong from us was a beautiful little islet begrown with graceful trees; on the slopes westward of us was a wood of varied growth overhanging the narrow meadow on the south side of the river; while to the north was a wide stretch of mead rising very gradually from the river's edge. A delicate spire of an ancient building rose up from out of the trees in the middle distance, with a few grey houses clustered about it; while nearer to us, in fact not half a furlong from the water, was a quite modern stone house—a wide quadrangle of one story, the buildings that made it being quite low. There was no garden between it and the river, nothing but a row of pear-trees still quite young and slender; and though there did not seem to be much ornament about it, it had a sort of natural elegance, like that of the trees themselves.

I disentangled myself from the merry throng, and mounting on the cart-road that ran along the river some feet above the water, I looked round about me. The river came down through a wide meadow on my left, which was grey now with the ripened seeding grasses; the gleaming water was lost presently by a turn of the bank, but over the meadow I could see the mingled gables of a building where I knew the lock must be, and which now seemed to combine a mill with it. A low wooded ridge bounded the river-plain to the south and south-east, whence we had come, and a few low houses lay about its feet and up its slope. I turned a little to my right, and through the hawthorn sprays and long shoots of the wild roses could see the flat country spreading out far away under the sun of the calm evening, till something that might be called hills with a look of sheep-pastures about them bounded it with a soft blue line. Before me, the elm-boughs still hid most of what houses there might be in this river-side dwelling of men; but to the right of the cart-road a few grey buildings of the simplest kind showed here and there.

There I stood in a dreamy mood, and rubbed my eyes as if I were not wholly awake, and half expected to see the gay-clad company of beautiful men and women change to two or three spindle-legged back-bowed men and haggard, hollow-eyed, ill-favoured women, who once wore down the soil of this land with their heavy hopeless feet, from day to day, and season to season, and year to year. But no change came as yet, and my heart swelled with joy as I thought of all the beautiful grey villages, from the river to the plain and the plain to the uplands, which I could picture to myself so well, all peopled now with this happy and lovely folk, who had cast away riches and attained to wealth.

News from Nowhere, chaps. xxix, xxx.

GLOSSARY

adze,   a cutting tool with an arched blade, used to trim off the surface of wood.

airts,   points of the compass. (Gael. *aird.*)

albeit,   although, notwithstanding.

alien,   foreigner. (Lat. *alienus,* of another race.)

arbalestier (arbalister),   crossbowman.

axle-tree,   an earlier form of *axle* which included the sense of *axis.* (AS. *eaxl,* the shoulder, on which the arm turns, and *treow,* a beam.)

bane,   destruction. (AS. *bana,* death.)

banker,   a covering, as of tapestry, for chairs or walls. (O.F. *banquier.*)

beck,   a brook. (AS. *becc*); cf. Trout*beck,* etc.

behoof,   behalf, advantage, profit. (AS. *behof,* behoof.)

bent,   a grassy slope.

beset,   to surround, inclose, urge, press. (AS. *besettan,* to set near.)

bested,   to put in peril, to beset. (AS. *stead,* a place.)

betid (betide),   to come to pass. (AS. *tidan,* to happen.)

bewray,   betray. (AS. *be-wregan,* to disclose.)

bill,   a long staff, terminating in a hook-shaped blade. (AS. *bill,* a sword.)

blood-wite, see *wite.*

boot,   help. (AS. *bote,* a remedy.)   *to boot,* in addition.

booth,   a shop, covered stall, shed. (Icel. *búth.*)

brazil,   red colour. (Pg. *braza,* glowing fire.)

briony (bryony),   genus of annual or perennial vines.

buckler,   a shield. (Fr. *bouclier.*)

burg,   a town or fortified place. (AS. *burg.*)

buttery,   originally *botelerie,* a place for bottles. The apartment where provisions are kept.

byre,   a cow-house, or group of farm-buildings. (Icel. *bær.*)

byrnie,   a coat of linked mail. (Icel. *brynja.*)

carle,   a countryman. (Icel. *karl,* a man.)

chapiter,   the capital of a column or pillar.

chapman,   a merchant. (AS. *ceáp-man,* a tradesman.)

china-aster,   a common hardy, free-flowering plant; called also the *Reine Marguerite.*

churl,   a freeman of the lowest rank; later a serf, or bond-man. (AS. *ceorl.*)

clerestory,   the row of windows high up along one or both sides of the hall.

cob,   clay mixed with straw.

coif,   to cover the head.

commune,   a small territorial division of France and Belgium.

crone,   an old woman. (Gael. *criona,* old.)

damascened,   ornamented with designs produced by inlaying or encrusting with another metal.

deem,   to judge, to think. (AS. *deman.*)

deft,   dexterous, clever, apt. (AS. *dæft,* fit.)

devoir,   duty, task, service. (Lat. *debere,* to owe.)

dight,   to dispose, arrange. (AS. *dihtan,* to order.)

doom-ring,   judgment-ring.

dorsar (dosser),   a cloth or tapestry, for covering chairs or walls.

dortoir,   a dormitory. (Fr. *dortoir.*)

duke,   a leader. (Lat. *dux.*)

fain,   gladly. (AS. *fægen,* well-pleased.)

fallow,   pale-gray, or yellowish. (AS. *fealo,* pale yellow.)

fell,   rock, hill. (Icel. *fell,* hill.)
Adj. savage, fierce. (AS. *fell,* sharp.)

fictile,   connected with pottery. (Lat. *fictus,* from *fingere,* to mould into shape.)

flitting,   removing. (Dan. *flytte.*)

floret,   a small single flower in a compact inflorescence, as in a composite flower. (Fr. *fleurette.*)

folk-mote,   a meeting. (AS. *mot, gemot.*)

forestalling,   purchasing goods before they come to market, with a view to raising the price.

forsooth,   certainly. (AS. *forsoð*, in truth.)

garth,   a walled inclosure outside the house, where the out-door work of the household was done. It contained the byres, stables, and outbuildings. (Icel. *garðr*, a yard.)

gate-thing,   see *thing.*

gild (guild),   the medieval association of men engaged in the same pursuits.

glaive,   a spear, lance, or a kind of halberd—a large blade fixed on the end of a pole. (Lat. *gladius*, a sword.)

handsel,   to give into one's hands, to make a gift. (AS. *handselen*.)

hauberk,   a coat of chain mail, without sleeves.

heckle,   to dress flax or hemp by means of a heckle, or metal comb.

hedge-priest,   a poor, illiterate priest—hedges were used as a shelter by the poor and lowly.

heft-sax,   haft, handle, and *sax.*

holm-oak,   evergreen oak, holly. (AS. *holm*, holly.)

hopple,   a fetter, chiefly used to prevent cattle from straying.

howbeit,   nevertheless.

hundred,   a division of a county in medieval England.

hundred, long,   the sum of 120.

jerkin,   a jacket or short coat. (Dim. of D. *jurk*, a frock.)

ken (the Swindling Kens),   a place where low and disreputable characters lodge or meet (a contraction of *kennel*).

knave,   boy, young man. (AS. *cnafa*, a boy.)

latten,   a kind of brass alloy, hammered into thin sheets. (Fr. *laiton*.)

leet,   the court of a manor or township.

leman,   a lover, mistress. (AS. *leof*, dear, and *mann*, a man.)

long-nebbed,   long-nosed. (AS. *neb*, face.)

losel,   a worthless person. (M.E. *losel*.)

luffer (louvre),   a dome or turret rising out of the roof of a hall or apartment in ancient domestic edifices, to allow the smoke to escape when the fire was kindled in the middle of the room.

madder,   a herb, used in dyeing.

mass-john,   the term *mass-priest* was frequently given in derision to a secular priest as distinguished from the regulars. *John* is a stock epithet, cf. *John Bull.*

mead,   a sweet fermented liquor. (AS. *meodo.*)

meet,   fit, proper. (AS. *gemet.*)

mote,   see *folk-mote.*

neat,   AS. *neat,* cattle.

nock (notch),   to place the arrow upon the string of the bow.

oleo-margerine,   Lat. *oleum,* oil.

parcel-gilt,   partially gilt.

peltry,   skins, or furs. (Fr. *pelleterie.*)

penfolds (pinfold, pindfold),   an enclosure. (AS. *pundfald.*)

pilchard,   a small fish resembling the herring.

plummet,   a lump, ball, or weight (of lead), as for a missile. (Fr. *plomb.*)

plump,   a cluster, group, crowd.

poll,   to remove the top or head. (L. G. *polle,* the head, top of a tree.)

poll-groat-bailiff,   the official appointed to collect the poll-tax, or tax per head, of a groat, the old English coin worth fourpence.

prepense,   deliberated or considered beforehand. (Lat. *præpensus,* weighed before.)

purblind,   originally *pure-blind,* altogether blind; now used as near-sighted, or partly blind.

queen,   a woman. (AS. *cwene.*)

quern,   a stone hand-mill for grinding corn. (AS. *cweorn,* a mill-stone.)

quick,   a live plant, especially hawthorn and hedge plants.

quit-rent,   rent paid by the freeholders of a manor in acquittance of other services.

rede,   counsel, advice. (AS. *ræd.*)

regrating,   buying to sell again in the same market or fair. (Fr. *regratter,* to scratch.)

rot-gut,	bad beer, or bad liquor of any sort.
ruffler,	a ruffian, or thieving beggar.
sackless,	guiltless. (AS. *sacu,* contention, and *leas,* loose.)
sax,	a knife, short sword. (AS. *seax.*)
scrivener,	a professional writer. (Lat. *scribere,* to write.)
shed,	in weaving, the interstice between the different parts of the warp of a loom, through which the shuttle passes.
sheepskin,	a bond, parchment of sheepskin.
shrowd (shroud),	to lop the branches from a tree. (AS. *scrûd.*)
shut-bed,	a screened recess, with a fixed bed, on the side of a hall.
sley,	a weaver's reed—the pierced rod of a loom through which the warp-threads are strung.
sling-plummet,	see *plummet.*
sooth,	truth. (AS. *soð.*)
stoup,	a vessel for liquids. (Icel. *staup.*)
summoner,	an official who summons, or cites by authority, especially one employed to warn people to appear in court.
surcoat,	the outer garment worn in the thirteenth and fourteenth centuries by both sexes. (Fr. *sur,* over.)
swathe,	a bundle or sheaf. (AS. *swethian,* to bind.)
tabard,	a short sleeveless coat. (O.F. *tabard.*)
teem,	to bring forth abundantly. (AS. *teman.*)
thing (mote),	a judicial assembly. (AS. *þing,* a cause.)
thing-stead,	AS. *stede,* a place.
thrall,	a serf, a slave. (AS. *thræl.*)
tie-beam,	a beam post, or rod, to hold parts together.
tilt,	the cloth covering of a tent or waggon. (AS. *teld,* a tent.)
tipstaves,	officers bearing staffs; constables, bailiffs.
troubadour,	the name given to the early poets and singers of Provence.
unbyrnied,	see *byrnie*

unruth, from AS. *hreow,* pity, mercy, compassion.

villeins, originally free tenants, but later serfs of the feudal lord. (L.Lat. *villanus,* from *villa,* a village.)

wain, a four-wheeled waggon or cart. (AS. *wægn.*)

warding, guarding, protecting. (AS. *weardian.*)

war-duke, see *duke.*

war-garth, see *garth.*

warp, the threads extended lengthwise in the loom and crossed by the woof.

wattle, to bind or interweave twigs.

welt, a hem, border. (M.E. *welte.*)

wend, to turn, to go. (AS. *wendan.*)

wherry, the name commonly applied to a light, shallow boat, seated for passengers.

wit, from AS. *witan,* to know. *wot* (pres.), *wist* (past).

wite, punishment, fine. (AS. *wite.*)

woad, a plant yielding the famous blue dyestuff.

wont, custom. (M.E. *wone,* accustomed.)

wot, see *wit.*

INDEX

Abbey of unknown Church, 46–7
Adam, 57
Alderman Iron-face, 28, 34, 35, 37, 40
Alftings, 4, 5
America in Utopia, 195–6
Apollo's bow, 62
Architecture, country, 102–3; English, 116; Gothic, 88; past, 78–9; principles of, 111–20; simplicity, 112; types of, 118–20
Art, artist and craftsman, 92; best, 148–52; craftsmanship, 84; Egyptian, 76; English, 79, 81, 86, 96; exclusive to few, 85; Flemish, 79; future of, 169–70; Greek, 79; happy, 83–4, 86, 106, 111, 116, 117, 140, 146; Italian, 78–9; neglect of, 97–103; past, 76, 81, 82, 83, 90, 94, 101, 114, 148; popular, 90, 115, 132, 140; Renaissance, 80, 85, 87; study of, 94; subjects of, 149; universal, 83–4, 97, 168–70; Venetian, 81; and beauty of life, 81–8; and England, 100–1, 104–8, 109; and labour, 91, 106; and lower classes, 99; and luxury, 98–9, 125, 137, 145–7; and morals, 143–8; in Utopia, 194–6
Arts, decorative, 108, 138–43
Athens, 108

Babylon, 200
Ball, John, 53–6, 66–75
Baptistry of Florence, 177
Beamings, 4, 5, 8, 10, 11, 13, 14
Bearings, 4, 13, 14

Bears-bane, 33
Blake, 87
Boffin, 173–6
Bokhara, 77
Borgias, 161
Bredon Hill, 102
Bride, the, 29, 30
Bridge, House of, 30, 43
Bristler, 37–40
Broadway, 102–3
Bull, House of, 30
Burgdale, 33, 34
Burgstead, folk-mote, 35–40; maiden ward, 41; market, 24–5; weapon-show, 26–35
Byzantine Empire, 89

Canning's Town, 203
Canterbury, 53, 55, 68
Carpet-gardening, 156
Chelsea pottery, 166
Churches of North France, 48–9
China pottery, 163, 166
Cities, 109, 200–8
Civilization, 81, 109; and art, 82, 98, 105, 106
Clement, St, 52
Coleridge, 87
Communal industry, 129
Competition, 98, 143
Constantine Palaeologus, 78
Constantinople, 78
Cotswolds, 102, 156
Craftsmanship, 84, 132, 139–40
Criminals in Utopia, 189–90
Crosby Hall, 171

Dalesmen, 25, 32, 40
Dale-wardens, 27–9, 39
Dallach, 29
Damascus, 166
Dandolo, 78

Daylings, 5
Decorative arts, *see* Arts
Derby pottery, 166
Devil's Manor, 59
Dickens, 175
Distribution of goods, 69
Doom-ring, 3

Easterlings, 59
Education, 103–5, 124–5, 131–2; in Utopia, 180–4
Egil, 5, 11, 13
Egypt, art of, 76
Elkings, 4, 5, 8, 10, 11, 13
England, love of, 96, 104–8; in Utopia, 200–8
English art, 79, 81, 86, 96, 104–8
English language, 87, 106
Environment, 128–9, 133
Essex, 58–9

Face, House of, 24, 27, 28, 31, 36
Face-of-god, 28, 29, 33, 34, 41
Factories, 134
Fellowship, 54, 55, 59–60, 73, 75
Fleece, House of, 32, 37
Florence, 65
Flowers, 153–7
Folk-beard, 31
Folk-might, 38, 39
Folk-mote, 29, 35
Fox, of Wolfings, 6; of Upton, 30
Freedom, 74
French Revolution, 87
Furniture, 157–62

Galtings, 4, 5
Galway, 77
Gardens, 152–7
Gate-thing, 34, 36
George II, 87
Gibbon, 76
Glittering Plain, 16
Gold-may, 43
Gothic architecture, 88, 177, 208
Gothic pottery, 164

Goths, 9, 10, 13, 14
Government in Utopia, 188–94
Granada, 166
Greece, art, 77; pottery, 163
Green, Will, 60–5
Greenbury, 32
Greensleeve, 36
Gregory, Long, 62
Grès de Cologne, 165
Guest House, 171–6

Hallblithe, 15–23
Hall-face, 32
Hall-Sun, 4
Hall-ward, 30
Hammersmith market, 176–80
Hammersmith Socialists, 173
Hammond, 189 et seq.
Hampstead, 203
Hampton Court, 208–12
Handicrafts, 92, 139–40, 144, 197–200
Hartings, 4
Hartsbane, 38
Health, 123
Heart of Midlothian, 87
Heriulf, 6–13
Hindhead, 208
History, 76, 89, 90, 93
Holm, 38
Hood, 202
Hostage, 21
Hosting, 34
Houses, 112–13, 159–60

Iceland, 77
Imaginative work, 119–20
Industry, change to Utopia, 196–200, 204–5; communal, 129; conditions of, 125–9; future of, 66–75
Iron-face, *see* Alderman
Ispahan, 90

John Ball, *see* Ball
Justice, 147

Kent, 57–8
Kirialax, 77
Knolls, House of, 31

Labour, conditions of, 130–38;
    future of, 66–75, 91, 170; and
    art, 91, 106–7, 117; in Utopia,
    194–200
Latakia, 185
Laxings, 5
Lea, River, 203
Leadership, 72
Leet, 51
Leisure, 125–6
Libraries, 125
London, 109–10, 200–5
Long-coat, 41
Louis XV, 161
Luxury and art, 98–9, 125, 137,
    145–7

Machines, 86, 121–3, 125–7,
    135–7, 197–200
Maiden Ward, 40–5
Majolica pottery, 165–6
Manchester, 110
Mark of Wolfings, 2, 3
Mastership, 67, 75
Mechanical art, 118–20, 150
Meissen, 166
Merton Priory, 72
Michael Angelo, 90
Micklegarth, 77
Morea, 78
Morsom, Henry, 197
Mote, 39, 178
Mote-stead, 40
Museums, 94

Nature, 94–5, 108, 139, 142, 155

Odin, 13
Ornament, 133, 139, 148–52
Oselings, 5
Otter, 5, 7
Oxford, 110

Pallas, 101
Parthenon, 101
Penny-thumb, 37–40
Pericles, 77, 108
Persia, pottery, 166, 168
Piccadilly, Utopian, 184–8
Plantagenet, 116
Plato, 90
Poor, condition of, 124
Population of Utopia, 172, 179
Portway, 27, 28, 41–3
Pottery, 162–8
Poverty, 70
Procrustes, 127
Profit, 134, 144–5
Punishment in Utopia, 191

Ravagers, 16
Raven, House of, 15, 19–20
Red-beard, 31
Red-wolf, 32
Renaissance, 80–1, 85–6, 166
Richard, King, 61
Robert the Weaver, 172
Romans, 5–15, 49
Roses, 153–4
Runnymede, 211
Rusty, 38–9

Santa Sophia, 102
Scott, 87
Scrivener, 28, 30, 31, 33
Senlac, 58
Sèvres, 166
Shakespeare, 90
Shepperton, 209
Shepherds, 25–37
Shooters' Hill, 203
Shopping, Utopian, 185
Sickle, House of, 31, 42
Silvertown, 204
Simplicity, 112, 145–7, 157–61
South Kensington Museum, 114–
    15
St Albans Abbey, 72
Steed-linden, 42

Steer, House of, 29, 30
Steinberg, 188
Stone-face, 31
Stone of Doom, 61
Stratford, 203
Straw, Jack, 61–4
Strongitharm, 32
Sun-beam, 41, 42
Swindling Kens, 202

Tewkesbury, 102
Thackeray, 159
Thing-stead, 3
Thiodolf, 5–13
Thorn, House of, 32
Thorp, 45
Throng-plough, 10–11
Toti, 10
Towns, change to Utopia, 200–8
Tyr, 9, 11

Undying, House of, 16, 19
Unknown Church, 45–8
Upton, 30

Vallings, 4, 5
Valois, 116
Venice, art, 81
Villeins, 67

Vine, House of, 31

Wain-burg, 11
Wall decoration, 148–52
Wallingford, 196
Walton, Isaak, 203
War, 127
War-well, 30
Wat Tyler, 53
Weapon-show, 26–35
Weaving, 67–8, 121
Weltering Water, 26, 27
Westminster Abbey, 95
Westminster Hall, 95
Wildlake, 26–7
William III, 209
William, Duke, 58, 59
William of Wykeham, 143
Wolfings, 1–13
Wolf's-sister, 9, 10, 13
Wolfstone, 29
Woodlanders, 25–34
Wood-wont, 39
Worcester, 102
Work, conditions of, 129–38;
    claim to, 126; rough, 137–8;
    in Utopia, 194–200
Wormings, 14
Wright, Hob, 65